Research and Teaching

Universities into the 21st Century

Series Editors: Noel Entwistle and Roger King

Research and Teaching   *Angela Brew*
University Teaching and Student Learning   *Noel Entwistle*
The University in the Global Age   *Roger King*
Teaching Academic Writing in UK Higher Education
   Lisa Ganobcsik-Williams (Editor)
Managing your Academic Career   *Wyn Grant with Philippa Sherrington*

Further titles are in preparation

Research and Teaching

Beyond the Divide

Angela Brew

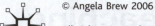
First published 2006 by
PALGRAVE MACMILLAN
Houndmills, Basingstoke, Hampshire RG21 6XS and
175 Fifth Avenue, New York, N.Y. 10010
Companies and representatives throughout the world

PALGRAVE MACMILLAN is the global academic imprint of the Palgrave
Macmillan division of St. Martin's Press, LLC and of Palgrave Macmillan Ltd.
Macmillan® is a registered trademark in the United States, United Kingdom
and other countries. Palgrave is a registered trademark in the European
Union and other countries.

ISBN–13: 978 1–4039–3435–2
ISBN–10: 1–4039–3435–5

This book is printed on paper suitable for recycling and made from fully
managed and sustained forest sources.

A catalogue record for this book is available from the British Library.

A catalog record for this book is available from the Library of Congress.

10   9   8   7   6   5   4   3   2   1
15   14   13   12   11   10   09   08   07   06

Printed and bound in China

Contents

Figures and Tables

▶ Figures

▶ Tables

Acknowledgements

This book has arisen from the many conversations I have had with colleagues in many universities in different countries. I should especially like to thank the following colleagues in the University of Sydney, who have contributed ideas, resources and time to my research for the book: Paul Ramsden, Michael Prosser and all my colleagues in the Institute for Teaching and Learning; Henriikka Clarkeburn and undergraduate student researchers; members of the University of Sydney Working Group on Research-Led Teaching and the Scholarship of Teaching; also Stephen Cheung, Chin Moy Chow, Alistair Davidson, Brett Green, Jim Kitay, Manfred Lenzen, Suzanne MacAlister, Gaynor MacDonald, Chris Morgan, Erica Sainsbury, Neil Southorn, Chris Stewart, Charlotte Taylor and Amanda Warren-Smith.

I am also indebted to the many people who have participated in conversations in workshops and seminars in a number of countries and who have responded to requests for information. I have drawn directly on ideas from: Sue Jones, Tasmania University; Margaret Hicks, University of South Australia; Stephen Kemmis, Charles Sturt University; and Paul Wellington, Monash University, Australia; Caroline Baillie, Queen's University, Canada; Chris Button and Gert-Jan Pepping, Otago University, New Zealand; Sue Birkill, Maria Donkin and Steve Gaskin, Plymouth University; and Sheila Ollin, Gloucestershire University, UK; Maria Murtonen, Helsinki University, Finland; Lyn Sorenson, Brigham Young University, USA; and many people, too numerous to name who have sent me papers and course outlines and website addresses. Where I have drawn directly on such work, my acknowledgement comes in the form of a reference to their work. I am grateful to them all.

During the preparation for this book I was fortunate to be invited to attend a number of meetings of groups of people interested in bringing research and teaching together. I would like to thank Roger Zetter and Bridget Durning (Oxford Brookes University) and members of the FDTL project group on Linking Teaching with Research and Consultancy in the Built Environment; the LTSN Project group on Linking Research and Teaching in Departments; Brenda Smith and many members of the Learning and Teaching Support Networks (LTSNs) whom I visited; Members of the UK Research and Teaching Group; Su White, colleagues and student researchers at Southampton

University; and Paul Blackmore, Glynis Cousin and student researchers at the University of Warwick.

I have been privileged to spend time in other universities during periods of study leave. I am grateful to the University of Sydney for opportunities to do this and would like to thank Dai Hounsell and staff in the Department of Higher and Community Education, also other colleagues in the University of Edinburgh for talking with me about their views on research-led teaching. Similarly, thanks are due to Stephen Rowland and colleagues in the Department of Education and Professional Development, as well as Hasok Chang, Katherine Jackson and Jason Davis, University College, London. I should like to express my appreciation to Graham Gibbs, Keith Trigwell and Harriet Dunbar-Goddet in the Institute for the Advancement of University Learning at Oxford University for providing an environment for me to complete the book in 2004.

Finally, I would like to thank Noel Entwistle and Roger King for inviting me to prepare a book for the series, and to express special thanks for ongoing encouragement, support and advice to Roger Brown, Lewis Elton and Alan Jenkins. Also, and especially, thanks to my friend and partner David Boud.

Series Editors' Preface

The series is designed to fill a niche between publications about universities and colleges that focus exclusively on the practical concerns of university teachers, managers or policy makers and those which are written with an academic, research-based audience in mind that provide detailed evidence, argument and conclusions. The books in this series are intended to build upon evidence and conceptual frameworks in discussing issues which are of direct interest to those concerned with universities. The issues in the series will cover a broad range, from the activities of teachers and students, to wider developments in policy, at local, national and international levels.

The current pressures on academic and administrative staff, and university managers, mean that, only rarely, can they justify the time needed to read lengthy descriptions of research findings. The aim, therefore, is to produce compact, readable books that in many parts provide a synthesis and overview of often seemingly disparate issues.

Some of the books, such as the first in the series – *The University in the Global Age* – are deliberatively broad in focus and conceptualisation, looking at the system as a whole in an international perspective, and are a collection of integrated chapters, written by specialist authors. In other books, such as *Research and Teaching: Beyond the Divide,* the author looks within universities at a specific issue to examine what constitutes 'best practice' through a lens of available theory and research evidence.

Underpinning arguments, where appropriate with research-based conceptual analysis, makes the books more convincing to an academic audience, while the link to 'good practice and policy' avoids the remoteness that comes from an over-abstract approach. The series will thus appeal not just to those working within higher education, but also to a wider audience interested in knowing more about an organisation that is attracting increasing government and media attention.

NOEL ENTWISTLE
ROGER KING

Introduction

I have discussed the relationship between teaching and research with numerous people in different countries, sometimes in seminars and workshops and sometimes in research interviews and in meetings and with people in my own university, including students. In this book my aim is to explore the sorts of things that we've been talking about. I like to think of the book as an extension of the conversations about research and teaching that people in higher education seem increasingly to be having and how we can bring them together to enhance higher education. My hope is that it will contribute to enhancing such conversations.

My fundamental belief is that ideas about how research and teaching can be brought together are going to be different for each person in higher education and that developing these ideas rests on discussions that people have in their tea rooms, in departmental meetings, in research groups and course teams, in discussions with students and general or support staff, and with others outside the university. I think it is only by talking together in a spirit of inquiry about what a research-enhanced or a research-based higher education might mean in any particular context that thinking will advance.

In my conversations in universities, some people have told me how they understand this relationship as if that were the only way it is to be understood. I hope that this book will open up a wider set of possibilities, and provide a conceptual framework for understanding the range of different perspectives about how research and teaching can be brought together.

I am concerned to present a spectrum of different views including many examples of ways in which research and teaching are being brought together in different disciplinary areas and different countries. I have worked for many years in central academic departments, so have had lots of contact with people right across the university community. I am going to be drawing on the large research literature, where people have tried to correlate research and teaching, and decide whether there is a connection, but I do not want to rehash old arguments about whether or not there is a correlation between some kind of measure of research performance and a measure of teaching or teaching effectiveness. I want to go beyond them to develop understanding of what is really involved if we are serious in bringing research and teaching together.

I suggest that an ultimate goal of the integration of research and teaching is the creation of inclusive scholarly knowledge-building communities in universities. I explain what I mean by this, why I think it is important, and I explore how to do it.

The book is divided into three parts. In the first part my aim is to introduce key concepts. I explain in Chapter 1 why I think bringing research and teaching together is a focus of attention at this particular time and why it is important in terms of the education of students; why students need research. In Chapter 2, I examine different ways teaching, research, knowledge and scholarship are understood. This is a preparation for presenting a new model that takes the relationship between teaching and research beyond any kind of divide. I argue that we need to break down the divisions between separate categories of people that exist within our universities: academics, students and general or support staff.

In Part 2, the focus is on learning, teaching and curriculum. I have chosen to focus on undergraduate education because this is where I believe the greatest challenges and opportunities lie. In Chapter 3, I consider a number of assumptions that create boundaries and possibilities for how to think of bringing research and teaching together. Then there are two chapters which look at cases where research and teaching are being integrated in some way. The first of these begins by examining examples of limited integration of research into teaching and progresses towards fuller integration. However, these cases stop short of developing scholarly knowledge-building communities. In the cases presented in the second (Chapter 5), research and teaching are more firmly integrated, but here again, academics are still stopping short of engaging students in their world. Students do research but this tends to be separate from the research the lecturers are doing. Some exceptions to this are specific undergraduate research schemes. They are considered at the end of Chapter 5.

Attention then turns to research on learning and teaching because one way academics can and do integrate their research and their teaching is by engaging in the scholarship of teaching and learning. In Chapters 6 and 7 I draw on my experiences, and those of my colleagues, of teaching academics in our university how to engage in researching their teaching. I argue that developing a reflexive, critical, inquiry-based approach to learning and teaching can point up some of the value conflicts in today's higher education, and that this can provide an impetus for change. I further argue that involving students in this process is an important step towards the development of scholarly knowledge-building communities.

Finally, Part 3 moves away from a primary focus on learning and teaching to examine, first of all (in Chapter 8), how teaching informs and can be used to enhance research, and then in Chapter 9, to look at the institutional and social context in which all of this is taking place. My concern there is to explore what factors inhibit or enhance individuals', faculties', schools', departments' and institutions' abilities to integrate research and teaching including, for example, institutional strategies, research assessment and government funding. Finally, in the last two chapters, I bring the arguments together to first of all set up some dimensions to evaluate progress in moving towards the development of inclusive scholarly knowledge-building communities, and then, in the final chapter, to explore the implications for a new research-based higher education. I suggest that moving towards inclusive scholarly knowledge-building communities goes beyond the integration of research and teaching to embed inquiry-based approaches into academic practice more generally.

I am passionate about bringing research and teaching together because I believe that this is the key to the inquiry-based higher education that I think we need for the future. If we are going to prepare students for an unpredictable future; a future where they will have to solve problems that we cannot at this moment even dream of, then they need to develop the skills of inquiry, and if we are going to get anywhere near tackling some of the world's big problems, then we have to think about how research needs to change and who needs to be involved in doing it.

In many contexts, discussions about the integration of research and teaching are being driven by people interested in, or with responsibility for, learning and teaching. The challenge then is to engage the research community in seeing this move as of benefit to them. I like to see myself as representing both the teaching and research communities. I am an academic developer with a responsibility in my university for curriculum change, and that positions me on the teaching and learning side of things. But I am also a researcher and someone who has investigated and written a good deal about how research is understood, so I trust I also speak from a research perspective. As I indicated, everyone has their own ideas about how research and teaching can be brought together. So to portray different orientations and points of view, sometimes I use a conversational style of writing and sometimes present specific conversations to give voice to some of the ideas and people with whom I have been talking. Ultimately, however, this book represents my perspective. It is offered as a resource for reflection and hopefully to inform and stimulate further conversations.

Part 1
Exploring the Research and Teaching Relationship

A long tradition of studies has looked at whether there is a relationship between research and teaching at the level of the individual faculty academic, or at a departmental or disciplinary level, whether there is a relationship at institutional level or across institutions. Such studies have used a variety of measures of research, (e.g., publication or citation counts, number of research grants, peer review, etc.) and a number of measures of teaching (such as student evaluations or ratings of teaching effectiveness, personality, colleagues' ratings, etc.). In addition, attempts have been made to suggest underlying elements that both research and teaching share, such as learning, critical reasoning or scholarship and a number of models showing inter-related variables have been proposed.

Alongside this there have been some attempts, the most notable of which is by Boyer and colleagues at the Carnegie Foundation in the United States, to transcend the research and teaching divide by redefining the nature of academic practice, or, as Boyer (1990) calls it, 'scholarly work'. Boyer's resulting four types of scholarship have been influential in encouraging people to think differently about the work of universities. Outside of the United States, considerations of the scholarship of teaching, in particular, are having considerable impact in changing how people think about teaching and, specifically, teaching development.

Boyer's intention was to 'break out of the tired old teaching versus research debate and define, in more creative ways, what it means to be a scholar' (Boyer 1990: xii). Here, my intention is rather different. My aim is not to present a picture of how research and teaching ought to be understood, but rather to explore how the relationship has conventionally been viewed, to examine the external forces that dictate how academics and others in higher education conceptualise the relationship, and to surface some of the underlying assumptions they make about research and teaching and academic practice more generally. Part 1 therefore provides an in-depth exploration of the forces and ideas within the academic community that underpin discussions of the relationship between research and training. It relates ideas about academic practice to educational theory more generally, and leads to the development of a conceptual model where research and teaching are integrated. This incorporates a number of suggestions for transcending the research and teaching divide, which provide a framework for explorations in the remainder of the book.

Chapter 1 puts the relationship between research and teaching in its contemporary context, and examines why this relationship has become a focus of attention in universities at the present time. The chapter explores the ways in which political, cultural and economic factors have made the relationship particularly problematic and how the move to mass higher education systems has generated value conflicts, with universities needing to simultaneously balance elitist ideas with expectations that they should educate a democratic public. Mass higher education indicates a need to provide a new rationale for why the students of today need research, for it is now well recognised that only a very small minority will pursue careers where academic research is a key focus. Chapter 1 concludes by articulating such a rationale in terms of the professional demands of the twenty-first century. This provides a compelling case for why attempts need to be made to integrate research and teaching.

In order to comprehend how to move beyond the research and teaching divide, it is important to explore what is understood by research and by teaching. Chapter 2 begins by presenting a model of the way the relationship has conventionally been conceived. It is suggested that this model rests on particular views of the nature of teaching, of research and of the generation of knowledge. Drawing on research into how academics understand these activities, the chapter explores conceptualisations implied by the model. It is suggested that when individuals extend the ways in which they understand and experience teaching, research and knowledge, how the relationship between research and teaching is understood also changes. The chapter then presents a new model of this relationship, based on the ideas of inclusivity, knowledge building, new approaches to learning and teaching, expanded ideas of research and teaching as research, and ideas about academic professionalism with academics and students working in partnership within scholarly communities. The chapter concludes with a discussion of the challenges presented by this model for the future of higher education.

1 Why should we be interested in bringing research and teaching together?

The relationship between teaching and research is intricately embedded within ideas about what universities do and what they are for. It is fundamental to what is understood by higher learning and to ideas about the nature of the academy. Understanding this relationship raises substantial questions about the roles and responsibilities of higher education institutions, about the nature of academic work, about the kinds of disciplinary knowledge that are developed and by whom, about the ways teachers and students relate to each other, about how university spaces are arranged and used; indeed, it raises fundamental questions about the purposes of higher education. If we want to go beyond the divide between teaching and research, we have to face not just questions about how and what to teach and how and what to research, but also subtle yet complex power-plays involving political, economic and social as well as academic interests.

For a number of years I have been looking at various key aspects of higher education, how we do things and what the implications are. I have been examining the nature of research and how academics understand it. I have looked at the relationship between teaching and research, and between knowledge and scholarship, and how people conceptualise them. What drives this work is a belief that there are some fundamental contradictions in how we view higher learning and that if we are to cope with the context of twenty-first century uncertainty and what Barnett (2000) calls 'supercomplexity', we need to take a reflexive and critical approach to understanding the relationship between teaching and research and the complex of forces that act upon it. My aim is that by examining many of the facets of the relationship, this book will furnish a conceptual basis for better understanding of: (i) the role of research in teaching and learning; (ii) the role of teaching within research and scholarship; and (iii) how higher education might be transformed by bringing research and teaching together.

I shall explore a vision of higher education institutions as places where academics work collaboratively in partnership with students as members of inclusive scholarly knowledge-building communities; where teaching and research are integrated, and where both students and academics are engaged in the challenging process of coming to understand the world through systematic investigation and collaborative decision-making in the light of evidence. I want to look at pedagogical trends that are pointing in this direction. However, this means examining the political, economic and social factors that inhibit such developments.

I would like to think that the academy could become a place where both academics and students in their different ways develop the strategies, techniques, tools, knowledge and experience needed to solve complex, important and yet unforeseen problems; where the distinctions between teaching, learning and research break down as both teachers and students explore and share the issues that confront them. Yet this means facing up to elements of the academic environment that work against the integration of academics and students.

We shall see in this book how teaching is becoming more like a process of inquiry; how research is becoming more like inquiry-based learning; how learning is becoming more akin to research, more focused on inquiry with students being involved in learning through their own inquiries and teachers through investigations into their own teaching. On the other hand, we will notice how conflicts in values, entrenched hierarchies and a lack of critical reflexivity confine academics' ability to go beyond the divide between teaching and research to establish new pedagogies and new research strategies based on such redefined relationships.

To explore the development potential of a close relationship between research and teaching and go beyond current practice to new forms of curriculum decision-making, new teaching and learning practices, and new forms of research, demands a critically reflexive examination of the way the academy operates. In this book my aim is to bring new conceptual tools to inform this process. I will argue that it is important to understand the relationship and its implications for research and scholarship and for students' learning in order to address difficult problems of the world today. I begin in Chapter 1 by exploring the factors that make the relationship between research and teaching of both particular importance and particular interest at the present time.

▶ Why teaching and research should be brought together

While the two activities of teaching and research have much in common (as we shall see in later chapters) the relationship between them is essentially asymmetrical. I have found the work of the French sociologist, Pierre Bourdieu helpful in understanding the mechanisms which sustain this assymetry between teaching and research in universities. If we are to transcend the divide that currently exists between research and teaching, we need to go beyond rhetoric to examine underlying assumptions and dispositions that, intentionally or unintentionally, direct current practice. Bourdieu's focus on the ideas that lie behind the ways in which people think and act in social contexts – what he calls the 'unthought categories of thought' (Bourdieu 1982: 10) and his concern to uncover the presuppositions that make academic life possible – make his work particularly relevant to understanding the relationship between research and teaching. In this book, where relevant, I draw upon Bourdieu's work to illuminate aspects of the research–teaching relationship which otherwise might lie hidden.

For Bourdieu, a social scientific analysis of a particular social space which he calls a 'field', in this case the academic field, is understood by examining the ways in which the different forms of power operate within the field (Bourdieu, 1998). He refers to the different forms of value within any given field as cultural, political, economic or intellectual capital. Applying this to the teaching and research relationship, it soon becomes evident that, however research and teaching may be measured for the purposes of analysis, they each carry different levels of academic capital. Research has relative kudos and is a highly valued asset; a point that has been the subject of much debate particularly in the American literature (see Chapter 2). It carries levels of prestige that teaching inevitably lacks, however effective or innovative the teaching is, or however well it is rewarded. This is what I mean when I say that the relationship is assymetrical. Debates about the status of research *vis à vis* teaching, and concomitant questions of the differential status and prestige of universities, are of crucial importance to considerations of the relationship between teaching and research.

Ramsden and Moses (1992) have suggested that there are three views of the relationship between teaching and research:

- the strong integrationist view which suggests that in order to be a good university teacher one must be an active researcher
- the integrationist view which is the belief that there are links between teaching and research at the departmental or institutional level but not at the level of the individual academic
- the independence view which says there is no causal relation.

Such perceptions are grounded within institutions with differing orientation and ethe. Indeed, all attempts to understand the relationship are located in a particular moment in the history of universities and, as such, are attempts to capture a dynamic ever-changing scenario (Brew 1999a).

While there have been a number of studies of the relationship carried out within particular institutions, many are focused on understanding the relationship over a population of universities and higher education institutions. Yet institutions differ in how they define the relationship. We shall see in

Chapter 9 how different research policies and departmental arrangements for teaching allocation affect the extent to which academics are able to integrate teaching and research activities. The point to note here is that the motivations to integrate research and teaching are inevitably different in different kinds of institution. Within research-intensive universities the motivation for an interest in developing the relationship between teaching and research may be considered to lie in the competitive advantage which comes from attracting students to an environment where they may be taught by some of the world's top researchers; the assumption being that this is bound to be better education (Ramsden 2001). On the other hand, within universities less strong in research, the motivation to strengthen the relationship between teaching and research is more likely to be aspirational; a desire to ensure that governments do not strengthen funding mechanisms which may divide teaching institutions from research institutions.

Yet these are not just two different orientations. Strong hierarchical mechanisms support and sustain research as a valued commodity both within and between higher education institutions. Historically grounded hierarchical relationships ensure that research intensive universities – such as the prestigious Russell Group in the United Kingdom, the Ivy League in the United States, the Group of Eight in Australia – maintain a larger measure of cultural capital in their respective countries as a whole. The result is that the aspirations of such universities to integrate research and teaching are viewed in quite a different way by policy-makers and academics alike, to the aspirations of academics in universities where there are not such strong research traditions. Yet there is a culture of silence on such issues. Bourdieu describes this as a kind of 'double consciousness'. The analysis of teaching and research relationships is treated in a rational manner, yet it exists only by masking the inequality between different institutions. This becomes problematic only,

> by the making explicit of the truth of institutions (or fields) whose truth is the avoidance of rendering their truth explicit. Put more simply: rendering explicit brings about a destructive alteration when the entire logic of the universe rendered explicit rests on the taboo of rendering it explicit.
>
> (Bourdieu 1998: 113)

Numerous discussions in the academic research literature have, for many years, been examining the teaching–research relationship, yet the power issues implied in this quotation have tended to be neglected in this work. Robertson (2002) usefully characterises existing work as being of three kinds:

(i)   quantitative statistical anlyses of the relationship between measures of research productivity and of teaching effectiveness;

(ii)   more recent qualitative studies designed to elucidate the relationship;
(iii)   and more theoretical or speculative pieces about the relationship.

Statistical studies have failed to establish the nature of the connection between research and teaching, or even whether there is one. Reviews of numerous studies in the United States have shown no statistically significant inverse associations between research productivity and scholarly accomplishment on the one hand, and teaching effectiveness on the other. While the relationships were always positive, generally they were not statistically significant (see, for example, Feldman 1987; Webster 1985). Feldman found that the small correlation which existed when research was measured using publication counts, indicators of research support and peer ratings disappeared when measured by citation counts. These, according to Feldman, appeared to be unrelated to teaching effectiveness. In a study of Australian academics, Ramsden and Moses (1992) similarly found negative or near zero correlations both at the individual and at the departmental level.

However, currently the most influential study is perhaps that of Hattie and Marsh (1996) who, following a meta-analysis of 58 studies of the teaching–research relationship firmly concluded that there was no correlation. Hattie and Marsh's subsequent work has served to underscore this finding, which in turn has been seized upon by policy-makers in support of calls to separate research and teaching functions and – most troublingly for those working to strengthen the synergies between them – by government agencies to support calls for the separation of teaching and research institutions. For example, a UK government paper setting out the future of higher education (DFES 2003) draws upon Hattie and Marsh's zero correlation to support their claim that cutting-edge research is not essential to good teaching in higher education. Marsh and Hattie (2002) point out that a zero correlation means that:

> Good researchers are neither more nor less likely to be effective teachers than are poor researchers. Good teachers are neither more nor less likely to be productive researchers than are [poor] teachers. There are roughly equal numbers of academics who – relative to other academics – are: (a) good at both teaching and research; (b) poor at both teaching and research; (c) good at teaching but poor at research; and (d) poor at teaching but good at research. These results clearly demonstrate that personnel selection and promotion decisions must be based on separate measures of teaching and research and on how academics provide evidence that their research and teaching are mutually supporting.
>
> (Marsh and Hattie 2002: 635)

As Mclean and Barker (2004) indicate, there is nowhere any evidence that separating teaching and research results in better teaching. Indeed, it has been found that perceptions of the nexus between teaching and research within the academic community are complex and subtle (Neumann 1992) and also that many faculty academics are unable to differentiate which of their activities are research and which teaching (Rowland 1996). However, it is clear that the belief that there is a relationship has been stronger than the evidence for its existence (Centra 1983, Neumann 1992, Webster 1985).

In spite of the prevalence of zero correlations, Hattie and Marsh (1996) concluded that, given that there is such a strong belief in the complementarity of research and teaching within higher education, the important task is to work to actively bring research and teaching together:

> The strongest policy claim that derives from this meta-analysis is that universities need to set as a mission goal the improvement of the nexus between research and teaching ... The aim is to increase the circumstances in which teaching and research have occasion to meet. ... We advocate that a desirable aim of a university would be to devise strategies to enhance the relationship between teaching and research, and all should be pleased when they increase the relationship positively beyond zero.
>
> (Hattie and Marsh 1996: 533–4)

Other researchers have come to similar conclusions. Shore, Pinkler and Bates (1990), for example, suggested that research may serve as a model for teaching, while Barnett (1997) called for teaching to become more research-like. Interestingly, while Hattie and Marsh's suggestion that the nexus between research and teaching should be strengthened has been quoted by those wishing to work to integrate research and teaching, and has demonstrably led to a number of qualitative studies designed to elucidate how the relationship is understood in the academic community, it has tended to be ignored in a policy context.

▶ Government intervention in higher education

It is now clear that in order to understand more about the forces at work that make the relationship between research and teaching particularly problematic, we have to consider the influences of political, economic and social contexts on universities. What is notable about the history of the respective roles of research and teaching in universities is how they are tied up with the social and political ambitions of institutions and, indeed, since the nineteenth century, with governments. As the idea of the university has grown and developed, so the relationship has taken on different characters. The early universities of Bologna and Paris were focused on teaching. When the scholar knew all that it was possible to know, teaching within a university community was the obvious extension of that knowledge. Following the period known as the 'Enlightenment', in the nineteenth century the development of empirical scientific research heralded the idea that research was essential in universities. In the German idea of the university, which stemmed from the ideas of Alexander von Humboldt, for example, teaching and research were thought to go together. The idea was that research teams located in a research laboratory would be led by a professor who would direct research and teach the next generation of researchers. Such research teams became very powerful and attracted researchers from far afield. The social and political ideals of the German government were subsequently well served by this strong research focus of its universities. State control, moreover, ensured that it could turn both teaching and research to its own ends, which it did with devastating consequences in the early part of the twentieth century. In Britain and in America, governments exerted less control, but the idea of a strong relationship between teaching and research established by the German universities also took hold.

For most of the twentieth century, teaching and research continued to coexist with very little intervention from outside. However, in recent times a number of political cultural and economic factors have contributed to critical questioning of the relationship and led to it becoming problematic. Intellectual crises have also challenged traditional conceptions of knowledge and led to crises of authority in terms of who defines what knowledge is, the nature of evidence, and the status of practical and applied knowledges –also with profound consequences for how both research and teaching are viewed.

It is now well recognised that governments have, over the past thirty years or so, been increasingly exercising control over universities. Through targeted funding and specific accountability requirements, they have been working to control agendas for research and teaching within institutions. Governments are now taking it upon themselves not only to make statements about the relationship between teaching and research, but are creating policy and funding regimes which are affecting whether academics are able to pursue both, and, further, which are affecting the ability of institutions to sustain both.

Another way of expressing this is to say that in recent years the political and economic fields have increasingly influenced the academic field. Deer (2003), influenced by Bourdieu and writing specifically about UK higher education, highlights how profound this shift is:

As the political elite has accumulated social resources, the political field has been better positioned to influence practice in the academic field according to its own values. It has accumulated financial power by restricting funding and imposing selective funding allocation for research and teaching. It has used legal resources to limit academic employment protection while restricting the financial independence of higher education institutions by forbidding the free setting of tuition fees. Finally, it has accumulated ideological power by promoting a discourse based on economic rationality toward the academic field. For the latter, it has been increasingly difficult, although not impossible, to initiate change or secure stasis in an autonomous way. To do so, agents within the academic field have had to increase their interactions with agents in other fields, and in particular those in the economic field, resulting in a greater submission of academic to economic values and practices. The English academic field emerges as a divided whole, the legacy of its increased heteronomy epitomized by the introduction of new managerial institutional practice, centrifugal professional interests and a multiplicity of value discourses.

(Deer 2003: 202–3)

Debates about the relationship between teaching and research are right in this melting pot. Deer suggests that the overlap and heterogeneity of different fields means that it is becoming more difficult to define the nature of the academic field merely by the habits and practices of those who inhabit it. The political field has, in fact, repositioned itself as an important player within the academic field, influencing academic practice and stimulating innovation (Deer 2003: 204–5). We shall see in Chapter 9 how this scenario plays out in the context of the relationship between teaching and research.

However, what has also had a profound impact on the relationship between teaching and research has been the move to mass higher education. Governments have been under pressure from electorates to increase the number of university places. Yet a mass higher education system, justified as it is on the grounds of equity and access, challenges traditional notions of the university as an elite institution.

Universities are historically hierarchical. The way in which they operate works to create and continually reinforce privilege (Webb, Shirato, and Danaher, 2002). They generate and maintain distance between academics and students, for example, through the use of rituals, by addressing students in formal ways in some institutions and departments, through the layout of university buildings and lecture halls, and through the use of esoteric language (Webb, Shirato and Danaher 2002). The accumulation of academic capital, Bourdieu argues, takes time, and, 'Since the positions of power are hierarchised and separated in time, reproduction of the hierarchy supposes a respect for distances, that is respect for the order of succession' (Bourdieu, 1988: 87). A range of assumptions within what he calls the academic 'habitus' keeps students waiting in submissive roles progressively allowing them to participate fully in academic life (Bourdieu 1988: 95).

> The exercise of academic power presupposes the aptitude and propensity, themselves socially acquired, to exploit the opportunities offered by the field: the capacity to 'have pupils, to place them, to keep them in a relation of dependency' and thus to ensure the basis of a durable power, the fact of 'having well-placed pupils'. . . implies perhaps above all the art of manipulating other people's time, or, more precisely, their career rhythm, their *curriculum vitae*, to accelerate or defer achievements as different as success in competitive or other examinations, obtaining the doctorate, publishing articles or books, appointment to university posts, etc. And, as a corollary, this art, which is also one of the dimensions of power, is often only exercised with the more or less conscious complicity of the postulant, thus maintained, sometimes to quite an advanced age, in the docile and submissive, even somewhat infantile attitude which characterises the good pupil of all eras.
>
> (Bourdieu 1988: 88)

Exercise of academic power was unproblematic when universities were elite institutions and it could reasonably be expected that a significant proportion of their students would end up in scientific or technical fields. However, in a mass higher education system; a system which includes major professions such as medicine, engineering and law, it is clear that only a very small minority will become career academics. This is not to say that students no longer need research skills. Rather, it points to the need to articulate a different kind of rationale for the integration of research and teaching. Increased numbers of students mean there is a tendency for the distances between the academy and students to be strengthened, rather than diminished. There is a conflict of ideals in, on the one hand, the tendency of universities to maintain their traditional adherence to an unexpressed elitism and, on the other, the requirements of a participatory democracy (see, for example, Zipin 1999: 30).

It is within these values' conflicts that questions about the relationship between teaching and research become particularly acute. Research has traditionally belonged with the elite. For many academics it is the culmination of the 'waiting'; the reward for the hard work, of progressively working one's way up the university system, from being a first year 'freshman' student, to becoming a postgraduate research student, a 'post doc' and finally a fully fledged academic. We shall see later how such rewards are now being challenged via new pedagogies which involve students in various forms of inquiry; but we shall also note the ways in which these initiatives, more often than not, stop short of fully engaging students in communities of researchers and how students are required to take on submissive roles until they are judged ready to carry out research.

With the opening up of higher education through a desire for greater access and equity in a mass higher education system, additional and different organisational demands are placed on institutions and, in particular, on academics. Teaching more students is typically more time consuming (for example, more time needs to be spent on organisation and assignment marking, see Gibbs and Jenkins 1992) and this affects the amount of time available for research. It also, along with a range of other factors, leads to the questioning of higher education's goals.

Governments have, on the one hand, to provide equity of access to higher learning, while simultaneously preserving the status of elite research institutions necessary to compete in the global knowledge market. One of the responses of governments to the challenge of creating a mass higher education system has been to create new universities from what were once polytechnics or colleges of higher and further education; to open up the concept of a university to embrace a wider range of institutions. This, together with the introduction of quality assessment exercises which have made the research and teaching performance of each institution public, has raised critical questions about whether research is an essential activity of a university. The diversity of higher education institutions, some of which are involved in world-class research with a substantial proportion of staff actively engaged in research and others where very few academics are so engaged, questions conventional ideas about what a university is.

An educated population is essential to a participatory democracy. However, governments also need to fund elite research which is internationally competitive and this conflicts with societal trends towards equity and inclusivity. Within universities there are fears that governments will fund some universities to do research and others to simply teach and this, paradoxically, has generated considerable interest within different kinds of institution in defining strategies to bring research and teaching together. Fears have also been expressed that, while higher education for the elite might involve engagement in research and research-like activities, the mass of higher education students will be given a broad general education. Such an outcome might fulfil some government aims, but it will not be sufficient to prepare students for the world in which they will find themselves after graduation. So we must turn now to a consideration of why research needs to become an integral part of higher education pedagogy for all students.

▶ **Why students need research**

It has now almost become a cliché to say that we live in a society characterized by uncertainty, uncontrollability and unpredictability. It is a world that we cannot at any particular time fully understand. Barnett (2000) suggests that the world is not only complex, but super-complex. We can cope with complexity, or we could if we had enough time and resources to put into solving complex problems. But supercomplexity arises when the very frameworks we have for making sense of complexity are in dispute. We have no idea how to solve super-complex problems (Barnett 2003). Barnett argues that the personal and professional studies in which the student of the future will be engaged will take place in the context of this uncertainty and super-complexity. So questions about the nature of higher education and about the role of research and science, and questions about the kinds of education appropriate for students are intimately related to questions about how we are to live in such a society. The students of tomorrow's society are going to face huge numbers of complex and important decisions throughout their lives. Higher education needs to teach them how to do it.

The more complex and important the choices that are facing people daily, the more they need to have developed the skills of critical analysis, gathering evidence, making judgments on a rational basis, and reflecting on what they are doing and why. These are the skills of inquiry. Inquiry is central to a super-complex society. Vital elements of a university education thus need to become focused on preparing students to solve a range of interconnected, frequently unforeseen problems which are going to continue through life, but especially when the student leaves university. 'What is required', says Ron Barnett, 'is not that students become masters of bodies of thought, but that they are enabled to begin to experience the space and challenge of open, critical inquiry (in all its personal and interpersonal aspects)' (Barnett 1997:110).

It is not only a super-complex world, it is also an uncertain world. We have no idea what is going to happen to us next. It is a world of acute ambivalence. Barnett argues that in an unknown world, questions of identity are central. We are constantly asking, 'who am I', and 'how can I make sense of the world in which I find myself?' Wenger (1998) provides a framework for understanding that it is useful to employ here. He describes the concept of identity formation and learning within a site of social practice as constituted of three distinct modes of belonging: engagement, imagination and alignment. Engagement, for Wenger is the 'active involvement in mutual processes of negotiation of meaning' (p. 173). Imagination is ' creating images of the world and seeing connections through time and space by extrapolating from our own experience'. Alignment, according to Wenger is 'coordinating our energy and activities in order to fit within broader structures and contribute to broader enterprises' (Wenger 1998). Engagement, imagination and alignment, Wenger argues, each 'create relationships of belonging that expand identity through space and time in different ways' (p. 181).

Individuals' personal and professional identities are bound up in that sense of belonging to a group of people they know well. Teachers and students develop their personal identities within the teaching and learning encounter; their view of themselves changes. Developing our identities, Wenger reminds us, may challenge our preconceptions; our prior understandings. Hopefully, if learning is to take place, it will challenge and change the ways we view reality, or at least some aspects of it. Research, teaching and learning may also go further and challenge our basic beliefs and values.

In this context we need to see teaching and learning as a shared encounter between individual human beings. Whether they are defined as 'academics', 'teachers', 'students' or 'participants', individuals enter into relationships within our higher education institutions. Disparate groups of people, with some shared interests come together, bringing all that they are to the encounter. Some of what they are is relevant to their interactions; other aspects are not. Some aspects they believe not to be relevant may later turn out to be so. Teaching and learning is a shared encounter.

For Bourdieu and Passeron (1977) this shared encounter rests on a power relationship. An educational institution delegates pedagogical authority and that involves what they call 'symbolic violence'; the imposition of meaning by one person over another. Currently we do not have anything like inclusive communities in our higher education institutions. We have separate communities of academics and of students and of general or support staff. Yet if we begin to take the ethic of inclusivity seriously, we begin to build different kinds of communities; to open out what are currently very closed communities into more loosely coupled, yet more inclusive ones. We shall see in Chapter 7 how engaging higher education teachers in reflective practice, causing them to examine the ways in which they exercise power and to examine their values and the values conflicts that underpin their pedagogical work can lead to changes in the ways in which power is exercised in higher education; particularly needed if teaching and research are to be integrated.

Acting within a context of confusion and ambivalence is an important task facing the higher education of the future and its students. It will be important to encourage students to be open to new problems and new questions and to finding new ways of searching for new solutions. The purpose of teaching thus becomes to induct students into various forms of inquiry so that individuals are able to live in a complex, uncertain world where knowing how to inquire is a key to survival. We are looking towards a higher education where inquiry can become centre stage for both academics and students. 'Inquiry, investigation, and discovery', says the Boyer Commission on reinventing undergraduate education in the United States, 'are the heart of the enterprise, whether in funded research projects or in undergraduate classrooms or graduate apprenticeships. Everyone at a university should be a discoverer, a learner' (Boyer Commission 1999: 9).

An improved understanding of how students learn in higher education contexts has shifted attention away from the lecture as the predominant form of university teaching to a more diverse diet of course offerings. Moves to evidence-based teaching and learning including problem-based learning, increasing development and use of research-based curricula as well as changes in research activity to include a greater involvement of students are indications that cultures of inquiry in the teaching and the research domains may be in the process of being integrated.

In order to educate students for a society such as Barnett suggests, we need to work with students to develop approaches to learning which teach both them and us how to live. This suggests a need to move to more inclusive, collaborative, inquiry-based models of research, teaching and learning. The distinction between teaching and learning breaks down if this happens because both teachers and students explore the issues that confront them. This is not just for those students who are likely to engage in further study or become academics in the future. Neither is it just for students in small elite research-based institutions. Rather, it is important to develop the ability to engage in a rigorous systematic process of inquiry in whatever field or institution they are engaged.

Students need to be fully inducted into the culture and community of researchers. They need to develop a knowledge of what it is to engage in the subject in a research-based way, to understand the key issues and debates in the subject area and know what researchers in the subject do, in general and specifically. They need to engage in activities which mirror the research processes that their teachers are engaged in. They need to learn methods and techniques used in research in the subject and have opportunities to practise such methods and techniques. This all implies that during their studies they should engage in building knowledge just like researchers. Bereiter (2002) describes knowledge building as starting with the questions that one wants to ask about the world as one perceives it. We build knowledge from that starting point. As we develop knowledge in relation to that aspect of the world so we learn about the knowledge that others are building, and in this way knowledge building becomes a shared and collective, collaborative process. But the equalisation of power suggests we must go further. Students will need to become involved as participants in ongoing research programmes with a sense of belonging to a community of researchers.

► Conclusion

My concern in this book, then, is to examine how higher education can develop a closer relationship between teaching and research. I will draw on research into the teaching–research relationship; research on conceptions of research, learning, teaching, knowledge and scholarship; as well as research examining how research-enhanced teaching is currently understood, to build a conceptual basis from which current and future practice can be discussed and evaluated.

First, however, it is important to be clear what we mean by research, what we understand by scholarship and how these ideas are related to conceptions of knowledge and approaches to teaching, for, as Neumann (1993:106) suggests, the difficulty of defining complex endeavours such as 'research' and 'scholarship' is 'a major issue to contend with'. Robertson and Bond (2001:16) similarly argue that 'fundamental questions persist about the definitions and shared understandings of such terms as knowledge, research, teaching and learning'. These different understandings are, I believe, important prerequisites for the development of a research-based theoretical model designed to provide a greater depth of understanding about the relationship between teaching and research. In the next chapter we will explore these different views and understandings.

2 Towards a New Model of the Relationship

Perceptions of the relationship between teaching and research are crucially dependent upon ideas about what teaching and what research is, how knowledge is conceived, and how we conceptualise scholarship. There is considerable variation in how people think about these ideas and this variation is significant to an understanding of how to bring all these facets of university lives together. So, in this second introductory chapter, I want to explore these different understandings. To do this entails considering two differing models of the relationship between teaching and research; one a traditional model, where teaching and research are in opposition, and the other a new model of the relationship, where we go beyond the divide. Thus the aim of this chapter is to establish the components of this model in order to provide a conceptual basis for discussions that follow.

▶ A traditional model

In much of the research on the teaching–research relationship, two elements, one representing a measure of research productivity and the other representing a measure of teaching or teaching effectiveness, have typically been correlated (see, for example, Webster 1985; Feldman 1987; Ramsden and Moses 1992; Hattie and Marsh 1996; Marsh and Hattie 2002). This kind of research has tended to presuppose a traditional model of the relationship between teaching and research (Brew 2003b). It is useful to look more closely at this model because it illuminates some views of both research and teaching, and indeed ways of thinking about knowledge which underscore many discussions of the relationship. In an earlier publication I drew the model as in Figure 2.1.

In this model, research and teaching inhabit quite separate domains. Research is viewed as taking place in what we might loosely call a disciplinary research culture, in which academics, researchers and postgraduate research students carry out the job of generating knowledge. Teaching is viewed as taking place within what I have called a 'departmental learning milieu'. The arrows are intended to suggest that research and teaching are

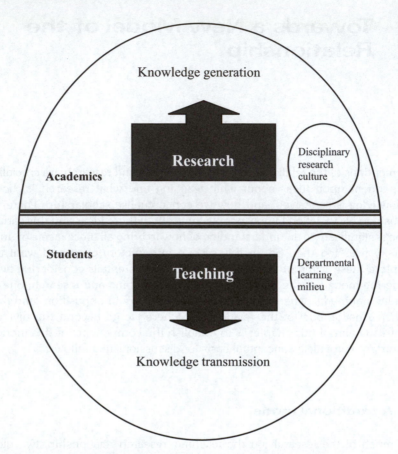

Figure 2.1   Model of the relationship between teaching and research
Source: A. Brew, 'Teaching and Research: New relationships and their implications
for inquiry-based teaching and learning in higher education', *Higher Education
Research and Development*, (2003) 22(1): 3–18.

pulling in opposite directions. The two lines in the middle of the diagram
represent the separation between the two. This separation tends to be
viewed in terms of the competition between time, resources and space for
research; and time, resources and space for teaching (see, for example,
Serow 2000).

While this model describes well the relationship between teaching and
research as it is conventionally conceived, as soon as we begin to unpack
what we understand by the terms 'teaching' and 'research', it becomes problematic because the model presupposes particular views of teaching and of
research and leaves out other important conceptions.

▶ Views of teaching and of research

On the basis of their research into how higher education teachers experience, understand and approach their teaching, Prosser and Trigwell (1999) distinguish between, on the one hand, an approach to teaching with an intention to transfer information from the syllabus to students, with a teaching strategy where the teacher is the focal point and, on the other, an approach to teaching with an intention to change the students' experiences of the phenomena of their study, which is associated with an emphasis on the student as central. They call the first approach an 'information transmission/teacher-focused' approach to teaching. They call the second, a 'conceptual change/student-focused' approach to teaching.

The sharp separation between knowledge generation and knowledge transmission in the above model is an indication that it is founded upon an information transmission/teacher focused approach to teaching. Prosser and Trigwell (1999: 143) suggest that in this approach the teacher's awareness is only on themselves and what they are doing, whereas in the student-focused/conceptual change approach, the teacher's awareness has been expanded to include, in addition to themselves, the students and how they are learning.

Importantly, it has been argued that these approaches have been found to be related to students' approaches to learning in that an 'information transmission/teacher-focused' approach to teaching has been associated with a *surface* approach to learning, and that of a conceptual change/student-focused approach to teaching with a *deep* approach to learning (Trigwell, Prosser and Waterhouse 1999). We shall see throughout this book that these different approaches to teaching have different consequences for how teaching and research can be brought together.

Work to establish how experienced academic researchers experience and understand the nature of research (Brew 2001b) has differentiated two key dimensions of variation. These are also important to considerations of the relationship between research and teaching. In some views of research there is an orientation towards external products and an intention to produce an outcome, such as, for example, a publication, a new drug or a robotic arm. Others focus on internal processes with an intention to understand, for example, the data, or to make sense of a newly discovered phenomenon or some experimental results. This work also distinguished between views of research where the researcher was as if absent from, or incidental to, their awareness, that is, not a focus of attention when talking of research, and others where the person of the researcher was foregrounded in ideas about the nature of research (Brew 2001b). The relationships between these different dimensions are shown in Table 2.1.

Table 2.1 Relationships between conceptions of research

Research is oriented towards	Research aims to	The researcher is present to, or a primary focus of, attention	The researcher is not a focus of attention
external products	produce an outcome	Trading view	Domino view
internal processes	understand	Journey view	Layer view

Source: A. Brew, 'Teaching and Research: New relationships and their implications for inquiry-based teaching and learning in higher education', *Higher Education Research and Development*, (2003) 22(1): 3–18.

So, for example, in the trading view, research is focused externally on a kind of social marketplace where there is a lot of interaction between people and where the exchange of products (research papers, grant applications, reputation, etc.) takes place. In the domino view, research is focused again on external products but here the process is viewed as synthesising a number of separate elements (tools, techniques, experiments, readings, etc.) to solve problems, to answer or to open up questions or to create an object. The layer view, in contrast, focuses on internal processes of discovering, uncovering or creating underlying meanings from data. In the journey view research is considered as if it were a personal journey of discovery, possibly leading to personal transformation, so it looks inward to the ideas of the person (Brew 2001b).

The person of the researcher occupies a central place in the trading and the journey views of research, but the focus in each is different. In the trading view it is the career of the researcher, their reputation and how it is growing that is the focus of attention. In the journey view, in the centre of a researcher's awareness are the personal issues and dilemmas that perplex them, and how these concerns relate to the disciplinary issues that are the subjects of the research. In the layer and domino views of research the person of the researcher is not a focus of attention; the researcher's presence is simply assumed.

Looking back to our traditional model of the relationship between teaching and research in Figure 2.1, we can deduce that the views of research which underpin this model are those focused on the solving of problems or the understanding of data and where the person of the researcher is not a focus of attention (the domino and layer views). Indeed, in this model the persona of the researcher is separate from their persona as a teacher inhabiting a separate domain from the students. The model leaves out views of research as a social phenomenon (the trading view). It also fails to consider views of research where the researcher, their career and their personal questions and issues are a focus of attention (the journey view).

These different views about what research is and how it is conducted, and about the nature and approaches to teaching to be adopted, have different consequences for how academics view the relationship between teaching and research. As we shall see in Chapter 3, possibilities for the development of different ways in which research and teaching can be brought together are enhanced or inhibited by these differing understandings. So we need a model of the relationship between teaching and research that can accommodate a wider range of experiences and understandings of the nature of research, including those that focus upon the personal and the social, and we need a model that encompasses more student-focused approaches to teaching.

▶ Knowledge

However, before developing such a new model, we need to examine the underlying assumptions about the nature of knowledge embodied in the traditional model in Figure 2.1, and we need to have some understanding of related views of learning and scholarship for these are also central both to questions about research and about teaching (Elton 1992; Brew and Boud 1995).

An information–transmission approach to teaching implies that knowledge is information to be transmitted. An Enlightenment objectivist conception of knowledge is therefore pre-supposed. Knowledge is viewed as 'absolute, specialised and unrelated to wider perspectives or experiences of life' (Rowland 1996: 15). From this perspective, the knowledge that is built through research is similarly viewed as objective and separate from the researchers who generated it.

It is true that traditional forms of higher education teaching include project work, assignments, tutorial discussions and practical work, all of which involve students in developing their personal understanding. However, as we have seen in relation to different approaches to teaching, there is a difference in how these are viewed. An information-transmission approach to teaching includes the idea that knowledge can be transferred from one individual to another. Prosser and Trigwell differentiate two variations within this approach: a teacher-focused strategy with the intention of transmitting information to students where:

the focus is on facts and skills, but not on the relationships between them. The prior knowledge of students is not considered to be important and it is assumed that students do not need to be active in the teaching–learning process.

(Prosser and Trigwell 1999: 153)

and a teacher-focused strategy with the intention that students acquire the concepts of the discipline:

> This approach is one in which the teachers adopt a teacher-focused strategy, with the intention of helping their students acquire the concepts of the discipline and the relationships between them. They assume, however, that their students can gain these concepts by being told about the concepts and their relationships. . . . they do not seem to assume that their students need to be active for the teaching-learning process to be successful.
>
> (Prosser and Trigwell 1999: 153)

The epistemology embodied in these ways of approaching teaching is widely infused throughout higher education teaching practice even though we know theoretically that ideas about knowledge have changed. Indeed there is a well-articulated view that knowledge is in crisis (see, for example, Barnett and Griffin 1997). Traditionally, university research defined what knowledge was and contributed the most to the stock of knowledge which it was thought we were building up. However, most knowledge is not now produced in universities and the generation of knowledge is no longer the sole preserve of university academics. Questions both of who owns knowledge and who defines it have become controversial.

Gibbons and colleagues (1994) distinguish between what they call 'Mode 1 knowledge', which is the traditional idea of disciplinary knowledge generated in universities, and 'Mode 2 knowledge', which is generated in practice and which, they argue, has now become a significant force in society. Society is characterised by what Nowotny, Scott and Gibbons (2001) describe as 'Mode-2ishness'. This derives from the similarities between what Gibbons and colleagues (1994) called Mode 2 knowledge production and the growth of complexity and uncertainty in various aspects of society, including politics and the economy. Science and technology are intimately implicated within what they call 'Mode 2' society, rather than being, as traditionally described, merely an outside contributor. Mode 2 society arises not through the existence of any one causal dimension of late modernity such as the dominance of the 'market', or through the pervasive use of communication technologies, or globalisation. It arises, they argue, through a number of processes underlying any or all of these dimensions: the generation of uncertainties, new kinds of economic rationality (for example, what is likely to be funded), the role of expectations (the future being viewed as an extension of the present), and what they call the 'flexibilisation' of distance (both physical and social).

A fifth important co-evolutionary process is the development of increasingly flexible and permeable social structures with a capacity for self-organisation. Mode 2 knowledge is trans-disciplinary, distributed over many sites of knowledge production and applied in numerous different contexts including business and industry. Theoretical knowledge, which is the traditional pre-serve of universities, has been subject to attack in favour of knowledge which can be of practical use. There is now, Gibbons and colleagues argue, a dynamic and intimate interplay between knowledge generated inside and that produced outside of the academy.

But the crisis in ideas about knowledge is not just about where knowledge is generated. It also and importantly arises from critical questioning of our ideas about what knowledge *is*. The traditional realist view of knowledge has come under attack from theorists who emphasise views of knowledge as 'ten-tative, open to reinterpretation or containing insights which can be applied more widely', which are likely to stimulate the lecturer's research when pre-sented to students (Rowland 1996: 15). Indeed, the most significant theoreti-cal influence on teaching practice in higher education over the past thirty years or so has been the move from a realist to an interpretive view of the nature of knowledge. We now know that knowledge is context bound, that it is defined by particular communities and that it gives expression to the inter-ests of powerful groups. We know that knowledge is individually and socially constructed within social groups and that it has an ambiguous and philoso-phically problematic relationship with what we traditionally call 'reality'. New conceptualisations of knowledge emphasise as primary, not objective knowl-edge, but the subjective and inter-subjective processes of individuals engaged in knowledge generation and understanding. It is a dialectical pro-cess of negotiation and communication within what Lave and Wenger (1993) call 'communities of practice'.

A move towards more pluralistic views of knowledge which take account of the interpretive nature of academic work means that research and teaching have the potential to be viewed as symbiotically related. Biggs (1996) argues that the most significant impact on teaching practice in higher education over the past thirty years or so has been the shift to viewing learning as a process of construction; as being about creating knowledge rather than simply absorb-ing it. Here the learner is viewed as developing a personal understanding of a phenomenon, building on pre-existing ideas by interacting with conceptions within the literature, ideas presented by teachers and others and by personal experience. As we shall see in Chapter 4, there is an increasing emphasis on encouraging students to take more responsibility, to become autonomous, independent learners. The emphasis on learning to learn and on reflective practice are all rational responses to understandings of the nature of knowl-edge as constructed within a socio-political context. Teachers and students increasingly hold beliefs about the nature of knowledge more consistent with Perry's (1999) concept of 'commitment in relativism'. Thus we are increasingly seeing teaching which is student-centred, negotiated, discursive and reflexive. A view of knowledge as built up in communicative acts implies a shift from an emphasis on teaching towards an emphasis on the facilitation of learning. This interpretive framework is embodied in Prosser and Trigwell's (1999) student-focused conceptual change approach to teaching. This draws attention to the way teaching takes account of how individuals develop their understandings and what understandings they develop (see, for example, Entwistle 1997; Marton, Hounsell and Entwistle 1997). Learning always takes place in a particular social and intellectual context and influences and is influenced by that context (Marton et al. 1997). It always takes place within a cultural tradition of knowledge much of which is derived from past research. The expectation is that students' understandings will, at least in some measure, reflect socially accepted understandings of the phenomenon. They represent a marriage between conceptions of a phenomenon which come from outside the learner and those emanating from within (Brew 1993).

Once we begin to see knowledge generation, learning and teaching in constructivist terms, we are led to ask questions about how that construction takes place. Such questions move us away from a focus on the individual teacher or learner, to viewing the teaching–learning process as a social phenomenon. Models of how individuals learn become subservient to questions about how they learn within social contexts.

While, as we have seen, some ways in which research is understood neglect to consider the persons doing the research and view research, as Feyerabend (1978) indicated, as if no human hands were involved in it, there is no doubt that the activities of research are carried out in social contexts. The proximity of other researchers and the ways in which they relate clearly vary according to the subject area (Becher and Trowler 2001). Nevertheless, research is a social process. Researchers make meaning; make sense of chaotic ideas, data and findings, and translate them into culturally accepted explanations in social groups, notwithstanding the power issues within such groups (see, for example, Watson 1969; Spanier 1995). Dominant interpretations then become the way in which society makes sense of particular phenomena.

In the process of sense making, and what Bereiter (2002) calls 'knowledge-building', researchers develop their personal understanding of the phenomena of their investigation, that is, they learn. Research thus provides ways in which individuals develop deep approaches to learning. Deep approaches to learning are about making personal meaning within socially accepted and culturally defined definitions. The emphasis is on understanding rather than on memorising and application. We now know from a body of literature examining teaching and learning in higher education that good teaching is defined as developing deep approaches to learning (Ramsden 2003a). So we can see immediately that engaging students in research is one way to do this. We shall see in Chapters 4 and 5 a number of cases where this is being done and Chapter 8 will explore the links between research and learning more fully.

Yet, as soon as we say that students should engage in research as a way of developing deep approaches to their learning, we are linking deep approaches to learning (conventionally conceived as an individual phenomenon) with engaging in cultural practices (i.e., a social phenomenon). Indeed, we inevitably move towards sociological understandings of the nature of learning as a dialectical relationship between individual, community and ideas. In this situation, Bereiter's concept of knowledge building provides a useful link between the personal and the social. Learning is an individual process, which may result from knowledge building as well as from other experiences of life but knowledge building, he argues, is a shared process. We look more closely at knowledge building in Chapter 5.

▶ Scholarship

These ideas move us away from the traditional model of the relationship between teaching and research towards a more discursive and collaborative one. However, before we can establish such a model, there is another element in the picture which provides additional glue binding research and teaching activities; namely, scholarship (Elton 1986, 1992).

> research and academic teaching are indivisible because – but also only just so long as – they share with the scholarship which should feed into both alike that spirit of active enquiry which is higher education's *raison d'être*.
>
> (Westergaard 1991: 28)

The ideal of the scholar is frequently associated with ideas about the essence of what universities are for. Scholarship is highly valued in higher education. It is therefore important to considerations of the relationship between teaching and research. Yet the concept of scholarship is shown to have a wide range of meanings and there is a good deal of confusion surrounding the concept. So how do academics think of scholarship and how are those ideas related to their ideas about teaching and research?

In the United States, unease about universities' role and mission in the 1980s and early 1990s centred around calls to redefine or to extend the concept of scholarship to incorporate both research and teaching. (See, for example, Boyer 1990; Rice 1992; Scott and Awbrey 1993).

Not only do our institutions have diverse missions – commitments to serving a wide range of scholarly needs within region, states and action – but also there is the special commitment to the education of an increasingly diverse population, to the intellectual preparation of the educated citizenry necessary for making a genuinely democratic society possible. Scholarship in this context takes on broader meaning.

(Rice 1992:128)

In America it was argued that in the changing context and climate of universities and their changed relationship to society, research had increasingly come to be viewed narrowly, in terms of publication of fundamental knowledge based on technical rationality (Rice 1992; Scott and Awbrey 1993; Schön 1995). Concern about the status of teaching *vis à vis* research arose from this (see, for example, Ruscio 1987; Leatherman 1990; Mooney 1990). As we pointed out in Chapter 1, research and teaching present an asymmetrical relationship because research embodies greater academic and social capital. Indeed, there was a very real concern in the United States about the different ways in which research and teaching were being rewarded in higher education. Boyer and colleagues (1990), in what was then the Carnegie Foundation for the Advancement of Teaching, suggested that: 'The most important obligation now confronting colleges and universities is to break out of the tired old teaching versus research debate and define, in more creative ways, what it means to be a scholar' (Boyer 1990: xii).

From their investigations into undergraduate education, they provided a framework suggesting a fourfold definition which, they argued, corresponded to different approaches to the ways knowledge is perceived and approached: the advancement of knowledge, its application, representation and integration in society (Brew 2001a). In their framework, research, scholarship, academic teaching and learning were all viewed as part of the same enterprise. The scholarship of discovery, Boyer (1990) suggested, came nearest to the idea of 'research'. It contributed to the 'stock of human knowledge' and also to the intellectual climate of the institution. The scholarship of integration was focused on making inter-disciplinary connections, interpreting and drawing out new ideas to contribute to original research (Boyer 1990: 19).

The third type of scholarship defined by Boyer and his colleagues was the scholarship of application. This drew attention to the way knowledge was applied in the wider community and envisaged an interaction between theory and practice where 'the one renews the other' (Boyer 1990: 23). Boyer (1996) subsequently called this the 'scholarship of engagement'. Finally, there was the scholarship of teaching. Consistent with the intentions of the Carnegie Foundation, yet drawing on Bourdieu's ideas, Nicholls (2004) argues that the concept of the scholarship of teaching is an attempt to give teaching symbolic capital, raising its status by aligning it with the scholarship that has high status. The scholarship of teaching was defined as well-informed teachers; teaching which was carefully planned, continuously evaluated and related to the subject taught; teaching which encouraged active learning and encouraged students to be critical, creative thinkers with the capacity to go on learning after their university days were over; and a recognition that teachers were also learners (Boyer 1990: 24). We shall see in Chapter 6 subsequent developments in the idea of the scholarship of teaching as initially discussed by Boyer, and Chapter 7 will examine what is involved for higher education teachers engaging in the critical investigation of their teaching that is implied by the scholarship of teaching and learning.

One of the effects of the Boyer framework is to separate out interrelated activities. There is then a problem of relating them back again. For, in spite of admonitions that all four scholarships need to be viewed together (see, for example, Healey 2000, Rice 2004), a tradition of discussing the scholarship of teaching has grown up independently of the other three of the Boyer scholarships in spite of a number of attempts to interrelate different conceptions. Paulsen and Feldman (1995) attempted to integrate different components of scholarship by taking a sociological perspective examining scholarship in terms of Talcott Parsons's four-function analysis. The scholarship of research and graduate training, they argued, performed the function of pattern maintenance in the 'scholarship action system' (Paulsen and Feldman 1995: 623); the scholarship of teaching performed the function of adaptation; the scholarship of service performed the goal-attainment function; and the scholarship of academic citizenship performed the function of integration for the overall scholarship action system. Comparing these four functions of scholarship with Boyer's (1990) framework, Paulsen and Feldman (1995) admitted that three of the categories were similar, but they argued that Boyer's scholarship of integration properly belonged within the scholarship of discovery, or in their terms, the scholarship of research and graduate training. The function of integration was performed, in their view, not by disciplinary integration. Rather, if the overall scholarship action system was to survive and remain effective, then the scholarship of academic citizenship was required. This, they argued, was missing from Boyer's framework (Paulsen and Feldman 1995; see also Brew 2001a: 44).

This work stresses the social interdependence of different definitions of scholarship. Indeed, this American literature uses the concept of scholarship to describe what those in some other countries, for example, Australia and the United Kingdom, would generally refer to as aspects of academic work; not necessarily scholarship. The US literature has suggested a wide range of traditional teaching, research and community service activities as important constituents of university scholarship (Paulsen and Feldman 1995). In contrast, in the Australian and UK contexts, in policy documents on research or promotions criteria, the phrase 'research and scholarship' is frequently used without qualification or explanation, and this American literature has been found helpful in identifying differences. However, to understand what academics in other countries understand by the concept of scholarship we have to look elsewhere.

In my study of Australian senior researchers' views of research, interviewees were asked to indicate what they thought scholarship was and how it related to research. From this data, five different ways in which these academics experienced and understood scholarship were identified (Brew 1999b). (See Table 2.2.)

Elton (1986, 1992) defines scholarship as the interpretation of what is already known; the primary work that feeds into everything else academics are supposed to do. He suggests that scholarship applies to, is necessary for, and supports good research and good teaching. Nicholls' (2004) study of the views of UK academics similarly identifies the production and

Table 2.2   Dimensions of conceptions of scholarship

Preparation view	Scholarship is interpreted as the preparation for research including reading background literature. This provides a context for the research.
Creating view	Scholarship is interpreted as the preparation for research including reading background literature which provides a context for the research but also includes the process of adding new knowledge to the existing literature.
Integrating view	Preparation and the addition of new knowledge are part of scholarship but scholarship is also interpreted as the process of making a contribution to society through the integration and dissemination of ideas and knowledge, for example through teaching and publication.
Quality view	Scholarship is interpreted as the way academics demonstrate professionalism through attention to detail, logic and critical thinking. Scholarship refers to the rigour and meticulousness of academic work. It includes possessing specific disciplinary-based skills and knowledge of specialist techniques to carry out work in a professional manner.
Research view	The concept of scholarship is interpreted as not making any sense on its own. It is viewed as synonymous with research and not a useful concept.

Source: A. Brew, 'Teaching and Research: New relationships and their implications for inquiry-based teaching and learning in higher education,' *Higher Education Research and Development*, (2003) 22(1): 3–18.

communication of new knowledge as key aspects of how academics understood the term 'scholarship'. These views capture the essence of the *preparation, creating* and *integrating* views of scholarship. These each share a basic orientation to key activities designated as scholarship with increasing complexity as one moves from preparation to creating to integrating, each view incorporating the activities foregrounded in the previous less complex one. The *creating view* includes the idea of preparation but adds the activity of finding new knowledge; the *integrating view* includes preparation and finding new knowledge but adds the dissemination activities. There are clearly some disciplinary differences in where the emphasis is placed within different views of scholarship. Nicholls recently found that:

> In Law scholarship was connected both to advocacy and practice, i.e. what Law does and the study of Law. . . . In Management scholarship was perceived differently from research but included research. Scholarship was seen as facilitating the engagement with ideas and being creative in the formulation of new and dynamic alternatives to established methodologies and processes. In the Health and Life Sciences equating scholarship to academic excellence that reflects depth of knowledge in understanding in a particular field was a recurring theme. In the Health and Life Sciences, as with Medicine, scholarship related to the ability to solve problems, discover new treatments/processes and disseminate such findings to peers. Peer acceptance was a dominant factor of scholarship. Understanding the need for process such as the experimental method and the equivalent need to exemplify the process, was a high prerequisite of scholarship in the scientific discipline domain.
>
> (Nicholls 2004: 39)

These views focus both on specific activities defined as scholarship and also on what I have called the *quality view*. This view is quite distinct. It relates, not to what is done, that is, to particular activities, but rather to the way things are done. In the *quality view*, scholarship describes the professional way in which academics work. This view is aligned with Neumann's (1993) suggestion that scholarship includes the idea of a quality describing the way research should be done. There is also some overlap here with activities Sundre (1992: 311) grouped as 'faculty members' professional characteristics and orientations'. The idea of professionalism is central to the quality view.

When they do academic work, there are some standards academics try to adhere to; things like being rigorous in reporting findings or experimental results. This refers to the qualities of meticulousness and rigour associated with academic reporting: for example, making sure footnotes are accurate and that all statements can be substantiated. It means making sure appropriate references to ideas quoted are given. It means not arguing more than data or results can claim and so on.

When you say scholarship, in my mind, that puts it on a bit of a higher plane and ... makes it sound as though we are ... really trying to be very thorough and very careful.

(senior researcher interviewee)

The quality view of scholarship also includes an emphasis on having the skills, knowledge and techniques to enable effective practice as a professional within a specific disciplinary domain. This view is holistic in that it can be applied to all of the activities mentioned as components of other views of scholarship.

No matter what profession students are being educated for, no matter what they do after they graduate, this quality of academic professionalism is a key attribute that will prepare them for a life of complex decision making (often in the face of incomplete factual information). In emphasising clarity, it is in some ways diametrically opposed to the *research view*. This latter view demonstrates the not inconsiderable confusion surrounding the concept of scholarship.

I have spent some time discussing ideas about what academics think constitutes scholarship because they are important to considerations of the relationship between teaching and research, and, specifically, they are crucial to an understanding of how and why we should bring them together to enhance students' learning.

Scholarship does not figure explicitly in the earlier model of the relationship between teaching and research where they inhabit separate domains. Yet clearly, we need to take it into account. Attempts to redefine scholarship, as we have seen, arise in part because of a concern that teaching and research have been differently rewarded. Redressing that balance, through a focus on an element they appear to have in common (i.e., scholarship) would locate scholarship both as an element within the disciplinary research culture and also within the departmental learning milieu. However, the focus in the work on scholarship that I have sketched above is always on scholarship as a function of the academics. It is viewed in individualistic terms as the ways in which academics function with the norms of professionalism directing what they do. The social context in which scholarship is pursued, however, is also important. Scholarship is not an individual activity. Even the view of the lone scholar, which characterises the stereotypical view of the humanities academic, needs to take account of the social context in which that person operates. The ways in which this context impinges upon scholarly work needs to be recognised.

Interestingly, what is called scholarship when applied to academics, tends to be relegated to the domain of 'study skills', 'generic skills' or 'graduate attributes' when applied to students. Much of undergraduate education is designed to encourage students to take on the mores of the academic professional: to write in a way consistent with the norms of the disciplinary area; to thoroughly investigate the literature; to develop the skills and techniques necessary to carry out rigorous investigations within a particular subject domain; to explore ideas and to behave in ethical and professional ways. Such behaviour exhibited by academics is recognisable as scholarship viewed as a quality of the way things are or should be done.

What this tells us about our model of the relationship between teaching and research, therefore, is that the concept of scholarship is as applicable to students as to academics. We are all in the process of developing academic professionalism. The new model needs to take this into account.

▶ A new model

The old model of the relationship between teaching and research was essentially a static one, focused on the individualistic actions and assumptions of academics. The new model, in contrast, is dynamic, focused on the socially related meaning-making processes of all participants as learners and knowledge-builders whether they are students or academics. The new model (Figure 2.2) is presented as a hexagon with radiating lines suggesting a network or a series of interwoven, overlapping elements. It is fluid so the lines are insubstantial. It can be interpreted at the individual, group or institutional level. So, for example, an individual may ask: 'How can my experience of higher education be developed to be like this model?' A group may ask: 'How can we ensure that our group works like this? A university may consider the model as a guide to how institutional policies and strategies for integrating teaching and research might be developed.

As well as expanded definitions of academic professionalism and scholarship, the new model has to take account of the shift towards inquiry or research-based modes of teaching and learning. It has to take account of views of knowledge as diffuse, constructed through communication and negotiation in social contexts. Our new model also has to be based on approaches to teaching focused on students. As well as the two different variations of the teacher-focused approach considered earlier in this chapter, Prosser and Trigwell (1999) specify two variations of a student-focused approach to teaching: one in which students should acquire the concepts of the discipline through engaging actively in the teaching and learning process, the other which is aimed at students developing and changing their conceptions, where:

> teachers adopt a student-focused strategy to help their students change their world views or conceptions of the phenomena they are studying . . . students are seen to have to construct their own knowledge, and so the

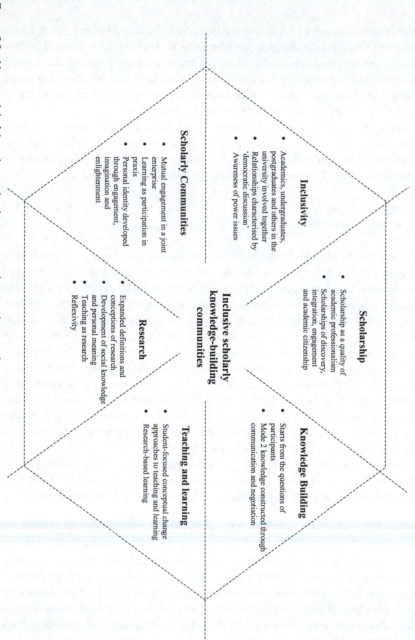

Inclusivity

- Academics, undergraduates, postgraduates and others in the university involved together
- Relationships characterised by 'democratic discussion'
- Awareness of power issues

Scholarship

- Scholarship as a quality of academic professionalism
- Scholarships of discovery, integration, engagement and academic citizenship

Scholarly Communities

- Mutual engagement in a joint enterprise
- Learning as participation in praxis
- Personal identity developed through engagement, imagination and enlightenment

Inclusive scholarly knowledge-building communities

Research

- Expanded definitions and conceptions of research
- Development of social knowledge and personal meaning
- Teaching as research
- Reflexivity

Knowledge Building

- Starts from the questions of participants
- Mode 2 knowledge constructed through communication and negotiation

Teaching and learning

- Student-focused conceptual change approaches to teaching and learning
- Research-based learning

Figure 2.2   New model of the relationship between teaching and research

teacher has to focus on what the students are doing in the teaching–learning situation. A student-focused strategy is assumed to be necessary because it is the students who have to reconstruct their knowledge to produce a new world view or conception. The teacher understands that he/she cannot transmit a new world view or conception to the students.

> (Trigwell, Prosser and Taylor 1994, quoted in Prosser and Trigwell 1999: 154)

It is this conception of teaching that needs to be embedded in the new model. However, as I suggested in Chapter 1, in considering a new model for the relationship between teaching and research we have to consider the social context of the educational process.

▶ Scholarly communities

Lave and Wenger (1993) argue that learning needs to be seen as a social practice. It consists of what they refer to as legitimate peripheral participation in communities of practice:

> A community of practice is a set of relations among persons, activity and world over time and in relation with other tangential and overlapping communities of practice.
>
> (Lave and Wenger 1993: 98)

They are 'informal groups of people that are contextually bound in a work situation applying a common competence in the pursuit of a common enterprise' (Schenkel 2002). As suggested in Chapter 1, individuals' social identities are forged and are tied up with their communities of practice (Wenger 1998; Roth 2003). Wenger describes 14 indicators of communities of practice:

1. sustained mutual relationships – harmonious or conflictual;
2. shared ways of engaging in doing things together;
3. rapid flow of information and propagation of innovation;
4. absence of introductory preambles, as if conversations and interactions were merely the continuation of an ongoing process;
5. quick setup of a problem to be discussed;
6. substantial overlap in participants' descriptions of who belongs;
7. knowing what others know, what they can do and how they can contribute to an enterprise;
8. mutually defining identities;
9. ability to assess the appropriateness of actions and products;

10. specific tools, representations and other artefacts;
11. local lore, shared stories, inside jokes, knowing laughter;
12. jargon and shortcuts to communication as well as the ease of producing new ones;
13. certain styles recognised as displaying membership;
14. a shared discourse reflecting a certain perspective on the world.

(Wenger, 1998: 125)

These indicators essentially involve mutual engagement in a joint enterprise with a shared repertoire, that is, shared ways of doing things, shared arte-facts and vocabulary, etc. (Schenkel 2002). The concept of communities of practice arose from studies of apprenticeships and is frequently associated with pre-existing relatively cohesive work groups with shared norms and practices. A common purpose is what binds the group together (Wenger 1998). However, the term has more recently come to be associated with informal, sometimes loosely coupled networks and groupings where the emphasis is on solving particular problems which may come in and out of being as the needs of problem-solutions demands (Wenger 1998). Some communities are relatively stable and exist over a long period of time. Others are more fleeting.

I have suggested that there is a need for scholarly communities to be 'inclu-sive'. There are several elements to the way I am using this term. First, inclu-sive means being involved. The idea here is of having permission to participate and/or initiate. In order for this to happen the other participants have to be 'allowing' in the sense of listening and respecting the contribu-tions of others. Second, participation needs to be as an equal. I do not mean that everyone is equal in the sense of having equal skills and knowledge. Clearly, different members of any community will inevitably bring different skills and knowledge, and at different levels. My concept of equality here is about treating individuals as fully participating human beings with things to contribute as well as things to learn. So this involves continually being aware of the power issues that serve to undermine the contributions of others. It also means exercising humility with respect to one's own views (Brookfield and Preskill 1999). Third, it involves democracy in the sense in which Dewey used the term, where education is about nurturing human growth and devel-opment. Democracy defines the quality of participation and leads to the development of collective wisdom (Brookfield and Preskill 1999).

In the old model of the teaching–research relationship (Figure 2.1), the dominant conception of knowledge was Mode 1 knowledge. In the new model, knowledge needs to be viewed as a process of construction in a vari-ety of contexts; Gibbons and colleagues' (1994) Mode 2 knowledge, which is created as much outside universities as within them. The emphasis in cur-riculum approaches in this model would be on the construction rather than the imparting of knowledge; encouraging a deep approach to learning and involving students in artistic and scientific production, emphasising uncertainty; in other words, in engaging students in inquiry. Conceptions of research to the fore here are those oriented towards understanding and the development of meaning. The researcher would be in the focus of awareness, for research in this model would include the growth not just of socially useful knowledge but also of personal meaning. Scholarship, as we have seen, would be viewed not simply as a set of activities, but as the quality of the way academic work is professionally done for both students and faculty academics.

The development of such inclusive academic communities where both students and academics engage could not take place without the relationships between students and their teachers changing and this is where we hit a snag. Students are not simply apprentices in this model; rather, they are viewed as equal partners bringing different levels of knowledge and understanding to it. A radical reconceptualization of higher education is implicated (Brew 2003b).

However, such a view does not take account of the asymmetrical power relationship between teachers and students highlighted by Bourdieu (Bourdieu and Passeron 1977; Bourdieu 1998). Academics have accumulated more academic capital and therefore have the power to cause 'symbolic violence'; that is, the power to impose meanings (Bourdieu and Passeron 1977) and exhort submission while at the same time masking the power issues that make such action possible (Bourdieu 1998).

For Bourdieu and Wacquant (1992) possibilities for change rest on the development of reflexivity, where reflexivity refers to the turning in of sociology upon itself. Research communities, by examining the unconscious social and intellectual processes embedded within practice, can surface the underlying assumptions, mores and values of such practice and this provides the possibility for transformation. We shall see in Chapter 7 how developing the scholarship of teaching and learning in academics and in students, in turn develops such a reflexive critique, opening up the possibility for transformation of the academic environment and creating the conditions for the establishment of inclusive scholarly knowledge-building communities such as I have described.

▶ Conclusion

The scene is now set. In Chapter 1 we examined the higher education context and some of the dilemmas facing those who would seek to transcend the divide between research and teaching in a mass higher education system which has raised some fundamental questions about universities' ability to sustain both research and teaching. I suggested that students need to learn to engage in research if they are to be prepared for an uncertain and super-complex future.

In this chapter a discussion of different conceptions of research, scholarship, teaching and knowledge has provided a basis for presenting two alternative models to explain the relationship between teaching and research in a changing higher education context, in order to take account of these different understandings. I have argued that a model which views teaching, learning, research and scholarship as social processes within inclusive scholarly communities can best be used to guide how we can bring research and teaching closer together to enhance both in the current context.

In the remainder of the book we will examine the challenges that need to be addressed for this model to become a viable reality and explore possibilities for overcoming factors that militate against it.

Part 2

The Domains of Research-Enhanced Education

It should now be clear that what academics think research is and how they perceive and approach their teaching are going to affect what they do if they want to bring research and teaching together. It should also be clear that if they had a different view of teaching and a different view of what research is, then they might do different things to bring research and teaching together.

There are a number of terms used to describe the bringing of teaching and research together to enhance learning and teaching and lots of initiatives to do this. These are the subject of this section. Such initiatives are sometimes referred to as research-enhanced or research-based education, sometimes as research-led teaching, but other terms are in common usage, for example, research-informed teaching, research-aligned teaching, research-enhanced teaching. Alternatively the focus may be on learning. Terms used might be research-led learning or research-based learning or research-informed learning. I want now to explore what we mean by these terms through a series of cases or examples where there is an attempt to integrate research and teaching in the curriculum.

I am not concerned here with what might be called teaching-led research. This refers, in contrast, to the influence of teaching on research. We come to that in Part 3, when we go beyond learning and teaching agendas to look at other dimensions of the research–teaching relationship.

Before that, in this section my concern is to examine different facets of research-enhanced teaching and learning and its assumptions, how it manifests itself in different curricula, the issues in its development and the contextual issues that shape it; in other words, all the different domains of teaching activities where research can inform and enhance educational experiences. I want to present a number of instances that I have come across in my travels where teachers are attempting to integrate research and teaching because I think these give a good flavour of what I have come to understand as research-enhanced education. I have had lots of interesting conversations with people about what they are doing and so I report some of those conversations. Through examining different examples in this section, we see how the different ideas about research, teaching, scholarship and knowledge that were discussed in Chapter 2 play out in the different areas where academics are able to integrate research and teaching. These domains include how academics prepare for teaching and learning, what they actually do in the classroom, how they reflect on what they have done, and how they learn about how to improve their teaching.

As we look at these different cases we shall note the extent to which students engage in the same or different worlds as their teachers. I have called Chapter 4 'Student engagement with research: at arm's length' and Chapter 5 'Student engagement with research: embraced into a community of researchers' because, as I said, we go from limited to fuller integration of research and teaching with the ultimate goal of developing inclusive scholarly knowledge-building communities.

I want to stress again that my primary focus is on undergraduates because I believe that presents the greatest challenges for us. If we are to develop inclusive scholarly knowledge-building communities we need to involve both undergraduates and postgraduates in the world of academic research. So I want to share some examples where this is being done. I include cases from a wide range of disciplinary areas and different levels of undergraduate education as well as large and small group teaching.

The focus in Chapters 4 and 5, then, is on cases where disciplinary research is being integrated into the education process in some way. This does not include examples of people doing research on their teaching; that is, engaging in the scholarship of teaching and learning. We come to a discussion of this in Chapters 6 and 7. In Chapter 6 I discuss some models that help us to understand different aspects of the scholarship of teaching and learning and in Chapter 7 look at the practicalities of engaging academics in learning how to research their teaching as a way of getting them to engage with critical reflection on learning and teaching. I am interested in how students can be involved in the scholarship of teaching and learning too. I want to suggest that all should be involved in critically reflecting on the teaching and the students' learning, and that ultimately this is what can lead to new ideas about higher education.

In Part 3 I return to the contextual factors that impinge upon ideas of research and teaching when I put the teaching and learning strategies into departmental, university and wider contexts, and consider factors that assist or inhibit academics from integrating their research and their teaching.

3 The Appropriateness of Research-Enhanced Education

Having established the framework for educational experiences that will take us beyond the divide between teaching and research, the question now before us is how we can move towards the new model. Since academics are key to the development of higher education curricula, their views of what is possible are critical in this. What academics think research-led or research-enhanced teaching and learning are, and how and whether they think it should be applied in university courses; their views of the appropriateness of research-enhanced teaching for different students and different contexts, and how they think it should be done; the kind of teaching and learning activities they believe it is possible to develop; their views of students and what they are capable of; what they consider possible within a particular disciplinary or institutional context; as well as their views of teaching, research, knowledge and scholarship discussed in Chapter 2, all influence how and whether research and teaching are integrated.

So, in this chapter, I want to explore these different understandings, their implications for the implementation of a research-enhanced higher education and how and whether they facilitate or limit the extent to which the development of inclusive scholarly knowledge-building communities is possible. The chapter begins by looking at what academics understand by research-led teaching and then addresses the question of what undergraduate students are considered capable of. The chapter then examines how different views of research translate into different ways of integrating research and teaching, and, finally, considers the importance to the development of scholarly knowledge-building communities of developing a reflexive critique of educational aims and values. This paves the way for the discussion of the ways in which academics are integrating research and teaching in Chapters 4 and 5.

▶ What do academics understand by research-led teaching?

What is understood by research-led or research-enhanced teaching will determine whether and how an academic chooses to engage with it and whether they think it is appropriate in any given context. For several years I have been presenting seminars in a number of institutions in different countries. 'Research-led teaching' being the term in common usage in my own university, at each of these seminars, prior to talking about what I understand by research-led teaching, I have asked academics to write an example on a post-it note. Having collected some 220 examples, my colleague Henriikka Clarkeburn and I carried out an analysis of what academics understood by research-led teaching as demonstrated in the examples they had chosen. Figure 3.1 presents the results of this analysis. The categories came from the data.

Figure 3.1 shows a clear differentiation in ideas about research-led teaching that are focused on students engaging in research activities: 'learning through research'; and those where the students are an audience for research: 'presenting research to students'. It also reveals that a number of academics think the term 'research-led teaching' refers to the scholarship of teaching and learning; that is, research into their own teaching. In other words their examples are focused on pedagogical research and not on their own or their students' disciplinary research. A few post-it notes did not present examples, but instead included reflections on the concept of research-led teaching, such as:

'[An] unanswered question is whether the student performance is enhanced.'

'Is this just student-centred learning and teaching or research-led teaching? ... So what if it is the same thing. If it engages dyed in the wool researchers in learning and teaching it's got to be good.'

'The relationship between research and teaching is much like sin and confession, if you don't do the former, you won't have much of interest to say in the latter.'

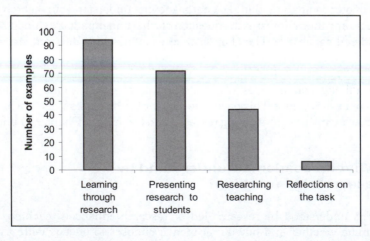

Figure 3.1   Academics' understandings of 'research-led teaching'

Approaches to teaching, according to Prosser and Trigwell (1999) are consistent with teaching intentions and experiences and understandings of teaching. The examples are differentiated, as I have indicated, according to whether students are an audience for research or are engaged in research activity (a distinction first made by Zamorski 2000). These approaches do not simply parallel notions of teacher-focused and student-focused approaches to teaching. Presenting research results to students is likely to be done through the medium of lectures or in web-based programmes and would normally be teacher-focused; that is, there would usually be an intention to transmit ideas or information to the students.

However, it does not follow that engaging students in research activity is automatically student focused. McKenzie (2004), in an extension of the Prosser and Trigwell (1999) model, distinguishes a teacher-focused approach to teaching where teaching is viewed as transmitting information to students, or organising explaining and demonstrating information for students to acquire disciplinary knowledge on the one hand, and, on the other, a teacher-focused approach to teaching where there is activity and interaction with and between the students with the intention of ensuring that they understand disciplinary concepts and techniques (McKenzie 2004: 4). This 'activity-based, teacher-focused' approach to teaching differs from a student-focused approach in that in the latter, students' understandings (including their prior understandings and misunderstandings) and the variation in their perspectives are taken into account. In the teacher-focused perspective, whether or not the students are engaged in activity, it is assumed that they will take on the disciplinary or the teachers' understandings.

The post-it note examples grouped together as 'learning through research' include both teacher-focused and student-focused activities. Clearly, these different understandings of the nature of teaching are important influences on what particular academics consider possible or desirable in relating research and teaching. We will examine examples of these different ways of viewing research-enhanced teaching in Chapters 4 and 5.

What is also interesting about the findings from the analysis of examples is that there were disciplinary differences with regard to how academics understood research-led teaching. The examples came from academics representing a number of disciplinary areas as demonstrated in Table 3.1.

There are clearly disciplinary differences in the extent to which examples were focused on engaging students in research activity (learning through research) and the presentation of research to students where students are an audience for research (Figure 3.2). In the education and humanities and social sciences areas, examples predominantly focused on learning through research, whereas in scientific and technological areas, while learning though research was clearly important, what dominated was the presentation of research to students. The examples are also distinguished by the

Table 3.1 A number of examples presented by discipline area

Disciplinary area	Number of examples
Education	43
Humanities, and social sciences (includes geography and law)	38
Medical and health related	20
Science and technology	72
Business and Management (includes accounting and economics)	42
Across university	5
TOTAL	*220*

numbers indicating that research-led teaching is perceived to be about carrying out research on teaching. For example, this is almost absent in the sciences and technology, but is the dominant view in the business and management area.

The relationship between the scholarship of teaching and learning (researching teaching) and research-led teaching is an intimate one. Research-led, or as I now prefer to call it, 'research-enhanced' teaching clearly includes both in the minds of academics. However, it is important to

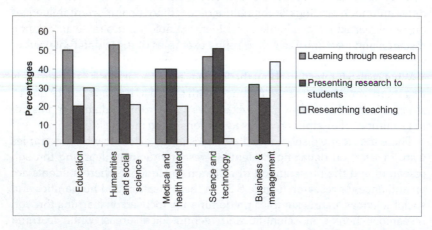

Figure 3.2 How academics from different disciplines view research-led teaching as exhibited by their examples

be aware of the distinction lest it be thought that research-enhanced teaching only involves the scholarship of teaching and learning or that it just includes aspects of disciplinary research used in teaching. At the University of Sydney, a working group consisting of representatives from all the faculties prepared a statement of what they understood by research-led teaching. Part of this statement clearly expresses this relationship:

> Research-led teaching refers to initiatives designed to bring the research and teaching functions of the university closer together. The aim is to enhance students' learning experiences by progressing the ways in which coursework teaching is informed by disciplinary-based research at all levels.
>
> Research-led teaching needs to be distinguished from the scholarship of teaching. Research-led teaching is about making our teaching and our students' learning more research focused in terms of what we wish our student to learn, while the scholarship of teaching is about drawing on and contributing to research and scholarship about the way we teach and learn within our disciplines.
>
> (University of Sydney 2004)

I believe that the development of inclusive scholarly knowledge-building communities depends on the development of both. Chapters 4 and 5 explore the integration of disciplinary research into teaching and Chapters 6 and 7 explore what is understood by the scholarship of teaching and learning more fully.

► Students and their learning

We turn now to another important area where academics' views are critical to the establishment of research-enhanced education: their views of students and their learning. The following is one of the many conversations I have had with groups of academics from different disciplinary areas:

> 'Surely students are engaging in research-led teaching every time they do an essay. They do this right from the first year. This is a normal part of teaching in the humanities. We've always been doing research-led teaching.'
>
> 'But you can't expect students to know how to do research right from the first year. They need to have a basis of knowledge before they can begin to inquire. In the final year, yes. Then they get to begin to do some real research. But you can't expect that at the early stages.'

'We do with our advanced engineering programme. The first years are given a problem, or they define a problem for themselves, and then they research it and set out to solve it.'

'Yes in the talented student programme that's different.'

'But you can't expect undergraduate students, I don't care what subject they're doing, you can't expect them to discover new knowledge. It just isn't feasible. They haven't learnt the techniques. They don't have access to the equipment.'

'The research we do is much too specialist to talk about at the junior levels. They don't have the basics. They wouldn't understand it.'

'Yet even first-year students can do an essay. We expect it. We assume they all know how to write an essay.'

Let us examine some of the assumptions being made here. There is a common view, particularly in the sciences, that research-enhanced teaching and learning is appropriate at the higher undergraduate levels and for post-graduates, but not in the early years except in the case of especially talented students. Zamorski found in her study that academics thought there was a relationship between students' intellectual maturation and the nature and amount of research they could or should be permitted to undertake. She found that this was related to their disciplinary area, concluding, 'such professional experience and beliefs impinged heavily on course design and pedagogy, and the role research-led teaching and learning was required or could be asked to play in them' (Zamorski 2002: 416). This assumption is seriously questioned by the fact that by the time students reach university, they have already had considerable experience in investigation, in project research and in inquiry-based learning at school. Indeed, Zamorski also found a good deal of evidence that academics' views on this were in contradiction to students' perceived expectations and desires.

Hierarchical institutional structures support and sustain the idea that knowledge is a staged process. Teaching students in year groups itself both reinforces and provides justification for a hierarchical view of knowledge. If, as I suggested in Chapter 1, research is viewed as a valued commodity; as a kind of reward for the 'submissive waiting' that Bourdieu (1988: 95) talks about, then it is possible to argue that undergraduates should not, indeed cannot, be involved in research in the early years. Yet this view is contested by the evidence. That students require to obtain a body of knowledge before they can progress has been demonstrably shown to be wanting in problem-based medical education, where realistic, authentic problems are set and the learning process is structured so that students are able to learn what is necessary to solve them.

There is plenty of evidence that given the right support and framing of questions, students – no matter what their level of education – can achieve a great deal through inquiry-based learning (Roth 2003). Indeed, it never ceases to amaze me that sometimes what academics say is impossible to do with university students appears to offer no difficulties to teachers of primary school children! (See, for example, Kellett, Forrest, Dent and Ward 2004; also http://childrens-research-centre.open.ac.uk.) As we shall see in Chapters 4 and 5 there are now numerous cases in many disciplines where students engage in some form of research right from the beginning of their university careers.

The idea that only talented students are capable of making the most of inquiry-based learning is often justified on the grounds that students are unable to create 'new' knowledge. But what do we mean by 'new'? There is a strong case to be made for students carrying out work which replicates well-established facts and theories. This requires a shift of thinking. According to Bereiter (2002), what is important is that students begin with their own questions. Often these are fundamental questions that relate to the world as the student experiences it. In interacting with others in the inquiry process, the student is able to integrate 'new' knowledge, that is, new for them, into their existing knowledge. There are some challenges in this when considering professional knowledge. However, Bereiter suggests it is the framing of situations in which the student is led to ask the necessary questions that creates the opportunity for them to develop their professional expertise (Bereiter 2002).

Another assumption that can limit thinking about how research-enhanced teaching might be developed, is the idea that 'we are doing it already'. It is true that there are currently many learning and teaching activities which lend themselves to being designated as aspects of research-led teaching. Student essays, laboratory work, field work, bibliographical exercises and project work, all in some sense involve students in research-based activities. However, research on students' views of research has shown that they often do not know how their work links with the research carried out in their institution (Jenkins, Blackman, Lindsay and Paton-Saltzberg 1998; Zamorski 2002). The challenge of exhortations to bring research and teaching together such as that contributed by Hattie and Marsh (1996) is, as I have argued above, to extend and make more explicit current ways of engaging students in research-based activities so as to enhance their learning; to go beyond simply reframing current practice as research-enhanced teaching and develop aspects of research-based learning that will more fully engage students in developing the skills of critical engagement with the subject matter that will be of use to them in the uncertain super-complex and pluralistic world in which they will live when they no longer have their teachers to guide them.

Academics frequently tell me that they are unable to engage students in inquiry-based approaches to their learning because of large student numbers. A mass higher education system creates major curriculum design challenges for research-based learning. The challenge is to design ways that groups of students can conduct authentic, realistic inquiries however many students are in the class. The idea of doing this is daunting, and a stumbling-block to even begin implementation, but I believe that it needs to be regarded as an opportunity for innovation rather than an excuse for stagnation. Examples where classes of up to 1000 first-year students engage in research-based learning are presented in Chapter 5.

Some academics have said to me that their work is too specialist, too difficult for junior year students to understand. Kirov (2003:13) quotes Ramsden and Moses (1992), and Elton (1992) as confirming that 'the closer research is to the frontiers of knowledge, the less likely it is to be directly quotable in teaching.' One of the challenges in a Mode 2 society (Nowotny, Scott, and Gibbons 2001) is that of finding ways to communicate research in a variety of forums. Scientists need to be able to explain esoteric research to as wide an audience as possible, undergraduate students included. However, Jenkins and colleagues (1998) argue that students should not simply have opportunities to benefit from their teachers' research, they should be more often involved in helping to carry it out. Neumann (1994) suggests that the earlier students are engaged in research, the better. Attention should be given in curriculum design to how staff research can benefit student learning.

It is clear from studies conducted in the United Kingdom, in Australia and in Finland that students have very hazy ideas of what research is. Research-enhanced education has to challenge and change students' conceptions of research (Jenkins et al. 1998; Zamorski 2002; Murtonen 2005; Petersson 2005). Changing such conceptions may challenge students' identity and also their ideas about what is going to be important in their future lives. It may question their relationship to the world and their ideas about the nature of reality, truth and knowledge. This makes research-enhanced education extremely challenging.

I have suggested that for all students, no matter what their ability or study motivation, the pursuit of professionalism embodied in the quality conception of scholarship can be a useful foundation for whatever the student engages in when they graduate. The ability to carry out a rigorous systematic process of inquiry and the capacity to apply the skills so acquired in a range of different contexts needs to be developed. As such the model I have proposed is a key to the future of a mass higher education system. As Barnett (2000) suggests, in a context of uncertainty and supercomplexity, research needs to teach us how to live.

If the task is to mentor students to become professional scholars, then the ways in which they are treated even in the early years of their study is crucial.

The Boyer Commission (1999) lays stress on the importance of students engaging in a keystone experience where they integrate their learning from different disciplinary areas. Brew and Boud (1995) suggest using resources to aid the process, using evidence, setting goals and planning, for both learning and research involve thinking and critical reflection. Hattie & Marsh (1996) stress the importance of emphasising uncertainty; encouraging a deep approach to learning; and emphasising the construction rather than the imparting of knowledge; and involving students in 'artistic and scientific productivity' (Hattie and Marsh 1996: 534).

▶ Views of research

Importantly, in developing research-enhanced education what is considered possible is going to depend on what academics think research is. Whether academics consider that integrating research and teaching is appropriate also depends on the nature of research being done and how that is viewed *vis à vis* the teaching being carried out. I have been using the terms 'research' and 'inquiry' almost interchangeably. However, some people see research as quite distinct from inquiry. Indeed, what academics think research consists in is clearly related to their discipline-led research activities and the theories that they draw on in their research. For some, the nature of research is simply assumed: it is what they do as research. For others it is highly problematic, as for example in a new discipline area where there are ongoing discussions among practitioners about the nature of research in that particular area, or when there are aspects of professional practice that dovetail with research, such as, for example, consultancy, performance or exhibitions. Some would argue that discipline differences make generic ideas about the nature of research-enhanced education virtually meaningless. As we saw when discussing the analysis of examples of research-led teaching, there were discipline differences in how this term was understood. This, in itself will lead to different kinds of implementation. In some of the newer discipline areas, for example, those that have recently become part of university life, such as nursing, performance studies and planning, there are likely to be discussions about the nature and role of research in the area taking place and those discussions may well include students. Where research is an established part of academic practice, the nature of research is more likely to simply be assumed:

> In a knowledge society, research is context specific and multidisciplinary rather than pure and discipline based; it has social relevance rather than being hypothesis led; it uses fuzzy rather than empirically based data; it is problem solving rather than deductive. In what might be termed the

commodification of knowledge, how knowledge is managed, synthesized and adapted become as important as knowledge itself. This requires not only a familiarity with the traditional academic research skills such as rigorous methods of inquiry and verification, but new skills, above all in organizing the deployment of knowledge in practical situations and using a knowledge base to derive solutions to new problems, rather than advancing the internalizing world of knowledge itself. Employers will increasingly demand that graduates have the skills to conduct appropriate research, the capacity to formulate solutions to problems based on awareness of research evidence, and the ability to critically assess that evidence; in other words knowledge creation and use.

(Jenkins and Zetter 2003: 11)

Griffiths (2004) writing from the perspective of built environment discipline areas argues that in applied fields, there is a weaker attachment to the concept of an academic discipline identity than in more traditional 'pure' discipline areas and more emphasis on multi or interdisciplinary thinking and on embedding knowledge in problem-solving, policy and professional contexts. Clearly, different forms of inquiry are appropriate to different subjects and hence what is appropriate in terms of research-enhanced education is going to be different in different areas. A key element in the development of research-enhanced education is that academics discuss these ideas and share their views about what is appropriate in their area.

The discussion of different ways of experiencing and understanding research in Chapter 2 highlights the importance of creating contexts for learning which provide opportunities for students to engage in activities that at times focus on the internal processes of research and at other times look outwards to external research contexts. We need too to bring the person into the research and to see courses as opportunities for students to develop their personal attributes, skills and understanding of self as well as their subject knowledge.

For example, if the focus of research is on utilising a number of techniques in a series of linear steps to solve a problem as in the 'domino' view of research (see Table 2.1), teaching may involve a series of separate techniques and then engage students in problem-solving activities in the laboratory, classroom or through field work. Where there is a 'layer' view of research with its focus on understanding, teaching may predominantly focus on collecting and interpreting data and on developing the skills students need in order to do this. If, on the other hand, a 'trading' view of research is the focus, students may be engaged in academic networks, team working, perhaps electronic discussions with students and academics in other countries and in peer review. Teaching may also focus on student products such as journals and conferences and other activities that mirror the social practices of research. Where the focus is on a 'journey' view of research, teaching may focus on the importance of students developing themselves as people through research and learning activities. This is not to suggest how these might be taught; we will come to this in Chapters 4 and 5. However, I suggest that it is important to develop a repertoire of teaching and learning strategies to take account of the full spectrum of views.

▶ Educational aims and values

The views of research-led teaching, about students and their learning as well as research, discussed in this chapter are all aspects of the academic environment or *habitus* that influence academics'capacity to implement research-enhanced higher education strategies. 'Habitus' for Bourdieu (1998: 7–9) refers to the set of dispositions or tastes which distinguishes one group of people from another. Such dispositions are largely unacknowledged. They are also likely to be distinctively different from any other group or class of people. So, for example, in the academic field, assumptions may be made which are unacknowledged explicitly, but which are understood by everyone who shares the same or a similar habitus, such as when someone does not come into the office until late in the morning it is automatically assumed that they have been working at home, or when an article is submitted for publication it is assumed that critical feedback will be given through a peer review process. This is not to deny that within any one defined social group there are likely to be competing perspectives. For Bourdieu, each social field is a field of struggles between those who have different kinds and levels of capital within the field (Bourdieu 1998: 32). Indeed, it is the conflict between different perspectives that creates opportunities for institutional change.

There is a good deal of discussion in the scholarly literature about the aims and purposes of higher education, and politicians and indeed university managers and administrators routinely express views in magazines such as *Change* and the *Times Higher Education Supplement*. However, although ideas about preparing students for a particular profession are well articulated within academic departments, ideas about the purposes of higher education in more general terms or even university education as a whole are aspects of the academic habitus that tend simply to be assumed (Barnett 1997).

Evidence about what academics consider to be the purposes of higher education have to be adduced from some of its taken for granted practices. According to Bourdieu, higher education has a regulatory and a transcendent purpose. Universities exist as a self-replicating field to produce and reproduce 'distinction' and reinforce privilege: for example, by maintaining social distance between academics and students; through teaching designed to convey the idea that the lecturer is sharing a secret kind of knowledge with students in lectures and through the use of the esoteric language of specific subjects. Indeed, despite arguments such as that by Nowotny and colleagues that universities have been forced to become integrated with society, there is still the idea (embodied, for example, in the very way university buildings are organised) that universities are set apart from society. 'It is this that gives universities a special kind of power' (Webb, Schirato and Danaher 2002:134).

Universities, according to Bourdieu, create knowledge not simply so that society can progressively understand the world, but in order to objectify forms of social organisation that sustain power relationships. That is, they are in the business of creating educated people who thus have access to capital; not just academic but also economic or political capital. The particular forms of address, the academic language that students are required to take on, the ways of thinking embodied within the notion of academic work, provide for students a set of generic skills that are useful to employers, that is, to a social context which values them. So they reproduce the social order. On the other hand, they enable the educated person to have a greater synoptic view than those without a university education. University educated people therefore have the capacity for reflexive critique of the situations in which they find themselves and they have the capacity to utilise theories to explain such situations. They therefore have the capacity to transcend their social class and to critically question the point of view of the dominant class (Bourdieu 1998).

This analysis serves to explain the inherent conservatism within the academic world. It suggests that reflexive critique is tied to the maintenance of academic prestige. That prestige, according to Bourdieu, is dependent upon relationships of patronage, even if it is only in terms of the granting of degrees, or commenting upon academic work. Creativity which may serve to threaten the livelihood of those who already have the academic capital is inevitably discouraged. Lectures preserve the views of those with the highest academic capital. Inquiry-based learning threatens to supplant it.

It also suggests deep ambiguities within the academic culture which are played out, as we shall see in later chapters, within attempts to transcend the divide between teaching and research. In Chapter 1, I argued that we need to bring teaching and research together in order to educate students for a pluralistic, super-complex, uncertain world. This suggests that recognising the capacity of higher education to lead people to undertake reflexive critiques of the society in which they live needs to be recognised and enhanced by academics, not in order to preserve distinction and privilege, but so that students can be educated for the kind of world we actually live in, not the one we would like to live in; for the professional demands they actually face, not the ones faced by their teachers when they graduated. There are big problems facing the world, and academics, together with their students, are capable of making important contributions to solving them. Initiatives that integrate academic research and student learning are currently tentative and small, yet it is only by integrating research and teaching in a climate of openness, trust and creativity that such problems can even begin to be tackled. Those academic teachers who have to date made valiant efforts to bring research and teaching closer together are pioneers developing pedagogies that begin to address the needs of a troubled, challenging world and, in doing so, heroically contribute to critically questioning the old privileged hierarchies that provide their own livelihood.

4　Student Engagement with Research: At Arm's Length

Given the differing views and perspectives on teaching, on research, on scholarship, on knowledge, on the nature of research-enhanced teaching and learning, and different ideas about students and their learning, it is not surprising that we find a multiplicity of different ways in which research is being used in teaching. Indeed, there is unlimited scope for enhancing teaching by incorporating research into it (Sainsbury 2003). The aims of this chapter and the next are, first, to see how the traditional model of the relationship between teaching and research discussed in Chapter 2 is changing through innovative uses of research in teaching and, second, to explore how far practice has moved towards the development of the inclusive scholarly knowledge-building communities which characterise the new model of the teaching–research relationship. I have given this chapter the sub-title 'at arm's length' and the next 'embraced into a community of researchers' in order to highlight the progression from limited integration of research into teaching where students engage in research tasters discussed in this chapter, towards fuller integration where students become part of research communities as discussed in Chapter 5.

I want to illustrate typical ways in which research is being integrated into teaching and student learning, so this chapter and the next present a rather idiosyncratic collection of cases from a wide range of subject areas. I have often found when talking to groups of academics, both in my own institution and in many others, that definitions and discussions and models of research-led teaching are all very well, but people's eyes really start to light up when I share examples of research-enhanced teaching and learning. Sharing and discussing cases where discipline-based research is being used in teaching and learning practice is a great way to generate ideas. Such cases are eclectic and often highly original, but each provides a resource for reflection. They may be related to the discipline or they may lend themselves to more widespread applications. All the cases in this and the next chapter have been presented either in publications or during conversations as examples of research-led teaching or of the use of research in teaching. As I have heard about cases, and read web sites and numerous publications purporting to describe examples of research-enhanced teaching, some of them have, as it were, leapt out of the page at me. What I am concerned with here, however, is not simply to list colourful examples (there are numerous such lists already available to anyone with an internet search engine), nor merely to demonstrate the rich variety of ways in which teaching can be said to be research led. Rather my choice of cases is designed to inform an understanding of pedagogies to integrate academic and student research and scholarly activity. Hence, my chosen cases are illustrative, not prescriptive. I want to take a critical look at these and examine what they tell us about how we can create inclusive scholarly knowledge-building communities. We will consider what aspects of research and teaching are being integrated, and look at the extent to which students are being encouraged and supported in engaging with research communities.

What strikes me about many of the cases that present themselves as examples of research-led or research-enhanced teaching and learning is, first, that many are simply examples of innovative teaching. They may be excellent innovations, but that is not the focus here. We need to be careful to understand what distinguishes research-enhanced teaching so we can identify which are examples of bringing research and teaching together. What aspects of higher education are brought into focus when we think of research-enhanced pedagogies, as opposed, for example, to any other kinds of innovation in university teaching? There will undoubtedly be debate on these issues and not everyone will agree that the cases I have chosen to present are indeed instances of research-enhanced teaching and learning. However, my aim is to create material for discussion and debate, not to provide a definitive list. The development of research-enhanced education is manifested in a dynamic and continually changing scenario. As we come to understand more about the nature and scope of research-enhanced pedagogy, so it changes before our very eyes.

The cases in this and the next chapter come from a variety of sources. Where they are based on published material or where more detail is available electronically, a reference has been given. Where references are not available, I have included in the list of acknowledgements the names of people who have helped in developing my thinking about different cases whether or not they supplied an example that I have used.

▶ The domains of research-enhanced teaching and learning

If we think about what students are learning when they are engaged in some form of higher education that has been influenced by research, we see that there are a number of differences in what is to be learnt. It may be that students are expected to gain some disciplinary knowledge (the content of research) through exposure to research, and/or they may come to understand what knowledge is within that discipline, or how that discipline functions to generate knowledge. They may learn about the nature of research more generally (i.e., how it operates). Instead of a focus on the content of research, the teaching may focus on students learning about the processes of research. In this regard, they may be expected to develop research skills, and this may be related to the acquisition of a related set of graduate attributes. Additionally, both the content and the process of research may be the subject of students' learning. Students may be expected to engage in interdisciplinary projects, or to learn about research as critical analysis, or about the use of research in professional practice, or about research as a social practice. What are considered to be the processes and practices of research will clearly depend on the teacher's conception of what research is in general and in their specific discipline area, and what students are expected to learn will be related, amongst other things, to their ideas of what students are capable of (see Chapter 3).

Different views of teaching, research, knowledge, scholarship and views of research-led teaching are reflected in both what the students are expected to know and in how they are expected to learn. We know from research that how the teacher views teaching is a key aspect of how students perceive and understand their courses (Prosser and Trigwell 1999). If teachers view their teaching in a teacher-focused way, then students are likely to adopt a surface approach to learning; and if teachers view their teaching in a student-focused way, then students are more likely to adopt a deep approach to learning, so in this chapter we will examine what these different approaches to teaching look like in relation to research-enhanced teaching. We will look at some examples of the different ways students can learn, and different ideas about what is to be learnt.

We have already noted that whether the teaching is student focused or teacher focused, sometimes students are an audience for the research and sometimes they are engaged in research activity (Zamorski 2002). Sometimes students are using research and sometimes they are doing research. They may be presenting research. They may be collaborating to carry out research with other students. Less often they will be collaborating to carry out research with a staff member; being involved in the research community. We may see students discussing research or using research in professional practice. In some cases the curriculum mirrors research processes.

▶ Students learn what knowledge is and how it is generated

'Every essay is an opportunity for students to learn research skills. Every practical class is an opportunity for students to use and practise research skills' (Sainsbury 2003). Even traditional essays, problem classes and laboratory sessions have as their foundation the ways in which academic researchers and writers operate. Some would argue that this is what makes a university education 'higher' education. Through doing essays and laboratory reports students learn about research and the way the discipline functions.

Essays and laboratory reports are most often used within a traditional teacher-focused, information-transmission view of teaching. Essays, for example, are perhaps one of the most frequent ways in which lecture courses are assessed, particularly in the humanities and social sciences. In the sciences, laboratory and problem-solving classes can be the main way in which lecture material is discussed, practised and assessed. There is scope here for linkages to be made with the research practices of academics; yet these are most often not mentioned. Essays, for example, engage students in a variety of research-based activities: investigating an idea or ideas, searching the literature, working through different sources of evidence, writing an academic argument and presenting it for review. The focus more often than not is the knowledge and how to write the essay (do the experiment) not on the parallels with work in the research community.

Countless students have written millions of essays but how many of these students, I wonder, have made the link to the kind of writing that their teachers do when they are preparing to write a scholarly article for publication. For myself, it was not until I wrote my first article for publication several years after graduation that I realised that I had developed the skills to do this through the essays I had written as an undergraduate. The question for us, I think, is how we can enhance students' essay experiences through what we know about how research proceeds. For example, when academics publish an article, it is rarely the first time the ideas are presented to an audience. They might, most usually, have already tried out the ideas in a conference paper. The first thing they write on the subject may therefore be an abstract for a conference. The conference committee then reviews this. When accepted, the academic writes and then presents the paper. They may try the ideas out on close colleagues in a departmental seminar before the conference. The conference presentation will provide them, if they are lucky, with some valuable feedback. It may mean a reorienting of the paper. It may mean that they need more data. Whatever the feedback, it is useful in developing the paper so that it is suitable for publication in a scholarly peer reviewed journal. Indeed, the feedback may suggest which journal the article would be suitable for. The academic may think that the ideas need a good deal more work, in which case they might develop it and present it again at another conference prior to working on a final paper for publication.

Rather than expecting students to work on the final paper (the essay) first, a teacher might, if thinking about how to develop research-enhanced teaching, ask students to first submit abstracts. There is a golden opportunity for them to try out a paper on their colleagues through the tutorial or seminar programme. How often do academics ask students to present papers in seminars unrelated to the essay they are working on? Within the normal processes of teaching and learning within essay-based subjects, there are lots of opportunities to extend research-enhanced education by mirroring the processes that are used when writing about research for scholarly publication. However, in traditional settings there is rarely any attempt to even begin to build a community and connect students with academics. Students are kept at arm's length. The connections with research, particularly in the early years of undergraduate education, more often than not are ignored.

An attempt to bring first-year students into contact with researchers is provided by Dwyer (2001). She describes a learning activity in the Geography Department of University College, London, where teams of five students first read three research papers by a staff member and then, when they have discussed and agreed a series of questions, interview the staff member about their research. Each student individually writes a report on what they have found. The purpose of the exercise is for students to learn about the aims, methods and ideas of a geographer doing research in the department, why research projects are started, and how they are carried out. The researcher may give students an unpublished paper as one of the papers students initially read, so raising issues of how research gets published. Students also develop their skills of critically reading in the subject. They develop some interview skills, and they develop skills of reporting their findings.

This student-focused activity may, like the essay or the laboratory report, still be conducted within an overall teacher-focused approach to teaching. However, here the students begin to get a sense of the community of researchers and the way knowledge is developed in the subject by researchers. It does not matter in this case whether the people co-ordinating the subject are researchers themselves, but it does matter that there is a sufficient number of active researchers in the department for students to interview. Jenkins (2002) reports a similar example at Rutgers University in the United States, where student teams interview community healthcare professionals about how their practice draws on research. This enables students to explore the role of evidence in their practice; a critical aspect of their undergraduate curriculum.

It is notable that the geography example concerns first-year students. Jenkins (2002) indicates that it is based on an integrative, what the Boyer Commission (1999) call a 'capstone', activity at Oxford Polytechnic reported by Cosgrove (1981), where third-year student teams interviewed staff about their research, their views about the development of the discipline, and how this was integrated into their courses. The difference in asking first-year students and final-year students to interview staff is quite crucial when we are wanting to see to what extent students are inducted into the community of researchers. There is a widely held view that students can become part of that community in the third or final year; witnessed by the number of final-year dissertation projects. Yet, until that point, students are more often kept at arm's length from the research community; a facet of the 'submissive waiting' that Bourdieu (1988: 95) talks about.

Dwyer (2001) indicates that the project is now part of a programme taking place over the three years of the degree, which is itself focused on geography as research practice and finishes with students doing their own research dissertations. However, there is no evidence in any of these examples that the students have any more contact with the researcher whom they interviewed. In terms of developing an understanding of research and how the discipline progresses, students occupy a separate domain. Their integration into the research community has barely begun.

A related example which looks not so much at research in one discipline area, but considers the nature of research as a social process comes from the University of Plymouth in England. Students are presented with an article from a popular magazine such as *New Scientist*. They research the original article on which this popularised version is based and write a report on the way the media has presented the research. They may contact the original author(s) to explore their perceptions of how their research has been represented by the media. In this example, students are not so much doing research as using research to understand about the nature of research and its relationship to society. Research is presented as an intellectual activity within a social context. The activity presents research as a process of knowledge production in Gibbons and colleagues' (1994) Mode 2 sense. Scientists and society (in this case via the media) are viewed as co-determining how we understand a particular phenomenon. Yet that co-determination does not extend to students. They learn how knowledge is generated but, more often than not, they are outside it – spectators, not players on the research stage.

▶ Generic graduate attributes

I suggested in Chapter 2 that students should be developing the skills of scholarship understood as a quality of the way professional academic work is done. I indicated that this kind of academic professionalism was important whatever students are going to do when they graduate. There is a direct link between this quality view of scholarship and the development of students' research skills because as they learn what is involved in doing research and learn how to do it, they must learn how to do it ethically and responsibly; that is, professionally. The development of research skills is central to the idea of students engaging in a research-based higher education, so it is important to discuss the issues associated with this, to examine some cases where this is being achieved within the framework of research-led teaching, and explore what these cases show us about how research and teaching are being brought together and about the engagement of students in scholarly knowledge-building communities of researchers.

When I was an undergraduate student of philosophy, there was one course called 'Methodology'. This was presented as a series of lectures on research methods. Most of the research papers I had read at that time were philosophical arguments, not empirical studies, and there was no suggestion that we should carry out any of the suggested research methods. The notes were useful when I came to carrying out some educational research in my Masters programme. Apart from that, I did not make much sense of them. This was a teacher-focused approach to the teaching of research skills. It now seems to me to be an absurd way to teach such skills. Yet lectures on research methods are still quite common in higher education.

Problems with teaching research methodology are widely recognised in the literature (see Winn 1995; Jaakkola 2003). They include students finding learning research methodology difficult and unpleasant; not possessing relevant subject skills and unfamiliarity with difficult concepts; negative attitudes including not knowing why they need research skills and possessing naïve conceptions of research; as well as superficial teaching and a failure to link theory and practice. Murtonen (2005) studied the views of students regarding learning research skills in Finland and the United States, reporting that about half of the students whom she studied did not consider that they would need research skills in their working lives. She, rightly in my view, suggested that this is cause for concern in the context of a knowledge society. Murtonen also demonstrated that students' attitudes to the learning of research methodology affect the approaches to learning that they adopt in courses on research methods. Students who were less sure they would need research skills in their working lives were more defensive, less task oriented and tended to adopt surface approaches to their learning. This suggests some of the reasons why teachers experience problems with teaching research skills and why we need to look at different approaches to research skills development.

Research skills do not exist in isolation but are frequently viewed as aspects of clusters of generic graduate attributes, such as the development of teamwork, communication and negotiation skills as well as skills of critical analysis. The teaching of generic graduate qualities or attributes gained popularity in the 1980s and 1990s following employers' criticisms of universities for failing to develop the skills of employability. Universities took up the gauntlet and many if not most now adhere to a strategic desire to improve the employability of graduates, develop what are known variously as key skills, transferable skills or graduate attributes, if not for the sake of the employers at least for the purposes of accountability, quality assurance or as a response to changing ideas of knowledge (Barrie 2003). Yet in spite of university rhetoric espousing the importance of such attributes, implementation is patchy and there is no coherent understanding even within departments let alone across universities or university systems of what is understood by generic attributes (Kemp and Seagraves 1995; Fallows and Steven 2000; Barrie 2003, 2004, in press).

Barrie (2003) provides a useful framework for examining how academics understand graduate attributes and how those understandings relate to different approaches to teaching. He found that academics in a research-intensive university in Australia understood graduate attributes in four qualitatively different ways:

1. Necessary basic skills which are a precursor to university entry (precursor view).
2. Useful skills that complement or round out disciplinary learning (complementing view).
3. Abilities that let students make use of or apply disciplinary knowledge (translation view).
4. Scholarly abilities that infuse and enable personal and disciplinary learning and knowledge (enabling view).

(Barrie 2003:105)

Related to these four ways of understanding graduate attributes, Barrie identified six different understandings of the processes of teaching and learning them:

1. *remedial*, where the role of the university is viewed as compensating for students not already having learnt such skills before entering university;
2. *associated*, where a separate course is used to teach such skills;
3. teaching of skills which forms part of the *normal teaching content* of the curriculum;
4. or, alternatively, are part of the *normal teaching processes*;
5. *engagement*, where the teaching of generic skills is not part of what is taught nor how it is taught but rather is viewed in terms of the way it engages students in their learning on the course;
6. and *participatory* which refers not to the way the student engages in learning, but rather to the way they participate in the broader learning experiences of university life.

(Barrie in press)

Barrie further found that there was a relationship between the way academics understood graduate attributes and the approaches to teaching and learning that they adopted. So, for example, the precursor and complementing views were associated with a teacher-focused approach to teaching, where such skills were either not taught at all or were taught in an additive way in a supplementary curriculum. The translation and enabling views could be associated either with a teacher-focused approach where the generic skills were taught in the context of disciplinary knowledge or through the way the course was taught. Alternatively, they could be taught in a student-focused way through the learning experiences of the course or through the way students engage with all the experiences of university life (Barrie 2003).

Since research skills form a significant part of graduate attributes, this analysis of academics' views of graduate attributes provides a way of understanding how research skills are being taught and enables judgments to be made concerning the extent to which students are being encouraged to develop the skills that will enable them to participate in discipline-based research communities. So let us now look at some of the ways students are being encouraged to develop research skills.

The development of effective skills that complement disciplinary learning usefully begins in the first year. For example, students of a *Social, Behavioral and Professional Pharmacy* unit of study, individually develop, in tutorial class time, an interview schedule to be used to interview a friend or relative who has experienced a significant 'health event' in their life. Material from the lectures, a book of readings and tutorial class discussions are used to formulate the interview schedule. Another example comes from medical radiation science. The lecturer provides a number of recent journal articles and asks students to answer a series of questions based on their analyses of these and other articles they have to find. He always tries to have a few questions where the conclusions that can be drawn from the articles are in conflict and asks the students how this should be resolved, thus producing a wide spectrum of discussion. Here a layer view of research underpins a view of research methods as developing in students the skills of interpretation which help them in their subsequent disciplinary study from lectures. Students develop the skills while learning the content of the discipline.

Another way of engaging students in critical analysis of academic writing is where students are given a paper which the tutor has written, but from which all means of identification (journal name, volume, page numbers, author name) have been deleted. The students are then asked to write an abstract for the paper. The exercise was used at Plymouth University, in geography tutorials, to develop the skills of writing, critical analysis, summarising information, and research design and planning. If a journal paper is chosen (as in this case) with plenty of data, the exercise also develops skills in data analysis and synthesis (Gaskin no date). Again, in this case, students are developing a range of useful skills to complement discipline content learning and that permit them to make use of or apply disciplinary knowledge (Barrie's 'complementing' and 'translation' views).

One development of this approach comes from Brigham Young University in the United States. The teacher collects the abstracts and puts them in a common format, then chooses the best four or five which are then put with the original abstract. Students vote for 'best abstract'. Then the teacher reveals the abstract's author, often to the surprise of the students!

Another development of this approach is a course on skills acquisition for sport science undergraduates at Otago University, New Zealand. Each student is required to complete a review of a stimulus research article from one of the four research themes introduced during lectures. The review of the article and its implications are presented to peers and teaching staff in the form of a scientific poster. The assessment of this work takes place within mock conference symposia aimed at coaches and sport practitioners. Prior to presentation of the poster, each student submits a 400–600 word abstract outlining their intended area of study. This abstract includes a brief review of the literature, the research question(s), the conclusions of the stimulus article, and the proposed implications for practitioners. Following the poster defence and subsequent feedback from staff and peers, a full abstract (up to 1500 words) is resubmitted.

Differing conceptions of research suggest that there are likely to be differing conceptions of what it is to develop research methods. Here, for example, the development of research skills includes elements of the process of conference submission and presentation (abstracts and poster presentation), reflecting a trading view of research (see Chapter 2); the teaching of generic skills being integrated into courses. A domino view of research might lead to the development of a set of distinct, relatively unrelated tools and techniques. A layer view might result in the development of the skills of data collection and interpretation.

Yet research skills are not developed once and for all through exercises at a particular level. We need to look for an integrated approach. First-year veterinary science students and second-year agricultural science students at the University of Sydney engage in a library retrieval skills and database searching workshop, which is reinforced in the second and third years by an advanced database searching session. There are assessments in several units of study where these skills are used to find research material to form a bibliography for an assessable assignment; for example, a critical review of a research paper by third-year agricultural students or a presentation to their peers of a recent research article on a defined topic by second-year veterinary science students. Fourth- and fifth-year students routinely search the internet and databases for information relevant to cases seen in the university clinic. What we see here is a progression from research skills (with a specific focus on information literacy) being taught as an add-on component in courses to a more integrated approach.

Yet, for the development of a knowledge-building community, we need to go further. Bereiter (2002), as we saw in Chapter 3, stresses the importance of students working from the questions that they personally identify so that they can build new knowledge. Thus, for the teaching of research methods to be successful, attention needs to be focused on the development of authentic questions in which students have an interest. Given the importance of inquiry to life after they graduate, it may not matter in the first instance whether questions that students begin to research are closely related to the subject matter of their study. What is important is that the teaching has to challenge and change students' conceptions of research. This will most readily happen where students are actively involved in learning not simply about the methods, but where learning about methods is integrated with the development of specific disciplinary knowledge.

Many of today's 'burning issues' in science are biological: controlling the SARS virus; pros and cons of genetically engineered organisms; consequences of clear-felling forests; the relevance of Darwinism to social policy. However media coverage of such issues is often limited and uncritical. How are our students, the biologists of tomorrow to develop the ability to assess the scientific evidence and develop an opinion of their own on such weighty topics? . . . we want our graduates to have the confidence and the skills to enable them to gather evidence and make sound judgements based on scientific evidence, even when the debate is not in their area of specialized knowledge.

(Jones and Barmuta 2003: p. 1)

The solution Jones and Barmuta devised was to develop a programme to develop research skills throughout the whole of the degree, beginning in the first year with a library searching exercise and ending in the third year with a 'research process experience' consisting of a major research project. In the second and third years there is a full unit of study with a focus on generic rather than subject-specific content. The unit develops research skills including synthesising and critically analysing research evidence, comparing and presenting scientific arguments. Students work in groups because 'cooperative learning opportunities model the collaboration that is the hallmark of scientific professional work' (Jones and Barmuta 2003: 2). The introduction to the course is an extension of the earlier example where students read and critique an article from a popular science magazine. Here the focus is ultimately on developing students' research skills. They first write a report on the abstract of the original article on which a *New Scientist* or *Nature* Australia article is based and then, following feedback, write a report on the main article. This activity provides the basis for further work where students in groups of ten work to evaluate research on a particular topic and then research aspects of that broad topic in pairs. The course culminates with the individual students writing a report focusing on the broad topic, including what they personally have researched and the bringing together of the research of the group as a whole, culminating with some reflective comments. Jones and Barmuta comment:

> we suggest that the teaching strategies and the assessment tasks developed for *Evolution, Ecology and Society* are effective in developing key generic skills in science undergraduates as well as stimulating students' interest in science through discussion of issues of major current significance. The overall outcome is an increase in the students' metacognitive skills: the unit helps them 'understand how they know what they know' (Etkina and Ehrenfeld, 2000 p 607), to extract meaning from readings and empowers them to evaluate and critique published literature. This fills an important gap left in many undergraduate science curricula'.
>
> (Jones and Barmuta 2003: 5)

Here the students develop a range of scholarly abilities and skills that enable them to develop their disciplinary understanding (Barrie's 'enabling' view of graduate attributes) by engaging in a range of research-based activities. In this fascinating and innovative approach to the teaching of research skills, students are engaged in and communicating within a scholarly knowledge-building community. We need to look further to see how and whether students' work dovetails with the research of their teachers and researchers; a point we will pursue in Chapter 5.

As we have seen, students' conceptions of the role and importance of research skills to their university study and in their lives will crucially affect whether they are motivated to develop such skills. Lack of motivation is inevitable if the teaching is unrelated to anything they may consider they will undertake either as an undergraduate (as in my example of lectures on research methods), or in their later careers. Students' sense of identity may not be bound up in notions of participation in academic communities of researchers, and, as we have seen, they may not consider research skills to be important to their future lives and work. If their conceptions of research skills parallel Barrie's 'precursor' and 'complementing' views of graduate attributes, and if the teaching reflects such orientations, then students are unlikely to be motivated. Such ideas need to be challenged if students are to engage fully with new ideas about the nature and role of research. This may require challenging students' sense of their personal identity and the values they ascribe to what is going to be important to their future lives.

Changing conceptions is not easy. Indeed, it is, I suspect, far more challenging than many teachers of research methods would recognise because it means acknowledging that the teaching of research methods cannot be done effectively without challenging the nature of the subject being studied and without questions being raised about what it means to study it. Conceptions of graduate attributes, and indeed views on how to teach research methods to students, are grounded in fundamental values about the nature of the disciplinary area and what studying it involves. Teacher-focused views of graduate attributes ignore questions about the relationship of research methods to epistemology. They treat such methods as a technical exercise; a set of skills to be mastered irrespective of disciplinary content. Yet questions about research method not only raise questions about the nature of research, they also raise questions about what constitutes a method for investigating it, and what the assumptions of that investigation are in relation to the nature of the reality being investigated.

So if students' conceptions of research are to be challenged, their fundamental beliefs about the nature of knowledge must be critically questioned. Developing the skills and understanding necessary to effectively carry out research may thus fundamentally question how they see their relationship to the world in which they live and their ideas about the nature of reality, truth and knowledge.

This illustrates the significance of, and also an important difficulty in, research-methods education. In order to fully engage students in developing an understanding of how to do research while engaging them in the process of developing an understanding of disciplinary content, big picture questions about the nature of disciplinary knowledge, and about its relationship to reality inevitably need to be addressed. Further, for such education to be effective, students' sense of their personal identity and the role of research in their lives must be challenged. As we saw earlier, research is important for all students to develop irrespective of the future career they are going to pursue. The ability to carry out a process of investigation is important in professional life; not just to the lives of academics. This suggests that students should be involved in learning research skills by engaging in research and inquiry projects alongside professionals. Yet the examples of the teaching of the skills of research that we have so far witnessed in this chapter stop short of this ideal. It is an issue that we will take up again in Chapter 5.

▶ Learning disciplinary knowledge

So far in this chapter we have considered some cases designed to teach students what knowledge is and how it is generated within a disciplinary area, and where students learn about the nature of research. We have then looked at the learning of research skills in the context of generic graduate attributes. We now come to consider cases of research-enhanced teaching where students are learning disciplinary knowledge.

Ideas about using disciplinary research in teaching are frequently viewed from what Prosser and Trigwell (1999) call a teacher-focused perspective. This usually means that ideas and examples from disciplinary research are included in the content of lectures. For example, a lecturer told me that she had been able to introduce 'sleep' as a topic in the *Exercise and Sports Science* course because of her involvement in sleep research. She says she tries to make the material relevant to the exercise and sports science field. This is a teacher-focused example, where students learn the content of the teacher's research in a lecture. It is a typical way in which research-enhanced teaching is viewed.

Some teacher-focused strategies where disciplinary content is the focus of attention are, for example, said to be to engage students through the currency of material. That material may be the actual content that students need to learn or it may provide illustrative anecdotes. It is frequently viewed in terms of the 'glow' effect of expertise. (Professor Bloggs the world expert teaches all levels of students.) This 'glow' effect may even be attributed to the fact that students are physically in a building where research is taking place. The fact that the person teaching the lecture is a person doing leading-edge research is assumed to excite the students. One of the academics I interviewed in my study of research-enhanced teaching said: 'The structure of proteins is taught everywhere, but what is different and better (at this University) is the fact that people are actually doing it.' Rades and Norris (2003) have called this 'research illustrated teaching'. Students are, in Zamorski's (2002) terms, an audience for research. Nevertheless the view that it enhances student learning because it makes lectures interesting is not uncommon.

Unfortunately, however, as we have seen, research has demonstrated that students are frequently unaware of how the content of their courses relates to the discipline-led research being done (see, for example, Jenkins et al. 1998). Students often do not know what research their teachers are doing and there is more often than not a reticence among academics in talking about research. Indeed, it is debatable whether the fact that a particular professor is a world expert is of interest to students, unless research is indeed used in some way to enhance students' learning. This indicates that it is important not simply to assume that teaching is based on or links in some way to research. The teaching needs to be specifically designed to bring research and teaching together and teachers need to make explicit to students how the teaching and learning links with staff research. It also suggests that it should not be assumed that talking about research in lectures necessarily enhances students' learning.

Another way in which students' disciplinary knowledge is assumed to be allied to the research interests of staff is when they take electives or engage in projects closely aligned with the research interests of their teachers, However, here again the importance of making explicit the links with research cannot be too strongly stressed. In these examples, research is, as Griffiths (2004) remarks 'weakly embedded'. 'Where research is more strongly integrated it is used deliberately to shape the learning activities carried out by students' (Griffiths 2004:721).

Some students are engaged in learning disciplinary knowledge through specially designed research-based activities. For example, at the University of Otago New Zealand, students engage in an exercise to examine research evidence from a research project where a mystery shopper posed as a member of the public with a particular ailment and went into a number of pharmacies to examine how the pharmacist explained about the particular medication (Rades and Norris 2003). The students are not engaged in the research in this case, merely with using the data to learn about the content of their course. This is an example of a teacher-focused activity-based approach to teaching as described by McKenzie (2003) (see Chapter 3).

In another case, the content of research on climate change and sustainability is translated into a student activity. The activity arose out of a concern of the lecturers that their lectures were resulting in the important and far-reaching ecological consequences of global warming found in their research being treated in a cursory way by their students; the engineers of the future. Here is how they explain what they did:

The problem of climate change is complex, global, and long-term, and therefore difficult to grapple with for politicians, scientists, teachers, and students alike. One might ask, how can teachers present climate change in a way that is not abstract and distant, but that will raise emotions within students, and will make them feel involved? The key is to link climate change to students' individual lives. One way of creating such a relationship is the idea of a personal greenhouse gas budget, comprising all emissions caused by a student over one year. A personal greenhouse gas calculator was developed in the School of Physics in the form of a computer spreadsheet, and applied in university teaching. This calculator, which is based on research carried out in the School, does not only address emissions from energy use, but also emissions embodied in goods and services, which are often ignored. As its normative part, the calculator states a benchmark of 3.5 tonnes of CO_2 per person per year, based on the principles of global equity and ecological sustainability. First experiences show that most students agree with that benchmark, and accept responsibility for embodied emissions. However, their personal emission results usually exceed by far the equitable and sustainable budget. This experience triggers various feelings, ranging from surprise and motivation, to denial, defence, cynicism, anger, and frustration. In contrast to purely factual teaching, this personal and provocative approach creates emotions, which will ultimately lead to better learning.

(Lenzen and Smith 1999–2000; Lenzen and Dey 2001)

This presents a student-focused conceptual-change approach to teaching where students are learning about the content of their teachers' research.

▶ Doing research to learn about research

When academics are asked to think of examples of research-led teaching, they provide numerous cases where the students engage in the process of doing research in order to learn about research; where the content reflects research findings and the processes of doing research are also to be learnt. Such cases range from independent one-off activities where students carry out an aspect of research, to full-scale curricula where the whole course is organised to simulate a research process. In this chapter, we consider some issues associated with the former. In Chapter 5 we will look at more holistic examples.

There are numerous cases where students devise a questionnaire and go on to the streets to collect responses. For example, in their introduction to pharmacy, first-year students at the University of Sydney investigate the way different pharmacist shops are laid out. They pool their responses and in doing so learn about important aspects associated with the practice of pharmacy. In media studies at the University of Gloucestershire, England, students in groups of four or five first-year students undertake small-scale field research into student television viewing habits. Their findings are compared with available research findings on television viewing for a general youth audience.

Urban vulnerability is a key concept in the study of urban poverty and poverty alleviation programmes in the majority of the world. Urban planning students at Oxford Brookes University, England, engage with the particular agenda that has been the subject of research initially through reading an article on the topic. This is then used as the basis for a simulation. On the day the simulation is to take place, students are given roles in groups of three or four. With an hour to prepare, they have to present a position on behalf of a stakeholder group: World Bank, multinational corporation, central government, urban authority, non-government organisation (NGO) or the local community (Zetter 2003).

One case where journals or publications showcase students' work that I came across was at the University of Sydney. In a first-year undergraduate course in classical mythology, students individually research and write a 'Homeric Hymn' to a Greco-Roman god or goddess. They first have to research what a 'Homeric Hymn' is and then they have to research their chosen god or goddess and write the results of their research in such a hymn:

> At the starting point to their task, then, students needed to familiarise themselves with the nature and techniques of the traditional Homeric Hymn; its possible meaning as a mode of praise or petition, its form, shape and metre, its openings and closures, its use of narrative and the kind of subject matter the narrative conventionally addresses, its use of other traditional material not only relating to the narrative subject matter, but to techniques surrounding the employment of established epithets and scene description.
>
> Next, through their own self-directed exploration and research, students collected data on their chosen deity to stitch into a form and shape for their compositions the parentage, domains and territories, attributes and feats of that deity, her or his specific and related myths from all sources available just as 'Homer' in a sense 'names' a diversity of sources.
>
> (MacAllister and Pascoe 1999: vi)

The results of some of the best of this research have been presented in a series of booklets. In order to see what these first year students are capable of here is a brief extract from one of their Hymns:

HYMN TO HERAKLES FOR THE OLYMPIC GAMES[1]

by James Elliott

The mightiest of mortals, Muses, sing[2]
One whom the neat-ankled[3] Alkemene bore
In fair-lawned[4] Thebes, to Zeus the lord of thunder[5].
Hail! Dauntless spirit, champion at labours.[6]
Dread[7] Herakles, son of Zeus, blessed hero-god,[8]
How cam'st thou didst free Prometheus?
Verily 'twas Heakles who, in honour of his father,
In Pisa,[9] by Alpheus sloping banks,
the first Olympian context, established.[10]
Indeed all this he did on his return
from the last of his laborious tasks
set by Eurystheus, fetching the golden apples

From the Hesperides' sacred tree,[11] a gift
to Heaven from the life-giving Earth, mother of all.[12]

(continued for 155 more lines)

1. Although we do not have evidence about how exactly the opening ceremony took place, I cannot help imagining this being read before Pheidias' Olympian Zeus: a colossal statue of which Quintillian wrote 'it's beauty can be said to have added something to the traditional religion, so adequate to the divine nature is the majesty of this work' (Quintilian *Inst. Orat.* 7.10.9).

2. For this form of opening (without the 'of') see Shelley's translations of the Homeric Hymns in *Complete Works*.

3. Alkmene's epithet 'neat-ankled' (variously translated as 'fair-ankled', 'slim-ankled', 'shapely-ankled'): eg. Hesiod *Theogony* 526, 950.

4. Thebes is described as the city of 'of the fair-dancing places', or 'city of lovely dances': eg. *Homeric Hymn 15: to Lion-Hearted Herakles 2.*

5. Zeus as 'lord of thunder': eg. *Hesiiod Theogony* 839ff.

6. References to Herakles' labours: eg. Pindar *Olympian 3, Olympian 10, Pythian 9*; Apollodoros *Bibliotheka* 2.4.8–2.8.5.

7. 'Dread' or 'terrrible' Herakles: eg. Hesiod *Shield of Herakles* 52.

8. Herakles as 'hero-god': Pindar *Nemean* 3.22.

9. Pisa is the name of the district around Olympia, in the Peloponnese.

10. For Herakles as found of the Olympian games see, for example, Pindar Olympian 2.3–4, 3.9–38, 6.67–70, 10.24–30, 43–59, Nemean 10.32–3, 11.27–28.

11. 11. The order of Kerakles' labours differs from source to source, but Apollodoros gives the apples of the Hesperides as second last (Bibliotheka 2.5.11) Placing them last here assists narrative smoothness.

12. Homeric Hymn 30: To Earth, the Mother of All.

(continued)

(MacAllister and Pascoe 1999: 53–4)

The footnotes have been edited by the editors making this a lovely example of a scholarly collaboration between first year students, a final year student and an academic.

▶ **Conclusion**

We have seen that students are involved in research in many different ways, subject areas and levels. However, they are not always aware that their learning links to the research of their teachers and do not always find research to be sufficiently well taught to be considered useful or pleasurable (Zamorski 2002). The discussion in this chapter tells us quite a lot about how students are viewed in universities. Key questions we need to ask are: how far are students trusted to engage in research and if they are trusted to engage in research collaboratively with each other, are they trusted to become involved in scholarly communities? I have been studying the ways in which academics involve undergraduate students in research for a number of years now and what strikes me the more I look into this is the frequent separation between what students are doing and what academics are doing.

What is particularly striking about the examples in this chapter, is the way in which they confine students to the fringes of research action. Students are either spectators, or they engage in research tasters. I am not denying that they learn important things by doing so, nor that these examples are not good pedagogy. Indeed, I applaud the teachers who are pioneering these and similar approaches to undergraduate curricula. As some of the examples in this chapter testify, given the right conditions, undergraduate students are capable of engaging in research-based activities and achieving a great deal by doing so. However, I believe many of these examples present undergraduates engaging in what Bourdieu, as we saw, refers to as 'submissive waiting' before they are able to enter the community of researchers. There are a number of metaphors to describe this exclusive domain: the hallowed halls of academia, the dreaming spires or the ivory tower. Students do not belong to that community until they have proved themselves in their undergraduate courses, after which only the best of them may be permitted into postgraduate research.

The new model outlined in Chapter 2 posits, in contrast, a closer relationship between students and teachers as both engage in scholarly communities. Yet, in the cases we have looked at in this chapter, students are not, by and large, even peripherally involved in academic communities. They are kept at arm's length, inhabiting a separate domain. In the next chapter we shall look at what is needed in order to move into more inclusive knowledge-building scholarly communities.

5 Student Engagement with Research: Embraced into a Community of Researchers

In Chapter 4 we considered some cases where aspects of research were integrated into teaching and noted that many provided research-based experiences for students that were separate from the research of academics. We now go further and consider the extent to which students are being involved with academics in inclusive communities of scholars. In other words, to develop an understanding of how to frame the relationship between teaching and research within new pedagogical discourses; ones that construct students as able to define and pursue, with academics, lines of inquiry related to their discipline-based interests. So this chapter considers how students are collaborating in inquiry and some of the different forms this collaboration takes. It then considers issues related to how academics are working with students to understand how disciplinary knowledge is constructed and defined and cases where academics are involving students in the social practices of research, before finally considering schemes that involve students as participating researchers.

However, before examining specific cases where students are being encouraged to engage in inclusive scholarly communities, there is a need to consider the extent to which students are developing the knowledge, skills, tools and techniques necessary to being a member of a particular disciplinary community and the extent to which they are being encouraged to develop the ethic of academic professionalism embodied in the idea of scholarship as a quality of the way academic work is done. Chapter 4 considered how students are engaging in the development of research skills. Now we need to look further and consider how academics are engaging students in developing their ideas about the nature of knowledge and of research within the disciplinary area through joint discussions and activities.

It is also important to consider the extent to which students are engaging in knowledge-building processes. Knowledge building, as we saw in Chapter 3 arises from the questions that students identify. For Bereiter (2002) knowledge-building grows out of the actions of a community, while learning is located inside people's heads. Learning may result from knowledge building, but, argues Bereiter, it is not possible to predict what a person may learn from the knowledge-building process (nor from any particular piece of teaching for that matter).

In order to appreciate the importance of this distinction, I want to look a little further at Bereiter's concept of knowledge building. Bereiter takes Popper's (1972) idea that in addition to the external objective world of objects and the world inside people's minds, there is the world of ideas, of theories, explanations, historical accounts, interpretations, criticisms of literary works, academic concepts and so on. These exist independently of people's minds and of the world of objects. Bereiter, calls these 'conceptual artefacts' and suggests that when we talk of working with knowledge, these are the kinds of things we are talking about (Bereiter 2002). Bereiter's concept of a conceptual artefact comes close to what Nowotny, Scott and Gibbons (2001) call a Mode 2 'knowledge object'. They suggest that negotiations amongst interested individuals and organisations within what they call 'transaction spaces', may grope towards a concept of what it is that is to be explored (e.g., the Human Genome Mapping project) or there may be a chance discovery, (e.g., the discovery of superconductivity) which defines a new field of investigation. The Mode 2 object cannot be decided in advance, but once it is conceptualised, research and, especially, funding attention can coalesce around it (Nowotny et al. 2001).

Each conceptual artefact according to Bereiter is a product of a process of inquiry: '[Scientists'] objective is to produce a piece of knowledge which is likely first to find embodiment in messages exchanged with peers, before it ever finds its way into a public display' (Bereiter 2002: 294). Bereiter argues that students should similarly be involved in the process of creating conceptual artefacts through the knowledge building process, and that knowledge building should arise spontaneously from the questions that students bring about an aspect of the world that they want to understand.

Roth (2003) provides an example of middle-school children taking part in just such a knowledge-building project. The idea was that they would learn science by participating with professionals and other adults to design research projects and participate in knowledge building in relation to the development of the understanding of the local community with respect to problems with its water supply. The students were introduced to the issues via newspaper articles and a talk given by the leader of the group of environmentalists working on the creek that supplied the water. They volunteered to help clean it up and to investigate its various facets. The children then became involved in a range of different projects working with different members of the community in diverse ways to understand and then to help solve the water problems. They framed their own investigations and chose how they would measure and represent their findings. For example, some students decided to conduct a study relating creek depth to the speed of the water, others sampled different sections of the creek to find what organisms lived in the different sections.

Roth provides this example to demonstrate the way in which learning is related to participation, and arises naturally and spontaneously from participation in the activities of a community; in this example, a community that has grown up through the interests of people with different knowledge and expertise to understand the issues associated with the health of this waterway in British Columbia, Canada. By participating in a particular material and social world, learning, he suggests, can be thought of as 'changing participation in the ongoing but changing collective praxis' (Roth 2003: 27).

▶ Collaboration in inquiry

Engaging students in such collaborative team-based inquiries in their courses is one of the most frequently cited examples of research-enhanced teaching. The development of teamwork skills is related to the development of generic graduate attributes discussed in Chapter 4. Participation in such team-based exercises can range from separate projects carried out for or during a tutorial situation or for a particular coursework assignment, to driving the way a whole subject, module or unit of study is organised and studied.

At the University of Sydney, teams of four to six pharmacy students undertake a project entitled *Analytical Profile of a Drug Substance* over a period of five weeks. The project involves a scenario where teams of students prepare a new drug formulation report on behalf of a pharmaceutical company, as if the report were to be submitted to the relevant Australian government department for approval to market the drug. Each student group is allocated a drug and each group member is assigned a different analytical technique. The practical is first explained to the students and the drugs and analytical techniques are assigned. This is followed by a library session, where students look up information on both the drug and the analytical technique. The students then discuss the information that they have found with the demonstrator and technical staff, and decide on the conditions to use for the analysis. They then do a preliminary analysis, checking that their methods are valid. In the third week each student is given a sample of their drug. They then determine how much drug is in the sample using their assigned method. The following week each group presents a 20–25 minute presentation on the drug that they were assigned, including its uses, pharmacology, toxicology and pharmacokinetics as well as their analytical results. Finally, a report is submitted in the style that would be submitted for drug registration, including information which they need to have researched from the literature.

In order to carry out the necessary tasks this exercise requires a variety of individual and group skills to be developed and practised. The learning experience includes developing information-gathering skills and the application of many pharmaceutical analytical techniques. The authors of this approach comment:

> teaching and outcome objectives of the approach have been most satisfying. Students now understand the relevance, have become more investigative and have applied problem-solving skills to their work without prescriptive guidance from laboratory exercise notes. . . . Overall the students responded favourably to this practical, they value the fact that they get to learn database and literature skills.
>
> (Wong, You, Baker and Duke 2001)

What we see here is students working within a community of students and mirroring the work of professionals in their practice. The academics define the problem and set up the structure to ensure appropriate learning takes place. They participate as advisors, and ultimately assessors.

A direct relationship between research and teaching is seen in a case where the research of an honours student, has been used as the basis for inquiry-based learning scenarios. From 1999–2000 Kathryn Refshauge and Christopher Maher (2001) supervised an honours student, who investigated the prevalence and identification of depression in patients with low back pain. The student found that depression is extremely common in patients presenting to physiotherapists for treatment of low back pain, a high proportion of which was classified as extremely severe depression on a Depression Anxiety Stress Scale. Since physiotherapists are typically poor at detecting depression in their patients and since depression is both a risk and prognostic factor for lower back pain, adequate recognition and treatment of depression by primary care professionals was thought to be essential. So they developed a major case study for fourth-year physiotherapy students to help them learn how to recognise and measure depression, and when to refer patients with depression. The case study was of a patient with many complex problems, potentially including depression, and the teaching and the independent inquiry conducted by students was based around this case study. While this case clearly shows the integration of research and teaching, the students who experienced the case study do not participate in furthering the research. They learn in groups of students within a separate academic domain.

Another case where students work within a tight-knit community group is a unit of study designed to provide high achieving first-year engineering students with an insight into engineering practice in industry. Student groups work on industrial projects and complete their project in one semester. They are expected to provide details and insight into how their findings could be used or exploited commercially. The emphasis is on the team members setting and achieving their own goals, and presenting their work in both oral and written form. By the end of the project students are able to:

- analyse an industrial problem
- carry out the background research required to fully define and solve the problem
- work effectively as a team member at all stages of the project
- write a coherent report, outlining the problem and its solution, as well as making an oral presentation
- prepare a business plan with respect to an industrial or research project

Although the students have a choice over the project that they wish to pursue, this is steered by the academic concerned. Senior faculty members supervise each project, which may or may not relate to their own research interests. Again we see, therefore, students inhabiting a separate domain where staff research plays an indirect and often unstated role.

Such research-based approaches to undergraduate education more often than not are implemented in the context of professional education and these examples are no exception. Although, clearly, knowledge of practice is important, these cases do not rely on the teachers or facilitators engaging in research directly on the topics studied, even though they do draw on research findings and the behaviour or attitudes of practising professionals. Although the students in these examples are engaging with learning about the research journey of academics, they are not engaging in the research community as practitioners in that community.

In the following example, again we see a direct relationship between teacher research and the way the student learning is structured within this professional practice setting. Yet again students are engaged in learning and researching within a community of their peers, not that of the academics. Within the unit of study, *Integrated Dispensing*, each student assumes responsibility for a group of pseudo-patient families, whose members 'develop' distinctive histories over the course of the semester-length unit. In keeping with an evidence-based approach, students use the skills they have learned to manage the medications of their families, and are required to undertake appropriate interventions and counselling when necessary, in particular using medication reviews and Consumer Medicine Information which has been shown through the research of the teachers to improve medication use in patients with complex therapeutic regimens (Chen, Crampton, Krass and Benrimoj 1999a, 1999b). Fourth-year *Integrated Dispensing* students have a family of patients. Each week they receive prescriptions for some of their families and they have to dispense, deal with clinical interventions, communicate with the doctor and patient, and provide counselling to the patient for each case (based on Sainsbury, McLachlan and Aslani 2001).

▶ Problem-based learning

Problem-based learning is a major innovation within professional education. It has become so widespread in professional education that it is now possible to find examples of problem-based learning being used as an organising principle for the way in which whole institutions (e.g., Maastricht University, the Netherlands), or whole faculties (e.g., the Faculty of Health Sciences, Linköping University, Sweden) are organised. There are now numerous degree programmes that take this approach. While problem-based learning was developed initially within medical and health-related fields, it is now practised in numerous disciplinary areas including social work, architecture, engineering and law (see, for example, Boud and Feletti 1997).

> The principal idea behind problem-based learning is . . . that the starting point for learning should be a problem, a query or a puzzle that the learner wishes to solve.
>
> (Boud 1985: 13)

> Problem-based learning is a way of constructing and teaching courses using problems as the stimulus and focus for student activity. While there are different versions of what constitutes PBL, it does not, as it is sometimes erroneously assumed, involve the addition of problem-solving activities to otherwise discipline-centred curricula. It is a way of conceiving of the curriculum centred around key problems in professional practice. Problem-based courses start with problems rather than with exposition of disciplinary knowledge. They move students towards the acquisition of knowledge and skills through a staged sequence of problems presented in context, together with associated learning materials and support from teachers.
>
> (Boud and Feletti 1997)

So for example in the problem based University of Sydney graduate medical programme, evidence based medicine is used to encourage students to formulate focused clinical questions, to search the literature effectively, and to find and appraise clinical research. One example of the use of evidence-based medicine is 'PEARLS' (**P**resentations of **E**vidence **A**bstracted from the **R**esearch **L**iterature for the **S**olutions of real individuals' problems), where the students find a patient in their clinical encounters and formulate a clinical question of relevance. In a series of tutorials, they develop their search strategy, conduct the search, find the best quality evidence, appraise it and present it to their colleagues and teachers in a formal presentation. There are similarities here with the 'seven steps' in problem-based learning used at Maastricht University, the Netherlands, which are now widely applied in a variety of contexts. The seven steps are:

1. Discuss and agree on working definintions of unclear words and concepts.
2. Identify one or more problems in the statement, agree on which phenomena require explanation or discovery of underlying causes.
3. Analyse problems into components, implications, possible explanations or solutions, and develop working hypotheses. This is like a 'brainstorming' phase with evaluation suspended while explanations or solutions are written on a flipchart or chalk board.
4. Discuss, evaluate and organise hypotheses and tentative explanations.
5. Formulate learning goals including how to resolve conflicting ideas, incomplete, incongruent or unclear explanations, what further information is needed; how can this information best be obtained?
6. Develop study plans to discover needed information; identify individual or sub-group study tasks, adjourn meeting to carry out these study activities.
7. Meet to consider and synthesize newly acquired information; try to apply it to the problem(s); test the results against alternative explanations or applications; agree on the best solutions.

(Schmidt and Bouhuijs 1980 quoted in Gilbert and Foster 1997: 245)

So, for example, in the Social Work division of the School of Community Health and Social Studies at Anglia Polytechnic University, England, inquiry-based learning is the basis for the first semester BA in social work – the qualifying award. There is a two-week induction and then three sequences of the inquiry-based learning cycle, using written scenarios of a complex social situation. With the aid of a social work tutor as a facilitator, students, working in groups of up to sixteen, go through a version of the seven Maastricht steps exploring the issues raised, grouping them in order of importance, identifying and checking out prior knowledge, researching new information and presenting it to their peers, and then applying their knowledge to inform their proposed intervention/care plans. They end each sequence by evaluating both the knowledge and skills gained, and noting how their values have been challenged, as well as reflecting on the learning process.

While graduate and professional programmes form the majority of cases of problem-based learning, the use of this approach in undergraduate education although less common is not unknown. One example is a first year undergraduate computer science course at the University of Sydney (Barg et al. 2000). Students engage in the design of computer software which requires simulation of a complex system; for example, planning and managing checkouts in a supermarket, managing a biodiversity survey, managing information for an entertainment advisor, managing activities for Olympic participants, managing the data for a school timetable, or managing a product inventory for a computer vendor. Students begin by working on a simple problem and learn how to work in teams. They then, in groups, research their chosen topic and the computer code needed to develop the simulation. Each simulation requires that students collaboratively write a small core of essential code and then develop it so that the simulation can cope with ever-more complex situations.

Problem-based learning has transformed learning and teaching, particularly in many professional areas, and has proved to be a highly effective pedagogy in higher education. It is a key way in which research and evidence-based approaches are being introduced into courses. However, from the point of view of the quest for research-based undergraduate education it becomes evident that problem-based learning, with its tight structure of problem solving and carefully designed sequence of steps to be followed, does not always set up opportunities for knowledge building in Bereiter's (2002) sense. For example, students do not tend to set the problems to be addressed. In addition, students are engaged in collaborative inquiry, but collaboration with each other. Teacher research again tends to occupy a quite separate domain. The research that students conduct in the case of problem-based learning is to enable them to learn, not particularly to contribute to the profession or the discipline itself. Consequently, there is frequently a separation between students' learning and professional practice even when the former replicates the latter.

Hence, there is a need to go further. In some cases, students act as if they were clients for particular bodies or organisations, or actually become clients. I came across an example of students acting as clients at the Faculty of Rural Management in the town of Orange in New South Wales, Australia. Students are required as part of a course in business finance, to carry out a financial appraisal for a business or land management project of their choice. Many of the students are employed in, or own, rural properties, so many of them are able to do a realistic project on a projected development in their neighborhood. The knowledge building arises out of the questions that they identify. For example: undertaking a major soil conservation project, purchasing an adjoining block of land, adding a mail order business to a nursery, choosing between alternative apple-juicing plant designs, implementation of a land management plan to return a degraded area to public use, establishment of a community waste disposal facility, re-establishing a fire-damaged plantation, and so on. To carry out the appraisal requires considerable research as well as knowledge of the chosen theoretical tools to be used.

On the same campus, in subjects designed to teach the application of engineering principles to development and restoration projects, students simulate the role of project manager and participate in the planning, design and implementation of an agricultural or land management project.

Graduates from these subjects might be expected to compile property management plans. They can explore the processes involved and practise planning in a safe learning environment. Some students carry out real projects with the property owner as the client. As well as gaining important generic capabilities, students have to learn about, and comply with, professional and industry requirements. This may involve interpreting maps and plans, measuring the dimensions of the project works, providing advice on the appropriate materials and specifications of a minor project, substantiating opinions with research, determining design criteria and appraising alternative options, identifying standards that the selected project has to comply with, identifying and evaluating appropriate sources of information, compiling a professional report, and also self-evaluating what they have achieved (Southorn 1999). Students may in this way go beyond community interests and involvement to provide technical expertise to a project that might otherwise not be forthcoming (Southorn 1999). In selecting and carrying out their chosen project, students have to negotiate and liaise with members of the community and with other professionals. In this way the students are working in a similar way to the students in Roth's study mentioned earlier. They build knowledge while contributing to a research undertaking with a defined outcome. The view of research that students experience when carrying out such professional tasks is of course quite different to the conventional view of research as carried out in the university (Smith and Coldron 2000). In this example students are engaged in Mode 2 knowledge building within professional communities of practice. If we are to follow Barnett (2000) in his belief that research has to teach is how to live within a super-complex society, then the type of research that these students are engaged in is extremely meaningful even though there is no evidence that their lecturer's research is involved in any way.

▶ Interdisciplinary inquiry

The Boyer Commission report (1999) suggested that the first-year undergraduate programme should be an interdisciplinary inquiry-based experience. Indeed, it suggested that universities should systematically remove barriers to interdisciplinary education; the main one being the way that universities are organised so as to create 'vested interests in traditionally defined departments' (p. 23). So, for example, semester-long modular programmes frequently do not provide adequate time for research-based approaches to be implemented and therefore tend to go against such integration. On the one hand, they may encourage multi-disciplinary thinking by enabling students to complete a range of (sometimes unrelated) subjects. On the other hand, they frequently do little to assist students to integrate their understanding from different areas. There is thus a need to define 'capstone' experiences to provide opportunities for integration that would not otherwise exist.

At the University of Calgary, an interdisciplinary team of engineering, design and communications academics have developed a first-year undergraduate course in engineering design for 600 students. Teams of four students work on real-life projects for real clients to create innovative engineering designs (Caswell et al. 2004). The course uses an environment with moveable desks with the teachers on hand in a 'central command' adjoining room to provide advice audio-visually. 'Coaches' from a range of different disciplines and from industry are also on hand to provide assistance. Students start with no more than a small motor and a stockpile of Lego and have to investigate concepts from engineering, art, robotics, physics and other disciplines to build robots. For example, students were asked to design robots that could ice skate, so that Olympic speed skaters might eventually one day be able to pit themselves against a robot that can skate faster than they can. There are no textbooks providing answers for students, and no examinations at the end of the course. Instead, students are in the kind of situation where they are asked to solve problems that they will encounter after graduation.

So far we have examined cases where teachers are active in the community of students as course designers, as advisers and as assessors, and may be separately active in the community of their researcher and practitioner colleagues as well. Research and teaching are coming together, but students are being tentatively involved in researcher communities of practice. In short, they are still occupying the distinct domain of the 'student'.

▶ Understanding how disciplinary knowledge is defined

When I was investigating examples of research-enhanced teaching during a period of study leave in the United Kingdom, I set out to visit a number of the staff involved in the UK Higher Education Academy's Learning and Teaching Support Networks (LTSNs). I was interested in how different communities of academics were coming to terms with the relationship between teaching and research in their disciplinary areas. What is considered to be disciplinary knowledge is going to depend, of course, on the nature of the discipline area and, as we saw in Chapter 3, there are going to be differences in how different areas attempt to bring research and teaching together. In some newer areas, for example, academics are working with students to explore how the discipline functions to generate knowledge and the ways in which knowledge is established. For those driving the LTSN network designed to develop teaching in the performing arts, for example, a focus of attention was the issue of what is research in the performance disciplines. Theatre studies, a relatively new academic area, has become a fusion of theory and practice. Engaging the student in discussion of this and how this relates to their own subjectivity is an important part of the student coming to understand the discipline. Reflective practice was considered to be an integral part of disciplinary knowledge. Research involved the practitioner as a person and this, it was considered, could not be left out of the teaching process.

In a course designed to take students on the journey that their lecturer, as a researcher, had travelled and to 'bring to them some understanding of my discipline, past and present   its history, methodologies and subject matter, and what challenges it currently and potentially addresses', Gaynor Macdonald at the University of Sydney seeks to provide for students a combination of a specific and personalised encounter with the discipline and a general understanding of its breadth and depth:

> I had been involved in the anthropology of Native Title in both academic and consultancy contexts and, as became clear in my own practice, it was necessary to understand, to be able to work with and to critique, a century of Australian anthropology in order to understand how to approach a Native Title case and to understand the theoretical as well as political and ethical issues it raised.
>
> (MacDonald 2001: 70)

This first-year course in social anthropology was developed in order to address these issues. It takes the topical, and often controversial, issue of Native Title as a means of engaging students with their contemporary society.

In the process of my LTSN visits I talked to Caroline Baillie, who at the time was Deputy Director of the Materials Science LTSN. Our conversation illustrates how the relationship between teaching and research is grounded in the problematics of academics' ideas about what is knowledge in the discipline area. She suggests academics should critically re-examine their ideas about the way knowledge is negotiated, and then bring students into that negotiation process. I've fictionalised our conversation for the sake of brevity and clarity, but essentially it went like this:

Angela: So tell me what you've been doing.

Caroline: Well there was a conference of materials scientists discussing a phenomenon in materials science. I had conducted research on students' conceptions of this particular phenomenon. When I presented this work at the conference, the researchers realised that there were different ways of understanding it.

Angela: So did this surprise them?

Caroline: Oh yes. When a community thinks it understands something, it thinks it is fact. One part of the academic, the researcher, believes that scientific knowledge is negotiable and uncertain, to be discovered and rediscovered all their lives and beyond. The other part, the teacher, appears to believe that scientific knowledge has one truth and that this truth can be taught to willing recipients of this wisdom without negotiation. Academics recognise that their conceptions of knowledge are multiple, but they just teach one of these conceptions. They aren't aware that they're doing this. I'm running a project on visco-elasticity. I started with the hypothesis that people have contradictory notions of visco-elasticity in research and in teaching, and I'm reviewing how visco-elasticity is taught. I'm interested in knowledge development. How do researchers think about knowledge and how do they learn about knowledge development?

Angela: So how do you understand knowledge development?

Caroline: The process of going from experiments to something becoming a fact, involves negotiations. Knowledge development is helping the person get from the data to the idea. I believe that by enabling scientists to reflect on the knowledge they negotiate and on the process of negotiation itself, they will be able to help students live the spirit of discovery. What students will learn within the university will then be more akin to how to be a scientist, rather than how to pass exams.

Angela: So how will you achieve this?

Caroline: Well there are two steps to the process. The first one is to identify the basic units of knowledge which constitute a particular branch of science that the student might want to learn in the course of a degree. In our research, this was carried out by in-depth, open-ended interviews of key researchers in a specific field (actually the field of composite materials) in several different countries, where the researchers were invited to choose the dimension of their research for discussion. A multi-dimensional presentation of the research field was then constructed and presented back to the research community in a technical conference.

Angela: So you're working with the researchers and their understanding of the domain.

Caroline: That's right. You have to ask, what are the barriers that prevent the development of an understanding of a scientific concept? What is it that blocks our way to scientific knowledge development? There are many factors: cultural, psychological, social, etc.

Angela: So the first step is to encourage a community of researchers to reflect within their specialist area on what are the most important effects and phenomena to be learnt by students?

Caroline: Yes. They then need to create collectively an 'outcome space' for each, which contains their many different ways of understanding these. The 'outcome space' then becomes the 'fact', which may be explained, labelled and tested, using the many and varied 'constructs' developed by the different skill sets and perspectives of the researchers from the far corners of the earth. What follows would be the responsibility of the research community to own their role as the 'guardians' of the knowledge they discover. At present there is no sense of awareness of this guardianship. The community decides what constitutes acceptable knowledge through peer review of grant applications (for the initial production of knowledge) and of journals and conference papers (for the dissemination of such knowledge) as well as through the textbooks and courses created for the next generation of scientists. However, what constitutes this knowledge base and the acceptance of the notion of a negotiated knowledge is not explicitly discussed.

Angela: I see. So what's the second step?

Caroline: Well the second step would be to bring into the undergraduate course some of the important aspects of the knowledge-negotiation process. This step involves considering the processes by which learning or knowledge building occurs. In order to uncover some of the basic blocks to the knowledge-building process, I organised a study. Interviews were arranged between academic researchers and art students. The intention was to ask individuals who were from very different disciplinary backgrounds, with no preconceived notions of knowledge in the areas studied, to interview the researchers about their objects of study. The ideal outcome of the knowledge-building process, intended to be developed during the interviews, would be a mutual understanding of the subject matter discussed.

Angela: The student could never understand the knowledge being discussed in the same way as the researcher. So it's not the purpose of the interview for the researcher to give the student knowledge, to explain and re-explain until the student 'gets it'?

Caroline: No, but it is necessary for the researcher to try to present their understanding of the subject matter, with as little jargon and assumed knowledge as possible. If they are able to do this, then they fully understand what they themselves are doing which is not always obvious. The student in their turn must intervene and feed back throughout the interview. If at any stage, they don't follow the line of reasoning they have to say so and to repeat back their own way of seeing the subject under discussion. The researcher can then alter the way they have been describing something, moving closer to the line taken by the student. In this way the perspectives of the students will now enrich the researcher's understanding. The students will have developed an understanding of the researcher's knowledge as seen from their own perspective.

Angela: And do you think that facilitation of knowledge building in this way would involve the breaking down of key barriers?

Caroline: Yes, it enhances the pathways through the barriers, for example, the implicit assumptions that are made. So someone might assume their way of viewing the world would be the same for everybody, and that's going to create a barrier if the other person doesn't see the world in the same way they do and if the assumptions are not made explicit.

(Baillie 2004)

Perhaps this case comes close to the possibilities where communities of students and academics work together, to which Bereiter alludes when he says:

Modern teachers need to be simultaneously active in two knowledge-building communities. One is the knowledge-building community they share with their students. Its object is building an understanding of the whole world. The other is a knowledge-building community they share with researchers and other practitioners. Its object is building a working knowledge of teaching and learning. Lying beyond the scope of what I have discussed here, but offering itself as an enticing possibility, is merging those two knowledge-building communities into a larger and more complexly dynamic one.

(Bereiter 2002: 417–18)

▶ **Research as a social practice**

So we are beginning to see students brought into disciplinary or professional communities. As we saw in Chapter 2, some academics view research as a social process; as a process of engaging with other researchers. They may view this as either working collaboratively to produce an outcome such as engaging in research networks, going to conferences, working in a research team, collaborating to produce an edited book for example; or competitively in terms of recognition through research grants, or some other kind of recognition or reward. In some of the cases discussed so far in this chapter students are engaged in mirroring aspects of these social practices of research.

While researching for this book, I attended a full conference organised and attended by students and staff involved in the second-year multimedia systems course at the University of Southampton (*see* http://mms.ecs.soton. ac.uk/mms2002/papers.php).

I park the car and easily find the building. There are not many people around so I know I must be early. I go up to the desk where a friendly person asks me my name and hands me a folder. There are some low, red chairs in the foyer so I sit down in a place where I can explore the comings and goings.

'Nervous?', one of the suited young people near me asks his companion.
'A bit.'
'You'll be fine.'
'It's the first time I've done anything like this.'
'Don't worry about it.'

I recognise a familiar face. It's Sue, one of the course leaders. I get up to go over to meet her. 'Angela, I'm so glad you could come. Can I introduce you to Andrew Farmer? He's one of our representatives from IBM.'
'Pleased to meet you.'

There is no time to do more than exchange pleasantries. By this time the foyer is humming with the buzz of eager conference participants.

The conference opens with a welcome from the conference committee. It's a committee consisting of students and academics and it is a student who welcomes us and introduces the opening keynote speaker, Professor Hey. He sets the scene for the presentations to follow, talking of the need for multimedia to be thought of on an international scale. Huge sums are being invested in multimedia and scientists all over the world have to collaborate.

Tom Weaver was the first student speaker. He talked about the gap between human and computer vision. He had researched the field and I found it an interesting presentation even though my knowledge of the subject was minimal. Alison Wade then gave a presentation about the legislation around the music industry. As a piece of research this was also an interesting presentation and it generated quite a lot of discussion. 'Memories of the future' was the intriguing title of the next presentation by Martin Wickett. This was a very technical overview of computer storage systems that are likely to replace current ways of storing information.

The students had chosen their topics and then presented an abstract for approval to the tutors. They had carried out their research and then presented their draft papers for assessment. This was done, as is normal for conference papers, through a process of peer review. Each student had reviewed six papers and had written a critical review of one of them. At this point the students chose who was going to present a verbal paper and who a poster presentation.

At the conference there were some very polished verbal presentations; interesting too. I'm still intrigued by the futuristic car navigation systems presented by Philip Ogunro. The posters too were generally informative. I was impressed by the enthusiasm that the students had for explaining about their chosen subject and I learnt a lot during the day. One student said that in doing the work for the conference he had developed a new research interest.

At lunch time I spoke to some students about the way that the subject had been taught:
'It's been good to do the research.'
'Yes, it's been fun.'
'Yeh, but when the conference is over we're going to have to face the exam.' This remark was followed by a groan from all three of the young people who were now sitting on the red chairs in the foyer. I asked: 'So what about the exam?'
'Well, it's a worry. It's hard to see what they are going to be like.'
'We've only studied one topic; only researched one topic. They said that the exam is going to be on what we learn at the conference.'
'How can they test that?'

It is clear that the conference was a significant learning event for these students. Some of the social aspects of research practice were being mirrored through this course. Not only the process of presentation, but the processes of critical evaluation, peer review and of learning through conferences – not something we academics do particularly well, I suspect – were all designed into the process. The involvement of managers from industry and a few other outsiders such as me as well as the academics made this course feel like a different kind of experience for the students. An inclusive scholarly community had been created.

▶ Involving students in the community of researchers

The main way in which students undertake research as an undergraduate is when they come to their final-year projects. In Australia this is likely to be in their fourth year if they continue to Honours, or the final year of a three-year degree programme as is commonly practised in the United Kingdom. There is no doubt that such projects provide important opportunities for students to integrate their studies, to develop a piece of sustained work and to exercise creativity. However, the question that we need to address is why such dissertation projects are used so extensively in the final year and not in earlier stages of an undergraduate's experience. Many academics would contest the idea that students are capable of carrying out research before that time. Yet this is clearly not true as we have seen in the many cases so far explored in this and the previous chapter, and as we shall see later. In Chapter 3 we noted the idea that students can only carry out research at the end of their undergraduate degree as a product of the kind of hierarchical thinking that Bourdieu talks about. Students are considered capable of carrying out research only when they have demonstrated a basic understanding of the subject.

A further question that has been asked in this chapter, namely, the extent to which students, including those in their final year, are carrying out research with their teachers or supervisors or whether the research is quite separate from them; whether students come to feel part of the community of researchers or whether they and the research they do is unconnected to other researchers. This will of course depend on the discipline. For example independent research will be common in the humanities but team-based research is more likely to be characteristic of the sciences. These questions can also be asked, of course, of postgraduate research and there will be as many different answers as there are students and academics supervising them. So, in order to provide food for further reflection, in the final part of this chapter I want to look at some other ways in which undergraduate students from more junior years are being involved in research.

One case where junior undergraduate students are involved in the research of the academic teaching them as a routine part of their undergraduate studies is a course and a research project on reinforcement in horses carried out by Amanda Warren-Smith at the University of Sydney:

Angela: So Amanda, tell me about the research you are doing.

Amanda: Well I use foals so that I can have completely naïve subjects.

Angela: So the foals are the subjects.

Amanda: Yes. Using foals is particularly important, not just from a research point of view but also because so many people do not understand what they are doing with reinforcement. So from the first exposure to training, the foals are then not taught anything clearly and this of course blurs any further work with them.

Angela: So how did you go about it?

Amanda: The methodology involved using negative reinforcement via aversive pressure on the head collar of the foal. Mare and foal pairs are kept together in the same yard during testing but the foals are given the stimulus to walk away from the mare. The treatments tested were varying the length of time the pressure was maintained on the head collar such that treatment Group 1 were reinforced just as the first step was taken; treatment Group 2 were reinforced as the second step was to be taken and the third treatment group were reinforced after two to three steps were taken. For this trial I used 14 unweaned foals, aged three to five months. I am in the process of doing it again with this year's foal drop as from the first trial I identified some minor things I can improve on.

Angela: That's an interesting line of research. I had no idea people did research on such things. Did you find any differences in the different groups?

Amanda: Oh yes. The results were interesting and not as we expected. The main thing to come out of it is that we should be reinforcing upon completion of the desired response, not just as they start to perform the response. That's normal in training. In fact this work challenges many of the traditional viewpoints in the horse industry and is not always readily accepted by those that feel they know all there is to know about horse training for all sorts of reasons. However, I feel that if I can have these breakthroughs with students and they then put it into practice, the more correct way of doing things will get out into industry, even if it takes a while for this to happen.

Angela: So the students were involved in the training.

Amanda: Yes. From the point of view of research-led teaching, I think the big 'ah-ha' for the students was the application of the aversive stimuli, get the response and then release immediately. Now that they have seen or heard of the foal work it really seems to have made much better sense to them and they have experienced first hand the difference in responses from the foals that I did the original work on. These foals are so much easier to deal with in every aspect. It really has made a difference and it says a lot about their learning too.

Angela: It sounds as if you could not have done this research without the students.

Amanda: One of the teaching units I have is about getting unfit horses to a significant level of fitness. Many questions always arise about various aspects of training and so we set up small trials to answer the students' questions. Last year I incorporated some standard exercise-testing methods and took different measurements to monitor fitness. The standard tests have been frequently conducted in lab environments using treadmills but they have not been done extensively out in the field, which of course replicates the real world environment. This year we are adding different dietary manipulations that should or should not be implemented prior to intense exercise in the horse. The students are so excited about it all, whatever happens it will be worth it just to have stimulated their enthusiasm. They are all set to measure feed and water intake; have research conditions in place (these are mostly first-year students) such as minimising variability, designing a randomised block design and thinking about statistics after it and so on.

(Warren-Smith, McLean, Nicol and McGreevy 2004)

What is being described here is an intimate relationship between the research and teaching. Students are not simply engaged in research activities in order to learn, neither are they simply collaborating solely in student groups to carry out inquiries. They are learning through the knowledge-building process that comes with carrying out real research collaboratively with a researcher.

An interesting aspect of this example is the fact that in order to be carried out at all, the research requires a number of participants who each work with one foal. Students are able to learn through participating in research because the research requires them. In a routine part of their course work, 1000 first-year biology students at the University of Sydney participate in research to simultaneously collect, grow and identify fungal spores throughout the Sydney metropolitan area. The information is then mapped and allergenic trends are identified. Students each write a report on their actions and observations, and the resulting overall findings are publishable in a scientific journal. Again this is research to develop new knowledge which cannot otherwise be carried out because it requires a large number of people to simultaneously gather data across a wide area. The large student cohort makes possible rather than impedes research experiences for students.

Another example where the research that undergraduates do is considered to be a part of their course work comes from Hasok Chang from University College London. The idea here is that all the students work on independent research projects that share a common theme, for example, the history of the chemical element chlorine. At the end of the year students' project work (reading notes, results of literature searches, photocopies of materials obtained, data, laboratory notes, annotated bibliographies, reports, etc.) is made available for the next year's group of students:

> To give a flavour of the work carried out so far, I will very briefly mention just two of the projects. One investigated the history of the 'chlorine chamber', a device that was apparently popular in 1920s America, based on the idea that breathing a low concentration of chlorine gas served to cure and prevent cold and flu. The students discovered that this was an idea promoted by the US Chemical Warfare Service as a beneficial application of chemical warfare agents, as it faced the prospect of closure due to adverse public reaction in the aftermath of the First World War. The other project investigated the initial discovery of chlorine in 1774 by the Swedish chemist Scheele, who did not think of chlorine as an element but as 'dephlogisticated muriatic acid'. One might imagine that this mis-identification was corrected once the phlogiston theory was overthrown, but actually the Chemical Revolution only resulted in the re-labelling of chlorine as 'oxygenated muriatic acid'. This was an excellent study of the arcane original papers, making sense of why the opposing camps of eighteenth-century chemists believed what they believed. Both of these projects went

considerably beyond existing secondary literature. The current phase of the course will run for one more year (2004–2005). Afterwards, we plan to collect the results into a book, provisionally entitled *An Element of Controversy: The life of chlorine in science, medicine, technology and war*.

(Chang 2005: 388)

Chang argues that in this course a community of researchers is created by, on the one hand, the fact that the students are all working on related topics and, on the other, by the way in which each year group inherits work from the previous set of students. Chang suggests that it is advantageous to choose a research topic in which the teacher is not a leading expert. Nevertheless, students are genuinely working to build new knowledge through their research; knowledge which will eventually be publishable in a book. We return to the issues raised by this example in the final chapter.

▶ Undergraduate research schemes

So far we have considered cases where undergraduate students engage in research as an integral part of their courses. However, another way in which students may be involved in research is through special undergraduate research programmes where students participate in the actual research being carried out in the university. 'Undergraduate research is an inquiry or investigation conducted by an undergraduate that makes an original, intellectual or creative contribution to the discipline' (Council on Undergraduate Research 2003). In such programmes selected students undertake research for a defined period of time, typically in a summer vacation, as part of a research team or alongside an established academic researcher. Most undergraduate research schemes appear to be targeted at the early years of undergraduate education; that is, in the first or second years. This is in contrast to the practice of engaging students in dissertation projects mentioned above.

It is difficult to estimate how widespread the practice of engaging junior students in undergraduate research programmes is. The Council for Undergraduate Research in America, for example, claims to have some 400 institutional members. Some universities have large programmes. For example, approximately 80 per cent of MIT undergraduates participate at least once in undergraduate research programmes during their time at university. The University of Arizona has 140 undergraduates participating in its biology research programme alone. In the United States, funding for undergraduate research comes from the National Science Foundation as well as from numerous private foundations and bursary schemes. Harvard, for example, has 700 students in one bursary scheme alone. In short, undergraduate research is a well established aspect of university life in the United

States. Numerous institutions have centres devoted to the organisation of undergraduate student research and many organise conferences and events and publish special journals to showcase students' work.

While the phenomenon of undergraduate students engaging in such real research projects in the junior years is commonplace in universities in the United States, elsewhere it tends to be relatively rare. This leads to the question as to why it is not prevalent anywhere else. As far as I have been able to tell, in Australia, for example, the practice of engaging undergraduate students on real research projects in this way is almost unknown, exceptions being the Summer Research Scholars scheme at the Australian National University and the Summer Vacation Research Scholarship programme at the University of Sydney. In the United Kingdom too, there is no history or tradition of this practice as there is in the United States. This may be because there is not a tradition of student employment while at university, 'working their way through college', in these countries. Yet the increased pressure on student finances does not appear to be an inducement to start such schemes. Engaging undergraduate students in research, particularly in the earlier years is more likely to be treated with suspicion. Exceptions to this are the schemes at Imperial College, London University and Warwick University, England, where the universities fund undergraduate students to work on 'live' research projects with academic staff either full time during vacations or part time during the semester as in similar schemes in the United States.

Real and perceived barriers to the development of undergraduate research schemes include academics' limited time for mentoring students, lack of laboratory space and equipment, constraints on the curriculum on the time needed to prepare students for an undergraduate research experience, insufficient rewards and incentives for academics to participate, and a research culture that is discouraging to young researchers (Morse 2003). The widespread practice of involving students in final-year dissertation projects may also be a factor. We might add, following Bourdieu, that attitudes of academics that confine undergraduate students to the fringes of academia and preserve privilege and status may also be influential. It is clear that in the United States, funding coming from the government's National Science Foundation is a considerable encouragement. Indeed, as we shall see in Chapter 8, the relationship between teaching and research is crucially affected by the policies of governments and research councils. The lack of stipends and bursaries to fund undergraduate research and an unwillingness on the part of such bodies to commit funds to this purpose must pose an almost insurmountable barrier.

So what are the benefits of students engaging in undergraduate research schemes? Do they take the role of low-level administrative assistants or are the students treated as part of a community of researchers? A study of undergraduate science research at four liberal arts colleges in the United States found that the two main benefits to students were a number of personal and professional gains such as increased confidence (e.g., in their ability to do research, contributing real knowledge as a scientist, or feeling like a scientist) and intellectual development in thinking and working like a researcher, including improved ability to apply knowledge and skills, development of critical-thinking and problem-solving skills, and a more advanced understanding of the nature of science/how scientific knowledge is built (Seymour, Hunter, Laursen and Deantoni 2004). These authors also note that nearly 20 per cent of the students reported improvements in skills, particularly communication skills, and some reported that the experience had clarified their career goals. Indeed, it was found that many of the students indicated that they thought the benefits that they had gained were transferable to a range of situations. Seymour and colleagues comment that in interviews with academic advisors it was clear that they were not aware of the significance of the personal and professional development among their mentored students and argue that this aspect of the undergraduate research experience is not well represented in the research literature. They comment that this may be a reflection of the unease that academics have about focusing on the affective aspects of experience. They suggest: 'Apparent disattention to the powerful impact of these experiences on young people – and their consequences for professional preparation – while focusing on such issues as how many of them choose graduate school is, perhaps, to miss the point' (Seymour et al. 2004: 531). It may also be a reflection of a view of research where the person of the researcher is absent from awareness (see Chapter 2).

Particularly pertinent to our discussion in this chapter is the finding that students valued the opportunity to work with academics in a one-to-one relationship. One of the most important gains for them was that they had the opportunity to work in a collegial way with academics and other researchers and the discovery that these people took their work seriously. For example, one student commented:

> When I was at the conferences, especially the one last year, I felt truly that I was a scientist. I was amidst scientists. I was just, you know, completely surrounded by them, – I was talking to them about my research and they were talking to me. And they, I could see them talking to me . . . not as if I was lower to them, but as equal to them. And that made me feel really good. – Some people even asked me if it was my doctoral work.
>
> (Male physics major quoted in Seymour et al. 2004: 509)

> I've gotten to know all the faculty . . . I actually see them more as peers. As a researcher, they are your peers; you're working with them. And you ask

them questions, and they are just as excited to know what I'm doing as I am to know how they're doing, or what they could help me with. . . . It gives a totally different aspect than being a student . . . and you don't have to be intimidated by them anymore.

(Male biology major quoted in Seymour et al. 2004: 510)

Commenting on the University of Warwick scheme, Blackmore and Cousin (2003) similarly report that students on this scheme appreciated the opportunity that it provided for them to participate in research communities of practice. They found that students appreciated being able to play a role in knowledge production through participating in the culture of inquiry. What such schemes do demonstrate clearly is that, given the opportunity to participate in research, students more often than not rise to the challenge and often achieve more than anticipated.

The findings of these studies raised a very important question about the ways in which students are treated when they become research scholars as opposed to when they are students. Both the students in the Seymour and colleagues' study and those at the University of Warwick reported that they were treated differently from how they are treated in teaching and learning settings. This made me wonder whether importing opportunities for students to engage in real research in this way into the curriculum would change the nature of undergraduate education, but would perhaps not necessarily result in changed relationships between researchers and students. We take up this point in Chapter 11.

There is also evidence in Seymour and colleagues' study that students were being inducted into the requirements of academic professionalism:

Students commented on the length of time involved, the care needed to make accurate observations and keep detailed notes, how much attention to detail was required, the tedium and repetition of some lab tasks, the long hours researchers worked, and their difficulties in achieving desired results:

You never really think that the scientist spends all this time . . . you never think anybody runs into a dead-end. Like the geniuses like Einstein, you never think that he ran into a dead-end, but he did. Many people did. And it gave me a better appreciation for it because, to get through all that and to know what we know today in the sciences, is just amazing.

(Male physics major)

This was much more than an intellectual appreciation of what goes into research. These students had come to understand that a high incidence of setbacks, errors, repeated procedures, and failed experiments is a normal part of the research process.

(Seymour et al. 2004: 516–517)

The University of Warwick scheme also demonstrated the ways in which engaging students in research can develop important skills, for example, of structuring one's workload, time management, a wide range of research skills including bibliographical searching, organisation of data, experimental skills and so on. Students commented upon the need to be able to focus on a number of tasks simultaneously. The experience demonstrated the complexity of research work and the need for patience and meticulousness; important aspects of academic professionalism. Baxter Magolda, Boes, Hollis and Jaramillo (1998) report similar findings in a larger study of students who had engaged in a ten-week summer research experience. They found students had increased confidence as learners, developed more capability for thinking independently, more awareness of learning as a life-long process and more capability for achieving career goals. In addition, they found that students had developed more complex conceptions of knowledge as a consequence of engaging in the research experience.

In another UK initiative, Zamorski (2002) invited 12 final-year undergraduate students to participate in a research project to examine students' experiences of research at the University of East Anglia in the United Kingdom.

This method offered a privileged access to data from the major constituent group researched (the student body). It also tested a model of student learning that was particularly distinctive in that it invited students to become integral to the whole process of research: to collaborate on the research design, on construction of the interview schedule, on early analysis work and in some of the dissemination and presentation activities.

(Zamorski 2002: 413)

The findings of this research have already been mentioned in Chapter 3. What is important to notice here is that the students were perfectly capable of and were treated as co-creators in the production of the research. I have subsequently carried out a parallel study working with second-year undergraduate students. What is interesting in respect to the present discussion is the way that, in discussing and agreeing the research questions and direction, one's language had to be tempered to address the students as junior collaborating colleagues rather than as student employees or helpers.

A number of different ways of involving students in the research process in order for them to learn have already been noted. Research-enhanced teaching may take the form of students working in collaborative groups engaged on problems defined by their teachers, and they may participate in the teacher's research. Yet care must be exercised. In so far as the students are engaging fully in a community of researchers, we must applaud attempts by teachers to involve students fully in their research. Yet this must be for pedagogical purposes. There are dangers that students may be used to carry out menial, repetitive research tasks that are perhaps irksome and time-consuming. I was alerted to the dangers of exploitation in a workshop I ran in which a participant talked about the way in which she and 30 of her classmates had been asked to work on computer printouts of species on coral reefs. The exercise would have been instructive had the class been asked to do this once. However, they did it for the whole semester. An enormous amount of tedious work was accomplished which the lecturer subsequently published without reference to the students' input. This is the dark side of research-led teaching, where students are exploited. Fortunately, such examples appear to be rare.

▶ Conclusion

In this chapter I have discussed a number of different ways in which undergraduate students are engaging in research and inquiry, and I have noted a wide range of attempts to provide research opportunities for students.

The key thing that has been noticed is how little academics are engaging students in their world; the world of research, and that apart from special undergraduate research schemes which, with the possible exception of North America, are very few in number, students are more often than not kept at a distance from the research culture. Many initiatives stop short of involving students in academic communities of practice which involve their teachers. Collaborative research is encouraged, but frequently this is collaborative research among students. More often than not, teachers define the questions that students enquire into. This may be justified on the grounds that it is necessary to ensure that students learn relevant disciplinary knowledge. Indeed, students in today's higher education institutions are more often than not required to learn what is specified in unit or subject outlines for them to learn. Indeed, the modular structure of today's degree courses, with their clearly specified learning outcomes, I suggest, meets accountability requirements but goes against the capacity for students to engage in the critical challenge of open exploratory inquiry. Students' capacity to engage in inquiries that go beyond the outcomes specified in course documentation is curtailed, limiting their ability to engage in knowledge building in Bereiter's (2002) sense. The challenge in thinking about how to change this is to design opportunities for students to explore the necessary disciplinary knowledge from the questions that they themselves generate, and to provide opportunities for students to devise learning outcomes that they themselves particularly want to achieve.

It is also worth noting that many cases of students engaging in inquiry processes in order to learn within their courses come from the professions. As professions become increasingly evidence based, valuing the use of research as an integral part of professional practice, so students are being required to engage in inquiry in order to learn and are, in the process, learning how to inquire into aspects of practice. We noted variation within different areas in the extent to which students are being encouraged to join in discussions about the nature of knowledge. This is particularly noticeable in newer discipline areas.

When students are treated as students, it appears that they are kept in a subordinate place. This helps to ensure the mystique of academia. However, when students are thought of as junior colleagues, the dynamic of their relationship to their teachers and to the university changes. This suggests that if we are to go beyond the divide between research and teaching, the discourse of teaching and students needs to change. We shall pursue these ideas in Chapters 10 and 11, but we now turn to examine the process of teaching and learning as itself a research process.

6 Teaching as Research

One of the ways academics are attempting to go beyond the divide between teaching and research is by turning teaching into research. As we saw in Chapter 2, the recognition that the academic community valued research more than teaching has led scholars to redefine the nature of scholarly work to include teaching. The scholarship of teaching and learning movement is a consequence of such work. In Chapter 3 we noted that when asked to give an example of research-enhanced education, a number of academics gave examples of research on teaching. So this and the following chapter considers how teaching can be made to resemble research by examining what is understood by the scholarship of university teaching and learning, and exploring its implications.

A close scrutiny of the scholarship of teaching and learning and its achievements (actual and potential) inevitably leads to an understanding of some of its challenges. I want to argue that there are some conflicts in its purposes and its implementation is not as straightforward as scholars would have us believe, but that the scholarship of teaching could lead to the development of inclusive scholarly communities of inquiry comprising both academics and students. This chapter first considers what is understood by the scholarship of teaching and learning and then examines the research literature and the theories on which it draws. This leads to a consideration of issues related to different disciplinary orientations, to the dissemination of teaching scholarship and finally to some ethical issues. The key aim is to establish a basis for examining the implications for disciplinary academics of engaging in the scholarship of teaching and learning which is the subject of Chapter 7.

▶ Understanding the scholarship of teaching and learning

Boyer's initial formulation of the scholarship of teaching has captured the imagination of higher education teachers and faculty developers thinking about how to enhance the teaching and learning process. However, we have come a long way from the initial formulations by Boyer and colleagues considered briefly in Chapter 2. Fifteen years on from the publication of *Scholarship Reconsidered*, we now have a much better understanding of what it is and how we can use it (Kreber 2002). Despite some scepticism about whether the term 'scholarship of teaching' is generally understood by academics (see, for example, Nicholls 2004), there is now a substantial body of work analysing its meaning, including within specific discipline areas, many examples demonstrating how it is being used in practice, numerous examples of teaching developments that have been made under its aegis, and a number of arguments for how such developments are improving the quality of students' learning in higher education.

Boyer set out to broaden the notion of scholarship, but one of the effects of his new definitions, particularly the concept of the scholarship of teaching and learning as it has now become known, has been to broaden the nature of what is understood by teaching. The scholarship of teaching and learning challenges and changes what teaching is understood to be by locating teaching practice within a wider intellectual context. Yet the more it is understood, the more it appears to encompass and the more challenges it seems to lead to.

While early work on the scholarship of teaching and learning stressed ideas of recognition and reward of teaching as central, Shulman more recently placed it in a wider context arguing that:

> Our interest in engaging in such work was summarized by three Ps, our professional interest, our pragmatic responsibilities, and the pressures of policy. Scholarship of teaching and learning supports our individual and professional roles, our practical responsibilities to our students and institution; and our social and political obligations to those that support and take responsibility for higher education.
>
> (Shulman 2000a: 53)

Trigwell and Shale (2004) suggest that the scholarship of teaching has descriptive aspects (understanding, categorising, defining and describing what teachers and teaching are) and purposive aspects (a means to an end, namely, the improvement of students' learning). Most scholars now agree that while there are a number of formulations of the scholarship of teaching and learning, it includes ongoing 'learning about teaching and the demonstration of teaching knowledge' (Kreber and Cranton 2000: 477–8). These authors distinguish four components:

1. Discovery research on teaching and learning.
2. Excellence in teaching as evidenced by teaching awards or evaluations of teaching.
3. Reflection on and application of the work of educational researchers.

4. Reflection on practice and on research on teaching in the teacher's own discipline.

The scholarship of teaching and learning thus takes teaching away from a direct focus on what happens in the classroom. Teaching becomes not just about how these students are going to learn this particular content knowledge, but how the teacher can most effectively engage students in the learning process. In other words, teaching becomes in and of itself a form of inquiry. Hutchings and Shulman (1999) argue that before ideas of the scholarship of teaching and learning were developed, teaching did not have an automatic mechanism for renewal. Unlike research which develops in the act of doing it through the process of peer review and the challenge of co-operative team-work, teaching, without a scholarly approach, stagnates. They comment, 'a scholarship of teaching is not synonymous with excellent teaching. It requires a kind of "going meta" in which faculty frame and systematically investigate questions related to student learning' (Hutchings and Shulman 1999:13). Teaching becomes subject to an ongoing process of change and adaptability.

There are numerous anecdotal examples of teachers improving aspects of their practice as a consequence of engaging in inquiries into their students' learning. There is also anecdotal evidence that teachers initiated into the practice of scholarship of teaching and learning are becoming leaders in teaching developments in their faculties. At the University of Sydney, for example, such teachers are able to challenge ideas on teaching with reference to evidence from the literature and there are examples where, as a result, ideas in the literature are being used to underpin the way in which a whole faculty designs its courses (see, for example, Institute for Teaching and Learning 2001). There is some evidence that engaging in training in university teaching leads to increased student satisfaction and an increase in the use of student-focused approaches to teaching (Lueddeke 2003; Gibbs and Coffey 2004). However, it is not generally known whether such training is characterised by a focus on scholarly approaches. It is most likely to be focused on the development of teaching skills or the development of a specific teaching practice, for example, flexible and on-line teaching, assessment of student learning, post graduate supervision and internationalisation, such as was found in an Australian study of tertiary teaching award programmes (Dearn, Fraser and Ryan 2002). Actually, there is surprisingly little research evidence that the scholarship of university teaching and learning enhances learning (Healey 2000). However, I want to suggest that the importance of the scholarship of teaching lies not so much in its ability to directly lead to changes in teaching and learning practices, important though these are, but in its capacity to lead to the development among academics of the reflexive critique which Bourdieu and Wacquant (1992) recognise as important if systemic changes in higher education are to be achieved. It is with this in mind that, I believe, we must take it very seriously indeed.

The complex interplay of issues within conceptions of the scholarship of university teaching and learning has led some writers to develop theoretical models for it. Such models extend ideas about the possibilities for, and the scope of, the scholarship of teaching and learning, and enable judgments to be made about the extent to which it is being exhibited. They also relate the ideas of the scholarship of teaching to broader theory. I want to draw on three models that I believe are particularly helpful in developing understanding of the scholarship of teaching and learning and its application within institutions of higher education. They are the phenomenographic model of Trigwell, Martin, Benjamin and Prosser (2000) considered in this chapter; Kreber and Cranton's (2000) model derived from Mezirow and Habermas, and Kemmis and McTaggart's (2000) notions of social practice considered in Chapter 7. These models highlight the importance of the scholarship of university teaching and learning as a means of integrating teaching and research and raise some substantial issues in relation to teaching as research.

► Literature and theory

So there is now general agreement that the purpose of the scholarship of teaching is to infuse teaching with scholarly qualities in order to enhance learning (Hutchings and Shulman 1999; Kreber and Cranton 2000; Hutchings, Babb and Bjork 2002; Kreber 2002; Trigwell and Shale 2004). Trigwell and colleagues (2000: 156) say the aim of scholarly teaching is to 'make transparent how we have made learning possible'. In order that this can happen, they argue, 'teachers must be informed of the theoretical perspectives and literature of teaching and learning in their discipline, and be able to collect and present rigorous evidence of effectiveness'.

Acknowledging the influence of Boyer (1990), Glassick, Huber and Maeroff (1997) and the work of the Carnegie Academy, Trigwell and colleagues (2000) developed a model of the scholarship of teaching based upon, and located alongside, phenomenographic studies of teachers' and learners' conceptions of, and approaches to, teaching and learning carried out principally in Australia (see, for example, Biggs 1996, 1999; Prosser and Trigwell 1999; Ramsden 2003a; McKenzie 2003). They found five categories of description of ways academics experienced and understood the scholarship of teaching which, they suggested, range from less to more inclusive views:

A.   The scholarship of teaching is about knowing the literature on teaching by collecting and reading that literature.

B. Scholarship of teaching is about improving teaching by collecting and reading the literature on teaching.
C. Scholarship of teaching is about improving student learning by investigating the learning of one's own students and one's own teaching.
D. Scholarship of teaching is about improving one's own students' learning by knowing and relating the literature on teaching and learning to discipline-specific literature and knowledge.
E. The scholarship of teaching is about improving student learning within the discipline generally, by collecting and communicating results of one's own work on teaching and learning within the discipline.

(Trigwell et al. 2000:159)

They argued that, in the more inclusive views of the scholarship of teaching, the act of teaching in the light of the research literature on teaching and learning in higher education in general, and as specifically related to the discipline, contributes to the body of work on student learning generally and specifically. It helps to build a body of knowledge about student learning, about particular discipline content, and about learning in general (Trigwell et al. 2000).

These ways of understanding the scholarship of teaching were differentiated according to four dimensions where academics' understandings and experiences of the scholarship of teaching are combined. This created a multi-dimensional model (see Table 6.1). In each dimension there were different levels of engagement enabling judgments to be made about the extent to which the academic is engaging in the scholarship of teaching and learning.

The preparation of courses necessarily involves scholarship. It is part of the professional ethos of academia that courses and curricula should be up to date; should reflect the latest developments in a subject area. The academic discourse around notions of course validation, quality assurance and quality review all presuppose that courses will be up-dated on a regular basis. This inevitably involves some element, if not of research, certainly of scholarship on the part of the teachers but it raises a number of questions about what academics understand by research and by scholarship, and these ideas vary significantly, as we have seen. Relating this to the above model of the scholarship of teaching and learning, we see that some of this work on teaching can be at the lower levels of each dimension. However, once an academic begins to critically reflect on their teaching, on teaching within their discipline area, or teaching in higher education in general in the light of the literature on how students learn, higher education moves away from just being a place where you work, to becoming a subject of study. Once teachers begin to critically reflect, their teaching becomes an example of teaching more generally. How does what they do relate to what other people do? What assumptions do they make about the nature of students and what they are capable of? What do

Table 6.1 Multi-dimensional model of the scholarship of teaching

Informed dimension (*The extent to which the teacher is informed about teaching and learning*)	**Reflection dimension** (*How the teacher reflects upon their teaching in order to improve it*)	**Communication dimension** (*How and where they communicate their knowledge about teaching and learning*)	**Conception dimension** (*How teachers conceptualise teaching*)
Uses informal theories of teaching and learning	Effectively non or unfocused reflection	No communication about teaching and learning	Sees teaching in a teacher-focused way
Engages with the literature of teaching and learning generally		Communicates with departmental/faculty peers (tea room conversations, department seminars)	
Engages with the literature, particularly the discipline literature	Reflection in action	Reports work at local and national conferences	
Conducts action research, has synoptic capacity, and pedagogic content knowledge	Reflection focused on asking what do I need to know about X here and how will I find out about it?	Publishes in international scholarly journals	Sees teaching in a student focused way

Source: K. Trigwell, E. Martin, J. Benjamin and M. Prosser, 'Scholarship of teaching: A model', *Higher Education Research and Development*, 19: 2 (2000): 163.

they think knowledge is and how do they think it is obtained? What theories of learning do they base their teaching on? Engaging in the scholarship of teaching and learning inevitably leads discipline-specific academics to these kinds of questions. It is no longer simply a question of which teaching and learning techniques to use or whether, for example, to employ flexible approaches to teaching and learning. It becomes a question of what is the overarching theoretical approach that drives decision making with respect to the curricula for which they are responsible. Teaching becomes recognised as a theory-driven endeavour. The scholarship of teaching and learning, by engaging teachers in the process of inquiring into their teaching, leads teachers to articulate a pedagogical framework or philosophy of teaching (see, for example, Schönwetter, Sokal, Friesen and Taylor 2001; Brew and Peseta 2004) in which specific approaches to teaching are viewed as instances of a broader theoretical approach.

Trigwell and colleagues place a significant emphasis on grounding teaching developments in phenomenographic theory. This is a body of work from mainly Northern European or Australian contexts which, over the past 30 years, has developed an understanding of teaching and learning and how it is perceived and practised in a wide range of disciplines. However, the extent to which knowledge of this particular body of literature on teaching and learning is necessary is hotly debated. There are both advantages and dangers in tying discussions of the scholarship of teaching to the phenomenographic tradition. The advantage is that work that individual academics do can readily be related to a body of work in the field. The danger is that the scholarship of teaching and learning becomes tied up with the dark side of phenomenography: for example, its 'cult-like' status (see, for example, Haggis 2004). Indeed, it is perhaps curious that reference to this work is almost entirely absent from the American literature. Theories that have been developed, particularly in the social sciences and in other areas of education, including theories of social change, theories of transformative learning, actor network theory, critical theory, activity theory and so on, provide a rich source of ideas on which teachers engaged in the scholarship of teaching and learning can also draw.

▶ Disciplinary issues

In the North American context there has been a focus on disciplinary variation because, it has been argued, the discourse on the scholarship of teaching and learning is coloured at all times by pre-existing notions of what constitutes research and scholarship and the nature of teaching within particular disciplines.

In some disciplines, teaching is something you do not want to have a problem with:

> In scholarship and research, having a problem is at the heart of the investigative process; it is the compound of the generative questions around which all creative and productive activity revolves. But in one's teaching, a 'problem' is something you don't want to have, and if you have one, you probably want to fix it. . . . Changing the status of the problem in teaching from terminal remediation to ongoing investigation is precisely what the movement for a scholarship of teaching is all about.
>
> (Bass 1998–99, quoted in Hutchings and Shulman 1999:14)

The issue then becomes, not how discipline-specific academics can be led to do educational research and to ground that in theory, but rather how academics can be encouraged to adopt methods and approaches that arise from and build on the methodological traditions in their own disciplinary areas. How can new forms of scholarly inquiry in relation to teaching be encouraged? Huber (2000), Diamond and Adam (1995) and others have argued it is necessary for the different disciplinary communities to define the scholarship of teaching and learning for themselves.

A key question is whether a disciplinary community builds on existing research and practice in teaching and learning in higher education, or whether it works in isolation. In 1999 when the United Kingdom's annual Improving Student Learning Symposium discussed how to improve student learning through the disciplines, I remember sitting in on a number of discussions that started from the premise that since we were all in different disciplines, teaching and learning would essentially be different. More often than not, however, we found that there was more shared than unique ground. Disciplinary journals on pedagogy bear this out. Weimar (1993), following a review of disciplinary journals on pedagogy concluded that such publications discussed issues which were transferable across fields, but that the journals included very little material from other disciplines. She also found that disciplinary journals were preoccupied with teaching techniques, not, for example, with broader theoretical issues (Weimar 1993). The challenge for individual discipline areas is to be able to communicate across disciplines to build up a shared understanding of teaching and learning practice, building on the shoulders of giants, as it were, rather than rediscovering the wheel in seperate local communities.

A focus on teachers using new methods of inquiry based on their own discipline-led methodologies tends to neglect taking account of the fact that educational research has been developing for many years, and that this tradition has developed an understanding of what is, and what is not, an appropriate method of inquiry in particular circumstances. I do not deny that there may be much to be gained by cognate disciplines developing new methods of inquiry which may ultimately benefit the discipline of education itself. One example is anthropology, which has much to teach us from using anthropological methods to inquire into teaching and learning. However, some methods are less appropriate. For example, 'double-blind cross-over trials' are common practice in medicine and have become routinely used to examine the effects of medical training. Yet, in the educational field, there is a literature showing that as a method of educational evaluation, this is problematic. It is important for teachers in all disciplinary areas, to understand the strengths but also the limitations of the approaches being adopted.

It has increasingly been recognised that focusing exclusively on teaching and learning in a particular discipline and the questions and methods that arise from that, while it is a useful starting point, is not enough. It is particularly a problem in areas where views of the scholarship of teaching and learning are limited by teacher-focused conceptions of teaching or a conception of the scholarship of teaching focused on recognition or reward (Lueddeke 2003). Huber and Morreale (2003) have argued that it is at the borderland of the discipline where cross-disciplinary exchange takes place that teaching development can occur most readily.

> . . . these disciplinary styles empower the scholarship of teaching by guiding scholars to choose certain problems, use certain methods, and present their work in certain ways. But these styles also constrain one's willingness to read literature on teaching and learning from other fields, and they can limit pedagogical and scholarly imagination.
>
> (Huber and Morreale 2003)

Another recognition is that disciplines differ in the extent to which pedagogy has been developed either as an integral part of disciplinary thinking, or as a distinct field of activity with its own specialist scholars. Healey (2000) suggests, following Colbeck, (1998) that disciplines may be differentiated according to how easily they are able to link research and teaching. His disciplinary affiliation is with geography which has a tradition of borrowing ideas from different fields of study. It is also, he argues, very open to innovations in teaching and learning. Social science disciplines are closer to educational ways of thinking, while what Biglan (see Stoecker 1993) calls the 'hard' disciplines may find the scholarship of teaching more difficult (Healey 2000:180–181).

In the 'hard' disciplines reflective practice in relation to teaching is not the norm. Huber and Morreale (2003) argue that the scholarship of teaching and learning challenges disciplinary styles of inquiry. Some academics will only consider work scholarly if it is, for example, quantitative, objective, and presented as if independent of the people who are studying it. Disciplinary academics frequently have a view of education research that it is waffly, vague, long-winded, subjective or unscholarly. The scholarship of teaching and learning requires the person doing the teaching to do the inquiry into that teaching. This may require a combination of quantitative and qualitative approaches. Indeed, reflective practice grounded in the scholarly literature on teaching and learning in higher education has lead to an emphasis on action or practitioner research on teaching in accounts of the scholarship of teaching and learning. This is in line with developments in the professional practice of teachers in other areas of education (see, for example, Groundwater-Smith and Hunter 2000; Sachs 2002), yet some areas of the research community have difficulty in accepting such methods of investigation as research. Engaging the academics of particular disciplines in the scholarship of teaching and learning involves encouraging them to re-evaluate the discipline of education in order to value it. Chapter 7 looks more closely at the challenges of doing this.

▶ Dissemination

Hutchings (2002: 15) suggests following Shulman (2000a: 50) that the scholarship of teaching and learning carries with it a moral commitment to ' "pass on" what we discover, discern, and experience'. Dissemination of the findings of research on teaching and students' learning is thus an important aspect of the scholarship of teaching and learning, and indeed there is evidence that teachers who engage in it are increasingly demonstrating scholarly outcomes; for example, through publications in the generic as well as subject-specific pedagogical literature.

Rice (1996) argues that the scholarship of teaching and learning has to be seen alongside and as integrated with the other three scholarships. Healey suggests:

> The scholarship of teaching can involve all four forms identified by Boyer: discovery research into the nature of learning and teaching; integration of material from several disciplines to understand what is going on in the classroom; application of what is known about how students learn to the learning–teaching process; and teaching, 'not only transmitting knowledge, but transforming and extending it as well' (Boyer 1990: 24). The advantage of thinking of the different kinds of academic work all as forms of scholarship is that it emphasises their common features, rather than their differences.
>
> (Healey 2000: 171)

One of the dangers of viewing the scholarship of teaching and learning on its own is that of assuming that it is just something that those with a particular interest in teaching can do, leaving the 'real' researchers to do disciplinary research; that is, scholarship of 'discovery' in Boyer's terms. In my travels and talking to academics in many universities as well as those I teach in a graduate certificate in higher education programme, I often encounter academics who say that they are experts in their subject discipline and cannot possibly be expected to become expert and to publish in teaching as well. I used to believe that those in a faculty or department who would take to publishing research on their teaching would be those academics who were more interested in teaching than research. However, in contrast, what I have since found is that the academics who successfully integrate elements of inquiry into their teaching, using an evidence-based approach to curriculum decision making, and are strongest in publishing their teaching research tend also to be strong in disciplinary research. Remarkably, some people manage to excel at both. Yet we should not be surprised. This is surely the mark of a rounded academic who has both teaching and research responsibilities. As Pat Hutchings remarks:

> Rather than a new research specialty for a few faculty, it is, I would argue, an aspiration for the work of all faculty – one that enacts responsibilities both to current students and to future generations; to colleagues, whose work we build on and contribute to; and to the profession of teaching.
>
> (Hutchings 2002:15)

However, there is a tension between a focus on the scholarship of teaching as a means by which teaching can be more publicly accountable, and the aim of the scholarship of teaching to improve student learning. A focus on account-ability leads to a focus on documenting existing practice and this can stay at what Habermas (1987) calls a technical knowledge interest; that is, at the lower levels of Trigwell and colleagues model (see also Chapter 7). A focus on improving student learning, on the other hand, is likely to go beyond exist-ing understandings to develop new ones and change the teaching in the light of new knowledge. Depending on which orientation is taken, teachers' and academic managers' energies can be focused in two quite different directions. On the one hand energies may be focused on changing institutional struc-tures for promotion, setting up awards for university teaching and develop-ing criteria for judging teaching effectiveness. On the other, an orientation to changing learning would lead to implementing a variety of institutional stra-tegies for teaching development. Both orientations are needed. However, we know from studies of the relationship between teaching and research that time spent on research can be time taken out of teaching and vice versa (see, for example, Serow 2000). So there is a potential conflict in where aca-demics place their energies.

▶ Some ethical concerns

Taking what they have learnt in examining teaching and students' learning out of the realm of the classroom and into the domain of academic publica-tion raises some important ethical issues in relation to how academics treat students and their work. Ethical conflicts arise, for example, when the class-room becomes a site for educational inquiry; when students' reactions to courses not only provide information on their learning, or on how the course should be improved for the next generation of students, but also become data for analysis and ultimate publication. Questions about the informed consent of students to use their accounts of their experiences or even their work as data in research on teaching are tricky. Hutchings (2002:12) asks whether the interactions that there are among students and academics and the work that they do are part of the kind of privileged private communication such as exists between lawyers or therapists and their clients, or are they, as Shulman (1993:6) suggests 'community property'? Do the students react differently to the course if they know, for example, that the teacher is studying their reactions? Hutchings (2002) argues that there is increasing awareness of the ethical issues that arise in the course of engaging in the scholarship of teaching and learning, and that these provide windows into considerations of our values. Our researcher role may conflict with our teacher role (Burgoyne 2002; Takacs 2002).

Going beyond the divide between teaching and research involves going beyond such conflicts to redefine relationships between academics and students. The ethical dilemmas thrown up highlight the importance of fully engaging students in the scholarship of teaching and learning. Hutchings suggests that we need to move away from seeing students as research 'subjects' to thinking of students engaging collaboratively in the research.

The scholarship of teaching and learning in this way thus provides opportunities for the development of inclusive scholarly communities of practice where both academics and students work on building knowledge of the educative process and how to enhance it. It can also, as we shall see in the next chapter, provide a basis for the development of an inquiry-based higher education more generally.

7   Learning to Transform Teaching

Evidence for teaching effectiveness or for how students experience their courses conventionally comes from a variety of forms of evaluation. Sometimes these are institutionally devised and may be mandated. They may be focused on aspects of courses of interest to the university, or they may focus on issues of relevance to individual teachers. They may involve the collection of quantitative or qualitative data. They may be driven by explicit hypotheses or theories or they may purport to be theory free. Without wishing to deny the value and usefulness of a variety of evaluation data which comes from students, colleagues or sources external to the university, it has to be acknowledged that the existence of evaluation does not of itself constitute a scholarship of teaching, nor does the process of acting on that evidence to effect changes in teaching. For the development of an evidence-based higher education embodied in the concept of the scholarship of teaching and learning, reflection on evaluation data has to be done, as we have seen, in the light of the literature on teaching and learning and preferably in the context of focused questions posed within an action research framework (Trigwell et al. 2000).

Chapter 6 introduced a discussion of the scholarship of teaching and learning. In this chapter I want to look more closely at what is actually involved in learning to engage in the scholarship of teaching and learning and how doing so changes teachers' understanding of the nature of the educative process. As suggested in the previous chapter, this is an important step in the development of inclusive scholarly knowledge-building communities. So my concern here is to examine what happens when academics come together in collaborative groups to ask questions and to develop knowledge about their students' learning and their role in fostering it. A number of the ideas developed in this chapter arose in discussions with my colleagues Kim McShane and Tai Peseta about teaching Graduate Certificate in Higher Education subjects, where we challenge participants to develop their capacity to engage in the scholarship of university teaching and learning (Brew, McShane and Peseta 2003). So I want to acknowledge their contributions and those of our course participants to the development of my thinking here.

▶ **Levels of reflection on teaching and learning**

Kreber and Cranton (2000) argue that different levels of reflection on learning and teaching related to Habermas's knowledge-constitutive interests are involved in the scholarship of university teaching and learning. Reflection may be focused at:

1. the instrumental or technical level where the focus is on an orientation to understand the facts in order to control the situation. Learning occurs through solving problems related to specific tasks;
2. the communicative level where the focus is on learning about and sharing others' ideas and perceptions, including negotiating meaning with them;
3. the emancipatory level where there is an intention to go beyond the existing situation through a process of critical reflection and reasoning. 'The goal is to overcome the limitations of self-knowledge and the social constraints on one's thought and actions'.

(Kreber and Cranton 2000: 484)

These levels of reflection provide the basis for a multi-dimensional model of the scholarship of teaching and learning related to three distinct, but interconnected domains of knowing about curriculum: instructional, curricular and pedagogical knowing. For each of these domains there are three levels of reflection possible: content reflection, in which the teaching process is questioned (i.e., what should I do in course design to select methods?); process reflection, in which the processes leading to particular strategies are examined (How did I do? Was my course design effective?); and premise reflection, which involves critical reflection at a deeper level, asking why the teacher teaches the way they do. The domains can then be differentiated according to the different levels described earlier (instrumental, communicative and emancipatory).

In a study of teachers' views on how they reflected on their teaching, Kreber (2004) found that although most indicated that they did reflect, very few could actually provide examples that demonstrated they reflected at the premise level; that is, questioned their basic assumptions. This level is closely related to the emancipatory dimension which is particularly important in the development of research-enhanced teaching and learning, as we shall see below, so this poses particular challenges for those who have the role of facilitating academics to develop their teaching and learning scholarship. Most of the reflection reported in Kreber's (2004) study appeared to be focused on reflecting on teaching content, with process and premise reflection being mentioned least often. This finding is similar to that of McAlpine and Weston (2002), whose distinctions between practical reflection, strategic reflection and epistemic reflection broadly parallel the three levels of reflection mentioned above. McAlpine and Weston similarly argue that the majority of the instances of reflection they found among the teachers whose views they examined were in the practical sphere, that is, focused on improving actions within a particular class, not examining generalisable aspects, nor focusing on the process of reflection itself. Kreber (2004) argues that for reflection to be the most useful, premise reflection (e.g., why do our goals and rationale matter? Why does it matter if I consider how students learn?) ought to provide the starting point for reflection. Yet this was the least mentioned form of reflection in her study.

Davies (1999) suggests that all educational practitioners need to be able to:

- pose an answerable question about education;
- know where and how to find evidence systematically and comprehensively using electronic (computer-based) and non-electronic (print) media;
- retrieve and read such evidence competently and undertake critical appraisal and analysis of that evidence according to agreed professional and scientific standards;
- organise and grade the power of this evidence; and
- determine its relevance to their educational needs and environments.

(Davies 1999: 109)

We can now see that even the kind of question posed by individual teachers is likely to focus at the more technical levels. The establishment of evidence, Davies argues, requires the teacher to rigorously plan, conduct and disseminate investigations into aspects of the educative process (Davies 1999). Depending on the level of reflection, the kind of investigation planned will vary as well. However, that is not all. Pedagogical research demands that we not only investigate educational phenomena, it also demands that we understand the nature of the kind of phenomena we are investigating, how that relates to other kinds of phenomena we might investigate, what kinds of truth claims we can make on the basis of our findings, and what the limitations of the approach we have adopted are. For some academics, as we can already see, this is highly problematic. Indeed, the scholarship of teaching and learning is likely to challenge teachers to examine their teaching in ways that are unfamiliar. Inquiring into approaches to teaching and learning turns out to be more complex than even the literature on the scholarship of teaching and learning recognises.

The nature of the questions posed, what constitutes evidence, how that evidence is evaluated and used is going to vary according to the theoretical assumptions that are made. In this regard, Kemmis and McTaggart's (2000) analysis of social practice is useful because it seems reasonable to suppose that how individual and collaborating teachers conceptualise the scholarship of teaching and hence choose to research their teaching and their students' learning is related to their views of practice. There are clearly

Table 7.1   Conceptions of practice following Kemmis and McTaggart (2000) and related to Mezirow/Habermas' views of levels of learning as described in Kreber and Cranton (2000)

Kemmis and McTaggart's (2000: 574) Aspects of social practice	Research approaches used	Mezirow/Habermas framework
1. Events, activities, etc. viewed as objective where practice is considered from the point of view of the behaviour of the individual	Quantitative, correlational and experimental methods, psychometric and various observational techniques, etc.	Technical/ instrumental
2. Practice may be considered not simply as the practice of individuals, but rather as having a social focus, which is again viewed from an 'objective' external viewpoint	Similar methods of investigation, and in addition systems analysis, sociometrics and social ecological approaches may be used	
3. In the third view of social practice, the focus is again on the individual but it is viewed taking a 'subjective' stance, with the emphasis on how the individual perceives the practice	Research approaches used here are likely to be qualitative and interpretive, with interviews, journals, diaries and self-reports used	Communicative
4. Fourth, practice is viewed as a process of social construction within a historical tradition and established discourses	Research approaches are again likely to be qualitative and interpretive and to include historical and discourse analyses	
5. This view of practice, Kemmis and McTaggart suggests, brings together objective and subjective views and sees practice both as an individual and as a social phenomenon. Practice is 'socially and historically constituted and as reconstituted by human agency and social action' (p. 576)	The use of multiple methods is appropriate here, including various reflexive methods, critical methods and dialectical analysis	Emancipatory

different views of the nature of teaching and learning as forms of social practice and Kemmis and McTaggart help us to understand why particular teachers may focus on certain aspects.

Kemmis and McTaggart (2000: 574) distinguish five aspects of social practice which they relate to five different methodological traditions. These provide indications of what methodological approaches are appropriate for each of the three forms of reflection that Kreber and Cranton (2000) argue must characterise the scholarship of teaching and learning. Table 7.1 illustrates this.

▶ Extending the levels of teachers' reflection

The implication of these ideas for disciplinary academics as they learn to engage with the scholarship of teaching and learning is that their views of the level and the focus of their teaching reflection is likely to need to change.

In order to engage in critical reflection on practice, teachers need first of all to have an idea of critical reflection. So there are particular challenges for teachers in areas where there is not a strong tradition of this; where teaching takes a technical knowledge interest and/or is focused on an information-transmission approach to teaching (Prosser and Trigwell 1999); and where, for example, it is assumed that teaching is about transmission of basic information to the students and learning is about absorbing information (facts and principles) about the discipline. Indeed, it is possible to have a higher education experience that has not at any time encouraged critical reflection on the nature of knowledge (Brew, McShane and Peseta 2003). As Quinn (2003: 13) points out from her experience of encouraging academics from different disciplines to reflect on the theoretical and epistemological assumptions of their own disciplines, not all academics were able to make explicit the 'truth foundations of their disciplines'. So this needs to be learnt. Indeed, the very idea that there are such assumptions can be quite alien.

When an academic begins to inquire into their own teaching, the first thing they are confronted with is what kinds of questions they can ask. For example, following Marton (1981), some questions are about what is the case, other questions are about what people perceive to be the case. Some educational questions are unanswerable because they require knowledge of what would have happened had circumstances been different. The challenge teaching scholars face is of recognising that there is a relationship between the kinds of questions asked and the resulting truth claims in respect to the outcomes.

In educational research the researcher needs to establish not only what the findings of the research are, but also what the status of those findings are as truths or as facts or as knowledge. In order to be able to do educational research, teachers therefore need an appreciation of not only the methods of inquiry, and of the particular methodological traditions in which those methods are situated – they also need to understand the epistemological assumptions of the particular methodology.

The teacher who wants to engage in the scholarship of teaching and learning has to come to terms with the idea that questions of methods and methodology are questions about the nature of knowledge within education. For many academics this opens up new ways of thinking. They come to realise that there are different ways of looking at knowledge, but this means that the scholarship of teaching and learning can challenge some peoples' notions of a verifiable, correspondence view of truth. Indeed, the idea that there might be different truths can be challenging. Even if teachers persist with the idea that, for example, the scientific method is the 'right' way to generate knowledge, they can never go back to the idea that it is the only way. For people with backgrounds in disciplinary areas where theories about the nature of knowledge and about the nature of reality are assumed rather than debated, this can be unsettling. So engaging in the scholarship of teaching can challenge how the academic views their own discipline and their disciplinary research.

Some people see social practice at Kemmis and McTaggart's first level and may have no conception of what is going on outside of their own disciplinary area in terms of the much more fluid notions of knowledge that have permeated the discourse (Brew and Phillis 1997) or other ideas of social practice. This is perhaps surprising given that there is so much discussion in the media and in the scholarly literature about the nature of science and knowledge (see, for example, Brew 2001a). A universe of discourse is opened up as a consequence of engaging in the scholarship of teaching and learning. Teachers are challenged to change their conceptions.

The idea that there are different perspectives on knowledge is fundamental to an understanding of how students learn. Having a notion of different perspectives, and an experience of opening up to new ways of seeing the world is a prerequisite for understanding what it means to challenge and change students' conceptions. Unless a person has had their own conceptions challenged and changed it is difficult, if not impossible, for them to imagine what this can be like.

The scholarship of teaching and learning requires a dialogic, constructivist view of practice as 'socially and historically constituted and as reconstituted by human agency and social action' (Kemmis and McTaggart 2000: 576). The bringing together of the objective conditions of the classroom, the teaching that sits within it, and students' learning with the subjective views of all of these are important aspects. Teaching as it stands today is to be transformed. Students' learning is continually to be enhanced. The scholarship of teaching and learning carries with it a value that it is something good; something to be applauded; something to be developed. It has emancipatory ideals. The direction of change is clear. It is towards student-focused activity-based learning in which inquiry becomes central (see, for example, Trigwell and Shale 2004).

▶ Teachers as learners

Learning to engage in scholarly critical reflection that will lead to new under-standings of the educative process is important to the development of an inquiry-based higher education. For the teacher whose experience of higher education teaching and learning has been predominantly of a tradi-tional lecture and tutorial type, learning to engage in the scholarship of teaching and learning provides the teacher with new experiences of being a learner in unfamiliar pedagogies; experiences that problematise teaching–learning relationships and the nature and forms of collaboration, that high-light different kinds of course structure and that trouble questions of power, authority and responsibility.

To engage in the scholarship of teaching and learning requires academic teachers to become learners. At the beginning of our graduate certificate course we tell academic participants that they will get as much out of the course as they put into it and that they have to take responsibility for their own learning. However, this is an alien concept to many people and the learning opportunities have to be carefully structured to support the challenging process of changing ideas.

When people put themselves into the position of being learners or teachers, they all bring their past experiences of being both a learner and a teacher into the course (see, for example, Boud, Keogh and Walker 1985; Prosser and Trig-well 1999). While the teachers may struggle with their identities as teachers and their role as facilitators of change, the participants in turn also struggle with their identity as learners, particularly in an unfamiliar inquiry-based course.

In a traditional lecture-based course, the patterns of control and authority are well established. However, the move to inquiry-based courses shifts the locus of control. In a curriculum where there is a high level of negotiation, it is important to establish what is and what is not negotiable (Brew and Barrie 1999). However, how the learner perceives what is and what is not negoti-able is not necessarily the way the teachers intended. When students move from an experience of teaching and learning which has a traditionally defined structure such as a lecture or tutorial, to an experiential learning environment, how that learning environment is structured may be a mystery. The discourse of higher education pedagogy appears to so socialise people into passive modes of learning that even academics who have themselves become teachers do not always take responsibility for their own learning when strongly encouraged to do so. What this tells us is how hard it is for people to shift to new ways of thinking about education. What is really important about this realisation is that the processes of learning are also being mirrored in the way participants teach their own students and, in turn, in the way their own students learn. Before anyone can think about changing students' perceptions or approaches to learning, they need to have experienced the sort of learning being implemented. The teacher has to have experienced being the learner. If academics see inquiry-based courses as unstructured when they engage in them, they are unlikely to have the capacity to implement such courses with their own students. Only by stimulating experiences of engaging in inquiry-based learning are participants likely to experiment with implementing similar processes.

▶ Values

As we have seen, there is general agreement on the importance of critical reflection as a key aspect of the scholarship of teaching and learning. In this connection, advocates have stressed the importance of the scholarly community in providing a base for peer review and collaborative team work. (Trigwell et al. 2000; Reeders 2000; Benjamin 2000). It is possible for a teacher to develop an evidence-based approach to their teaching in relative isolation, but it is unlikely that they will stay that way. The development of the scholarship of teaching and learning is not just an individual affair. Teaching is no longer private and *ad hoc*. The admonition to share ideas, to publish findings and to gain recognition for teaching demands that teaching development becomes a community concern whether that community is the department, the discipline as a whole (nationally and/or internationally), the institution in which the individual is placed, the work group or course team, or peer participants in a teaching development course or programme. At all these different levels, the scholarship of teaching and learning depends on the idea of a scholarly community in which individuals develop their expertise and their identity.

Rowland (2000: 99) argues that sooner or later inquiring into our teaching, particularly in the context of a collaborating group, will lead us to examine our values and specifically the values that underpin our teaching. Indeed, we cannot engage in the scholarship of teaching and learning without confronting our values about what it is to change our teaching and our students' learning, about the nature and direction of desirable change, and questions about why we should do this. Critically reflecting on practice is likely to highlight conflicts in values, or aspects of practice that are inconsistent with one's values.

The way that we teach and the way that we think about teaching and students' learning is dependent upon our fundamental understanding and belief in what human beings are and what they are capable of. Our values are at the core of our teaching whether we recognise them or not. Yet realising that teaching is value laden and that values come into the whole process is very challenging to teachers who think of teaching as an objective, value-free activity.

Many teachers in higher education institutions in Western countries adhere to the values of participatory democracy, respect for individual human life, for liberty, equality and justice. There are other shared values of course such as respect for disciplinary knowledge and the pursuit of truth (however that may be defined), but these are some of the overarching ones. However, as soon as one begins to examine one's teaching and learning practices in the light of an examination of one's values, conflicts emerge. A key realisation is that mature young adults, who are well able to take important decisions in their lives, who can participate in democratic processes within their own country are treated as a subclass of human beings when they enter higher education. They are kept on the fringes of decision making, often having little or no say in how courses are run or how they are going to be assessed. As we saw in Chapter 1, higher education is designed to reinforce privilege (Bourdieu 1988). Students most often inhabit separate domains of the university, with limited access to resources, including teachers. They are frequently diminished through the language of faculty academics who may refer to them as 'kids' – even when they include mature-age adults.

The value system lying behind teaching and learning practices in higher education, with its separate facilities and development for separate categories of people, is like an apartheid. While this is an emotive word, I believe it reflects the ways in which not only students but also other categories of staff are defined and treated in many institutions of higher learning. Indeed, when put into a similar teaching and learning context, even mature academics may themselves exhibit behaviour characteristic of students with expectations of subservience, reductions in personal autonomy and abdication of responsibility.

For people who share values of democracy and equality and who would not so much as buy a South African apple during the pernicious apartheid regime in that country, the realisation that we are working in a higher education that implicitly embodies similar values comes as a shock.

There are of course further implications of these value conflicts for the ways in which universities are organised and managed and there are confounding factors, such as students' and academics' needs for their own spaces (see, for example, Annan 1974), such as the fact that students typically spend three years in an institution and academics may spend a lifetime.

However, my concern here is with implications for the relationship between teaching and research, not with these wider questions which need to be debated in other forums.

At the heart of the separation of teaching and research is the divide between academics and students. It is not just a question of differences in levels of disciplinary knowledge. It is a question of how we treat other human beings. Since academics are the ones with institutional authority, it becomes a question of how far they are willing to open up their world to others. One of our graduate certificate participants, an experienced senior academic, for example, in his reflective statement at the end of a semester studying how to develop scholarship in relation to his teaching, said that he had realised that he didn't trust his students. It highlighted a conflict in values within his teaching. This is profound learning. It is this kind of learning that is essential if teachers are to move beyond the divide between teaching and research. Privilege comes with responsibility; and that means being true to our values in how we teach and how we assess and how we treat the adult human beings who put their trust in us by becoming students.

▶ Embracing uncertainty

Critical reflection on teaching means not just examining what we want to know about our teaching and our students' learning. It also means looking at the things that we do not want to know about our teaching. It means being challenged again and again when things that we think ought to work do not. When the disciplinary content is the main or the sole focus of teaching and learning attention, as in a typical lecture course, for example, it is possible to ignore the fact that there are, say, 200 human beings in front of us, each with their individual personality, their motivation, what they had for breakfast, the extraneous ideas going through their heads, and so on. The increasing use of critical reflection on students' learning, the trend towards collaborative, team-based approaches to teaching and the growth in evidence-based approaches to curriculum decision making means facing the things that we perhaps do not really want to know. It means facing one's fears about one's students' learning. 'When you begin to wrestle with people's deeply held, private, intuitive theories, you are engaging them in a process that is as deeply emotional as it is cognitive. This is why conceptual change is so difficult to negotiate' (Shulman 2000b: 131). This means, of course, also acknowledging the elation when things have gone well.

Working collaboratively can mean that we have to acknowledge that others have different views of the situation. I had this experience recently. I discovered that in one teaching session my colleague with whom I team-teach, interpreted the participants' reactions as angry. I interpreted them as interested engagement and a struggling to come to terms with difficult material. We shared our views and in doing so came face to face with ourselves. I had to acknowledge that I did not want to know that course participants may have been angry. She did not want to know that perhaps she was also angry. The scholarship of teaching and learning reclaims teaching as an emotional whole-person encounter between individual human beings trying to make sense of the world.

Earlier I suggested that we need to educate students for an uncertain and perplexing world; one in which there are no formulas for how to cope. Engaging in the scholarship of teaching and learning can cause academics to have just such an experience of uncertainty. The ability to live with uncertainty; to cope with that, is central. In times of confusion and uncertainty, we need guides whom we can trust. When there are no right answers and the decisions we take are inevitably based on incomplete perplexing, and even in some cases misleading information, trust becomes crucial to the teaching and learning relationship. Students need to trust their teachers and teachers need to trust their students. Yet traditionally, pedagogies of mistrust of students have dominated higher education; witnessed in the over-use of summative assessment, the 'covering' of course material in lectures, and the pretence of certainty and truth of propositional knowledge in some subjects. In contrast, in an inquiry-based education taking place within an inclusive scholarly knowledge-building community, the idea is that uncertainty is shared in mutual exchange of ideas, knowledge and strategies for investigation.

▶ Involving students in the scholarship of teaching

We can conclude that the scholarship of teaching and learning has become an extremely useful concept in drawing attention to the need for teaching to develop and in providing an organising concept around which teaching developments can cluster. Teaching within such a context can no longer be the *ad hoc* amateur trying out of methods experienced as a student. Instead, decision making comes to be based on evidence of what is effective as demonstrated in the scholarly research literature and as evidenced in the specific context. Decision making in teaching becomes founded on evidence of the effectiveness of different approaches. The teacher becomes capable of articulating their theories of teaching and of understanding the epistemological framework that drives their investigations. They are aware of the role that educational research and theory plays in their discipline. In this sense the scholarship of teaching develops a teaching professionalism.

We have seen that the scholarship of teaching and learning locates the teaching act within a broader intellectual context related to a social constructivist perspective, where knowledge is viewed as generated within a dialogic community and as serving emancipatory interests. It embodies values of community and communication and has at heart a student-focused view of teaching and learning. So it is important. Yet what is noticeably missing from this consideration of the scholarship of teaching and learning is the students. In Chapter 6 I indicated that they need to participate in the scholarship of teaching and learning, so what is their role in this?

As we saw in Chapter 5, there are many forms of teaching and learning where students could be inducted into the culture and community of academics. These include: developing a knowledge of what it is to engage in the subject in a research-based way, an understanding of the key issues and debates in the subject area, knowledge of what researchers in the subject do in general and what the researchers in the faculty do specifically; engagement in activities which mirror the research process through, for example, laboratory experiments, fieldwork, etc.; knowledge of the methods and techniques used in research in the subject and opportunities to practice such methods and techniques; involvement as a participant in ongoing research programmes with a sense of belonging to the community of researchers; and engagement in inquiry-based learning. However, if the aim of higher education is to induct students into forms of inquiry, we need to involve them in the decision-making processes in regard to their education. Then, for their teachers, it is not so much a question of whether they think the teaching and learning methods are appropriate, but whether their students do too. The scholarship of teaching and learning should result in a partnership where academics and students together engage in inquiry, not just about the disciplinary content of their learning but also about the teaching and learning process.

It is a small step from the recognition that teaching is a scholarly practice grounded in pedagogical literature and demanding an evidence-based approach, to the idea of learning as a scholarly practice grounded in the disciplinary literature and requiring the evaluation of evidence (Brew and Boud 1995). We need to frame our courses so as to engage students with us in reflecting on the nature of knowledge within the discipline, with an intention to collaboratively build knowledge in the area with them (Hutchings 2002). Suppose, too, that we incorporate reflection for both students and ourselves on the processes of learning in which we are all engaged, in the relationships we build in order to effect the knowledge-building process, and our emotions, desires, difficulties and joys as we grapple with unfamiliar ideas and situations. Suppose, too, that we critically challenge each other to provide evidence, to argue with astute logic, but at all times to take account of the perceptions of the other in a caring trustful environment:

In this sense, the scholarship of teaching and learning may be seen as a cousin to the undergraduate research movement – in which (at its best) students work collaboratively with faculty, and often with each other as well, to investigate and build knowledge about important issues in the field.

(Hutchings 2002:13)

When both teachers and students engage in the scholarship of teaching and learning the differentiation between academics and students begins to break down as both share the process of learning that comes from engaging in inquiry (Brew 2003b). In this way the scholarship of teaching and learning would be integrated into the generation of disciplinary understanding for both teachers and students. This is another aspect of participation in inclusive scholarly knowledge-building communities.

▶ Conclusion

I have endeavoured to demonstrate the challenges involved for higher education teachers when they learn to engage in the scholarship of teaching and learning. This analysis has shown that engaging in the scholarship of teaching and learning means confronting ideas about the nature of knowledge. It means confronting one's values and it involves confronting teaching and learning as a whole-person encounter with other individuals in an uncertain environment. Once teachers begin to explore such issues, they inevitably move from a view of practice as objective – Kemmis and McTaggart's first level – to a view of practice as both an individual and a social construction, where teaching and learning are viewed as socially and historically constituted. Engaging in the scholarship of teaching and learning inevitably moves individuals from engaging in the more technical or instrumental levels of reflection to reflecting at the more emancipatory levels. Transformation of teaching and learning practice is an inevitable consequence.

I want to suggest, therefore, that the scholarship of teaching and learning thus provides a means whereby teachers are enabled to develop the reflexive critique to which Bourdieu refers. For Bourdieu and Wacquant (1992) reflexivity involves, as we have seen, 'the systematic exploration of the "unthought categories of thought which delimit the thinkable and predetermine the thought" (Bourdieu 1982:10), as well as a guide to the practical carrying out of social inquiry' (Bourdieu and Wacquant 1992:40). The categories of thinking that are referred to here are those that are deeply embedded in the ways of thinking and acting that people take on because of who they are, including all of their prior experience, social class mores, dispositions and tastes; what Bourdieu refers to as the habitus. Thus reflexivity is not just a question of critical reflection on a topic in the light of the literature, nor is it 'benign introspection' (Woolgar 1988: 22). Rather, it refers to the process of becoming conscious of hitherto unconscious aspects of the ways in which we think, respond and act in society, in this case, in higher education. As mentioned before, this may mean confronting things that we do not want to know, and it inevitably involves an affective dimension.

Reflecting at these levels on taken for granted assumptions through engaging with the scholarship of teaching and learning inevitably involves considering the relationship between oneself as a teacher and one's students. It also raises questions about the ways in which knowledge is constructed together through social interaction. I have suggested that students need to be involved in the process of the scholarship of teaching and learning; in other words, in reflecting on the teaching and learning process in the light of evidence of what is effective for learning. In this chapter I have explored how reflecting on the process of teaching and learning, employing methods of investigation which require questions about the status of the findings of facts or as knowledge to be addressed, raises important questions about the nature of knowledge within the disciplinary content of the students' coursework. So the scholarship of teaching and learning inevitably raises issues for both student and academic concerning the nature of knowledge within the discipline. Learning becomes a process of inquiry. Teaching and research are brought together in a dialogic community consisting of the academics on the course team and their students. The scholarship of teaching and learning thus has the capacity to take both academics and students beyond the research and teaching divide.

Part 3

Going Beyond the Divide

In the first part of this book I set out a model for the development of inclusive scholarly knowledge-building communities and argued that working towards such communities is the key to going beyond the divide between research and teaching. I suggested that research-based learning needs to be based on expanded definitions and conceptions of research and teaching and that the development of disciplinary knowledge must go hand in hand with the growth of personal meaning. I further argued for the need to view scholarship as a quality of academic professionalism and suggested that this was important for both teachers and their students.

Part 2 explored attempts to bring research and teaching together within the undergraduate curriculum. It examined a number of assumptions about research-enhanced teaching and learning, and about student learning that influence the extent to which research-based learning is considered possible or desirable. Chapters 4 and 5 then examined a number of cases from a variety of universities and different disciplinary areas where there were attempts to integrate research and teaching. It was noted that although there were many interesting, innovative and engaging learning opportunities for students, more often than not there was a tendency to stop short of engaging students in participating with academics in the development of new knowledge. I argued that there was a need to extend research-based approaches to education that integrate students into the research communities of academics.

Chapters 6 and 7 examined the development and challenges of viewing teaching as research, arguing that academics and students should be jointly engaged in the scholarship of teaching and learning. It was suggested that this has the capacity to lead academics and their students to engage in a reflexive approach to understanding the hidden assumptions and mores that drive the academic endeavour.

Of critical importance to all of these attempts to change the higher education curriculum are the contextual issues that surround them. Topics that still remain to be explored are the influence of teaching on research, and the institutional and cultural issues that limit or facilitate the integration of research and teaching. The vision of higher education to which the idea of inclusive scholarly knowledge-building communities is pointing also requires further elucidation. These are the subject of Part 3.

In Chapter 8, I turn the tables to look at how teaching can enhance research; first examining what studies of the relationship between teaching and research say about how academics think teaching influences their research. The chapter then looks at how what we know about teaching could influence research and, finally, explores how expanded views of research and revised notions of who should be involved in doing it can lead to inclusive scholarly knowledge-building communities.

Chapter 9 considers contextual issues that shape the capacity of individuals, faculties and departments and institutions to integrate research and teaching. Governments and research bodies and the professions have an enormous influence on universities in general, and on the relationship between teaching and research more specifically. So Chapter 9 considers the ways in which they facilitate or limit the extent to which individuals and institutions are able to move beyond the research and teaching divide.

In the two final chapters I am concerned to spell out in more detail the vision of a higher education where academics and students work towards the implementation of inclusive scholarly knowledge-building communities. Chapter 10 considers seven interrelated and overlapping qualitative areas where progress towards the integration of research and teaching can be evaluated:

- research activity
- evidence-based teaching and learning
- a research based curriculum
- a culture of inquiry
- a community of scholars
- research aligned teaching
- learning- and teaching-enhanced research.

Exploring them highlights some important key challenges for the higher education of the future.

Chapter 11 recognises that there are some aspects of higher education that appear to be pulling in the opposite direction. It suggests that the development of inclusive scholarly knowledge-building communities implies not only the application of inquiry-based approaches within the pedagogical domain but also relates to academic practice more generally. I suggest that new forms of higher education involve democratic discussion, the development of new kinds of community involving all who work and study in higher education institutions, and openness to the contributions that students can make to the design of new approaches to higher education; in short, no less than a change in culture.

8 Teaching-Enhanced Research

So far this book has looked at the ways in which research may be integrated with teaching. Attention now needs to be turned the other way round, to how teaching is used in, and enhances, research. The focus of attention in this chapter is on the factors that facilitate or inhibit the influence of teaching on research and on what needs to happen to research if inclusive scholarly knowledge-building communities are to be developed. The chapter first looks at studies of the relationship between teaching and research and what they say about how academics think teaching influences their research. It then considers what we know about teaching to see how teaching could influence research. Finally, the chapter explores what we know about research and what needs to happen if, as I have argued, the higher education of the future is to encompass inclusive scholarly knowledge-building communities.

▶ How does teaching influence research?

Some academics manage to combine their research and their teaching activities. Doing this means that research and teaching can be 'mutually enriching' (Jensen 1988; Neumann 1992:161). However, while there are numerous studies of the relationship between teaching and research, very little of this work examines the ways in which teaching has an influence on research. More often than not the assumption appears to be that, and many studies only consider how, research affects teaching; not the other way round (see, for example, Jensen 1988). Where the relative influence is discussed, it is suggested that research does indeed have a stronger influence on teaching than teaching does on research. Yet why should that be? What is it that inhibits the capacity of teaching to influence research? Why should not research and teaching be mutually beneficial?

Smeby (1998) differentiates direct and indirect interaction between teaching and research. Direct interaction occurs, he suggests, when teaching generates specific ideas and problems that are then followed up in research. Indirect interaction occurs when teaching helps with understanding and maintaining the breadth of the subject, 'broadening the academics' horizons' (Neumann 1992:164) when it gives a better understanding of the whole field by putting research in a larger context, and thus becomes a source of inspiration (Rice 1992), or when it provides a way to get to know a new field or to identify gaps in knowledge (Jensen 1988; Neumann 1992:165).

Teaching, Smeby argues, helps the academic to think through research issues when responding to students' questions, or it provides opportunities for the academic to prepare and give a paper as a rehearsal for conference presentation. Kirov (2003) suggests that the act of communicating complex arguments in simple ways helps to develop skills that can be of use in the writing of grant applications. Moreover, since student questions demand an in-depth knowledge of the subject, they can directly or indirectly trigger new research directions (Shore, Pinkler and Bates 1990; Neumann 1992). Commenting upon the example where first-year students of geography interview researchers, Dwyer (2001: 363) notes that many researchers: 'commented that they liked the opportunity to reflect on, and be critical of, their own research practices and that this opportunity is stimulated by critical questions from students'.

Research can be lonely and may involve long hours of tedious work, for example, carrying out experiments, analysing data or writing up results, and so the interactions that occur with teaching can enhance job satisfaction and reduce alienation (Kirov 2003). 'Interruptions need not be negative. Research is often a lonely and psychologically stressing activity. Therefore teaching can often be a positive interruption which gives the possibility for direct feedback' (Jørgensen 1985, quoted in Smeby 1998:14).

'Doing research is so much working against the tide. Failures in research bog you down. It's nice to do something that works. It's a way to find energy for your research' (Stralfors, quoted in Calandra 2002:2). Stralfors also admits that his memory 'sometimes needs a boost'. Teaching provides an opportunity for him to review materials and has led to discoveries that would otherwise not have come to light. To see students' excitement is exciting (Lynn, quoted in Calandra 2002:3).

The extent to which teaching influences research appears to be related both to disciplinary area and to the level of the teaching. Smeby (1998) found, for example, that the Norwegian academics he surveyed considered that the higher the level of the teaching being considered, the more research was considered to be given positive impulses through teaching. Both he and Jensen (1988) found that more academics from the humanities and social sciences considered that teaching at a lower level had a positive influence on research than in other disciplinary areas. Jensen (1988) considered that research was more important for teaching at the undergraduate level, but that teaching was more important for research at the graduate level.

It is clear, as we saw earlier, that one of the ways in which teaching has an effect on research is in the supervision of research students. Kyvik and Smeby (1994) found that academics, particularly in the sciences, medicine and technology, viewed the supervision of graduate students as part of their own personal research whereas in the humanities and social sciences, supervision is more likely to be considered an aspect of teaching. They also found that there was a correlational relationship between such supervision and the research productivity of academics. Even when the analysis took account of the fact that the more senior academics supervised more research students, they found that there was a positive correlation between the number of graduate students supervised and the productivity of faculty as measured through publication counts adjusted to take account of multiple authorships. In the sciences, medicine and technology, it was the number of PhD students that had an effect and in the humanities and social sciences, it was the number of students studying a major subject (more or less equivalent to a research Masters degree) that had an effect. This is explained in terms of the fact that in the sciences, PhD students are more likely to work on topics related to the research interests of the academics than they are in the humanities.

Project work in the major subjects of the humanities, on the other hand may focus on collecting and analysing data for the supervising academic. Humanities and social science PhD students were more likely to pursue independent topics (Kyvik and Smeby 1994).

There are some useful pointers here as to how the influence of teaching on research can be enhanced. Where students carry out research in the course of their studies and where that research is related to or assists with the research of the academic, teaching is seen to benefit research. More often than not, this occurs at the higher levels of learning, particularly at graduate levels. Yet if, as Zetter (2002: col. 2) advocates, research projects are re-run with students, asking students to critique research methods or findings, then we have an argument for involving students in carrying out research at more junior levels. Discussing research with students, Zetter suggests, 'can lead to new insights, better ways of communicating research findings, or even developing the next research proposal'.

The studies discussed so far in this chapter examine the effects of teaching on research as far as individual academics are concerned. Yet, of course, the effects go further than that. Of importance, too, is the way in which the department operates to pursue both teaching and research agendas. The whole department may be organised around the research strengths and interests of the staff (including pedagogical research), and the curriculum may be aligned with those research strengths. It may be that the more research-led the faculty is, the more pervasive is the influence of the curriculum on the ways research areas are organised. So, for example, the School of Biology at Edinburgh University consists of three research institutes: environmental science, animal and plants, and molecular biology. Staff belong to research institutes and the Biology Teaching Organisation has overall responsibility for the teaching, bringing together the staff from the different areas to deliver the curriculum, which essentially follows the three-centre structure. At Honours level (i.e., fourth year), the students go into the institutes to do research. Here there is organisational alignment between research and teaching so that the mutual supply of researchers for teaching and students for research benefits both. In Smeby's (1998) study, physics academics also mentioned that undergraduate teaching provides a way to recruit graduate research students, who then work on research connected with the teachers' research. However, as we have seen, there are many examples, particularly in America, of undergraduate students employed on research projects, suggesting we should not limit thinking to the postgraduate sphere.

The discussion in this chapter so far has alluded to some of the cultural conditions that constrain the extent to which research is influenced by teaching. Undergraduate students are discussed in terms of their questioning and in terms of their need for broad explanations (verbal is assumed). However:

> the primary goal of research is to ask questions and create new knowledge. Students spent a lot of time answering questions and mastering old knowledge. It is not universally accepted that an important goal of undergraduate teaching is to train producers of new knowledge.
>
> (Shore et al. 1990: 33)

If, as I have suggested, learning in academic contexts is a process of collaboratively generating knowledge-building communities, the distinction between those who learn and those who teach or research can break down. Undergraduates and postgraduates are, of course, traditionally viewed as the learners in higher education and although some academics may sometimes say, 'oh I'm a perpetual student!', this is usually said as a joke. Yet we know that research is a vehicle for academic learning and there is a sense in which researchers remain students all their lives (Beveridge, 1927 quoted in Shore et al. 1990). We know that research proceeds by academics developing their understanding and knowledge of the subject through experimentation and investigation.

In a paper I published with David Boud in 1995, it was suggested that research and teaching both shared a common attribute; namely, learning (Brew and Boud 1995); that research and learning share a core of identical activities. In that paper it was argued that the learner develops a personal understanding of a phenomenon and:

> while the products of research may in the future add to the store of socially accepted knowledge, the process of discovery emanates in an individual's and/or a group's attempt to make sense of a phenomenon or a problem in their subject domain.
>
> (Brew and Boud 1995: 269)

Research is often a collaborative activity, but the learning which researchers do in the course of their work is individual to them. Deep approaches to learning are, like research, focused on making meaning. As far as research is concerned, the meaning-making of researchers may ultimately represent the way in which the culture subsequently makes sense of phenomena (Brew and Boud, 1995: 270).

Critical to this is the recognition that we, as people, learn through asking questions about the world or some aspect of the world around us. Students can be valuable resources for research, not just in the sense of employing them to work on data, but in the sense of aiding researcher learning. Involving students in critical questioning is the cornerstone of a knowledge-building community. The beauty of this is that undergraduate students are able to ask naïve questions; ones which on the one hand help them to understand, but which on the other may also help researchers to rethink their assumptions, their findings, or indeed any aspect of their research. 'Students have something of significance to contribute to the subject matter, albeit from a position of less experience' (Rowland 1996: 16). Students can be particularly helpful because they may ask basic or critical questions which those who are seeped in a particular tradition perhaps have overlooked.

Throughout this book I have stressed the importance of students learning through research. I have argued that students need to learn to engage in professional scholarship (see Chapter 2) and we know that there are now countless examples where students even at the lowest levels are engaging in research as part of their studies in a variety of ways. Graduate students and some privileged undergraduates participate in research projects including assisting with the research of their teachers. Research as a learning process needs to be shared with students and be reflected in learning environments that we devise (Shore et al. 1990: 23). Again the cultural division that defines students as inhabiting a separate realm, with the bachelor's degree as a 'rite of passage', protects the culture of the academy and denies access to the many hundreds of undergraduates who would learn more effectively through engaging in the knowledge-building process. On the other hand:

the constant contact with young intelligent people stimulates academics, keeping them alert, alive and 'on their toes'. Further, since the student body is a continually changing group, academic vigour and vitality is maintained. The students are a continually fresh source of contact with the wider world and are thus a means of preventing insularity and staleness.
(Neumann 1992: 165)

So once again we are confronted by the need to extend the opportunities for students at all levels to be involved in real research. Research needs new ideas and insights. It needs all the fresh questioning it can get. Researchers need to be able to explain why their research is important. They need to be asked and to answer the basic naïve questions as in the example given by Caroline Baillie in our conversation in Chapter 5. Research needs students.

▶ How could teaching influence research?

Teaching-enhanced research not only means that individual academics find teaching useful in their research, but it also suggests that there might be elements of teaching that, if integrated into research and the research culture, might enhance it. We have seen the importance of taking a research-based and scholarly approach to teaching, and we know that research is the way academics learn (Brew and Boud 1995), so what does the research on learning and teaching tell us that can be of use in enhancing research? Are there aspects of this literature that can help us to answer some of the bigger questions about the nature of research itself and tell us something that is likely to improve research in some way?

In what is perhaps one of the most commonly used texts on higher education teaching and learning, Ramsden (2003) suggests that there are a number of important elements of good teaching that have long been recognised. They are:

- a desire to share a love of the subject with students
- an ability to make the material being taught stimulating and interesting
- a facility for engaging with students at their level of understanding
- a capacity to explain the material plainly
- a commitment to making it absolutely clear what has to be understood at what level and why
- showing concern and respect for students
- commitment to encouraging student independence
- an ability to improvise and adapt to new demands
- using teaching methods and academic tasks that require students to learn thoughtfully, responsibly and co-operatively
- using valid assessment methods
- a focus on key concepts and students' misunderstandings of them, rather than on covering the ground
- giving the highest quality feedback on student work
- a desire to learn from students and other sources about the effects of teaching and how it can be improved.

(Ramsden 2003: 86–7)

All of these elements are important not only for teaching, but also for research. Some have to do with having a passion and enthusiasm for the subject:

- a desire to share a love of the subject
- an ability to improvise and adapt to new demands

Both of these are important for the success of research. But how far does the ability to improvise go? Can new understandings of the nature of research, for example, be enabled to influence the way the researcher views research? One of the difficulties encountered by new researchers is the existence of work that challenges old ways of working and draws attention to anomalies within a body of work. Yet it sometimes takes a generational shift for ideas and methods to radically shift direction. Research is inherently conservative at a time when there is a need for fast responses to changing circumstances (Brew 2001a). The ability to adapt to new demands is as important for research as it is for teaching.

Other elements in Ramsden's list are to do with the ways in which teaching is communicated. They also apply to research:

- an ability to make the material stimulating and interesting
- a facility for engaging with audiences at their level of understanding
- a capacity to explain the material plainly
- a commitment to making it absolutely clear and knowing why it is important
- disseminating research in ways that require people to consider the ideas thoughtfully, responsibly and co-operatively

Researchers are increasingly being called upon to communicate their research in a wide variety of media: TV sound-bites, news bulletins, the popular press, even health or women's popular magazines. Living in a Mode 2 society (Nowotny, Scott and Gibbons 2001) also means that they have to collaborate with people in business, industry and the professions. Research now permeates our everyday lives. Researchers need to use a variety of communication strategies for their research so that it can more effectively and more often be communicated to the wider community. This might involve developing researchers' communication skills or it might involve teaching research students to communicate their research to non-specialists. It might additionally involve setting up a reward system for the publication of popular books and articles. What we learn from research on good teaching is that the communication medium and message has to suit the audience. There are numerous critiques of the tendency of scientific writing to address itself principally to the scientific community and fail to meet the public's demands for information (see for example, http://psci-com.ac.uk; or http://wwwinfo. anu.au/cpas; or for a brief discussion, see Aldersey-Williams 1999). Adapting explanations to audience levels, explaining clearly without technical language is becoming increasingly demanded. As Nowotny and colleagues (2001) point out, everyone wants to have an opinion. Science has to be communicated.

Some aspects of what we know about teaching are to do with attitudes of mind. Again these can usefully inform the process of research, and indeed add to our notion of scholarship as academic professionalism as noted earlier:

- showing concern and respect
- commitment to encouraging independence
- giving the highest quality feedback on others' work

Research is full of examples where insufficient concern and respect either for the needs of people in society or for the environmental and social impacts of the work has been shown:

> Many of the taken for granted improvements in the quality of human life and many of the benefits of technological advance can be traced back to their origins in academic enquiry and exploration. On the darker side, physicists may share a particular sense of responsibility for the creation of atomic and nuclear weapons, and engineers for the dubious blessings of nuclear power. Chemistry has given rise to its own forms of weaponry: biology to the possibility of bacteriological warfare and, along another pathway, to the ethical uncertainties of genetic engineering. The pure and applied sciences are not alone in their openness to such accusations. The appeal to history lies behind some of the most bitter territorial and racial disputes; sociological theorizing has given birth to powerful and sometimes destructive ideological movements; economics shares some of the blame for disastrous financial policies as well as some of the credit for successful ones. All in all, the outcome of research must be rated as a mixed blessing to humanity.
>
> (Becher 1989: 132)

The more research has advanced, the more distrustful people have become of it. Nowhere is this more evident than in the debates about the genetic engineering of foods (Brew 2001a). The public is now wary. Researchers' assurances about safety or ethics and such subjects have become topics of public debate. Researchers have to learn to show concern and respect because the topics they are working on are too important to be decided upon simply because of the passion of a particular individual or group. Researchers also need to be encouraging people to make up their own minds on research issues, not blindly assuming that they know best. The point about feedback is a point about the fact that the research is part of a scholarly knowledge-building community and, as such, researchers have a responsibility to the research community to help that community to develop.

Ramsden's final point, the desire to learn from others, takes us back to the idea of critical reflection as a source of learning and professional development.

▶ Learning from critical reflection

In Chapters 6 and 7 we considered the importance of systematic reflection on teaching as an aspect of the scholarship of teaching and learning. We know that critical reflection on practice is becoming increasingly important as an aspect of professional practice and in the professional training of undergraduate and graduate students. Good teaching in higher education contexts nowadays embeds reflective practice into curricula (Ramsden 2003).

Critical reflection is also a feature of conventional research programmes; for example, when laboratory findings are put up to the scrutiny of colleagues or when ideas are shared in a paper and discussed with colleagues or sent for review when submitted to a journal. Research is a process of questioning assumptions and findings. However, what we think research is will influence the extent and the nature of that critical reflection. Chapter 2 considered different views of the nature of research. I suggested that research could be viewed from an internal perspective where the focus of attention is on the internal workings, such as making sense of data, or it could be viewed from an external perspective where the focus was on research as a psychological or a social process. Views of research were also seen to be varied according to whether the researcher was present to awareness or whether the researcher was as if absent from awareness. In other words, whether the researcher was conscious of their own self as they researched. These different orientations to research lead to very different kinds of critical reflection.

Where the focus of attention is on the techniques, the problems or questions or understanding the data or results, and where the researcher as a person is not considered as part of the research picture, critical reflection will focus on, for example, making sure that the techniques that are used are adequate, or on the creation of meaning, or the veracity of the findings. It may go further to seriously question, particularly in the newer disciplines, what can be called research and the role of the researcher in it. (For a fuller discussion of this see Brew 2001a). Where the researcher's focus of attention is on the social aspects of research, then critical reflection may include considering interpersonal relationships with colleagues and collaborators, issues of career development, reputation and status. Where the researcher considers research an extension of their psychological selves, then critical reflection will include personal psychological issues and their influence on, and relationship to, the research.

These different understandings of the nature of research translate over to postgraduate students. The extent to which research students will be encouraged to critically reflect, and use that reflection in their research, will depend on the ways in which their supervisors understand the nature of research (Pearson and Brew 2002). It will also depend on how and whether they are integrated into a community of researchers and encouraged to reflect as a group on their research in a variety of ways.

But there is another level of critique which is important here and which echoes the discussion of reflexivity in Chapter 7. We saw in that chapter the way in which learning about how to carry out research on teaching and learning led academics to look critically at aspects of the academic habitus; the ways of thinking that are deeply enshrined in what we consider to be 'normal' or 'natural' in higher education; what Bourdieu (1998: 8) calls 'generative principles of distinct and distinctive practices'. Such principles are what we use to distinguish what is acceptable and what is unacceptable practice. They determine our tastes and our desires. Yet they are largely unacknowledged and even less discussed. There is a growing interest in, on the one hand, enshrining the practice of reflexivity within new research methods and, on the other, developing a reflexive approach to understanding the nature of research as a social phenomenon. In this regard, the development of the scholarship of research – including, for example, seeking an understanding of the social and political influences on research and the way in which research sustains dominant discourses – is leading to critical questioning not simply of the assumptions of particular research methods and methodologies, but of the very nature and character of research itself (see, for example, Brew 2001a). To be beyond the divide between teaching and research, research needs to change and reflexivity in relation to what we understand by research is an important means through which it can do this.

▶ The changing nature of research

In this book I have been arguing that there is a need to shift away from a model of the relationship between teaching and research which depends on the idea of courses with knowledge presented as cut and dried, where research findings are put into lectures and transferred into students' heads as if undigested. I have examined some of the ways teaching is changing and moving towards scholarly knowledge-building communities. This discussion of the influence of teaching on research suggests some ways research also needs to change if the goal of establishing inclusive scholarly knowledge-building communities is to be realised.

I argued earlier that it is important for undergraduate courses to teach students how to live in the climate of uncertainty and supercomplexity which characterises twenty-first-century society. It is a society which constantly challenges us to change our ideas, where we are continually confronted with views that are radically different to our own. It is a society where we continually need to confront conflicts in values. It is a society where decisions are continually having to be made on the basis of incomplete evidence. It is not an easy society to live in. Professionals within this society have to be flexible and adaptable. They need to be able to identify super-complex problems and work out how to solve them. It is a society in which the students of today may have a number of different careers throughout their lifetimes and they will need to be continually ready to respond to radically changed circumstances.

As such, it is a society which is dependent upon research. Not only are research findings of crucial importance to solving problems of a medical, scientific or social nature, but new ways of thinking about problems are also critical to the ways in which people live in such a society. In a society which requires flexibility to change conceptions in the light of new and perhaps conflicting evidence, conservatism and dogmatism are out of place. It is important for those who research to be open to new problems and new questions and to finding new ways of searching for new solutions (Brew 2001a). Ethical dilemmas, conflicting values and the changed nature of knowledge mean that research processes have become as important as the products of research.

This is seen in the opening up of new types of research which are questioning the relationship of the researcher to the phenomena being researched. This is happening in many fields of study, including science and technology as well as the humanities and social science. I have argued in this book that there is a need to open up to a broad range of understandings of the nature of research to incorporate both understandings of it as a social phenomenon and understandings which include the development of the person of the researcher. This may mean opening up to new forms of research; ones where the researcher and their learning become an important aspect of the knowledge that the research is generating.

I have also suggested that there is a need to extend understandings of teaching, moving towards more inclusive ideas of teaching as the encouragement of research-based approaches where students develop knowledge, and where that knowledge is viewed as being generated within a wider social context than just in the university. Research is about knowledge building and that takes place in a social context. So that teaching and research come to share a common enterprise – knowledge building within social contexts; specifically, scholarly communities. In addition, I have suggested that both academics and students need to develop scholarship conceived of as a quality of the way academic work is done, for it is this that makes the process rigorous and professional.

While the way in which research proceeds may indicate how an academic learns, this does not necessarily correspond to how they teach (Shore et al. 1990). As we saw in Chapter 5, in the undergraduate years knowledge is often presented as absolute and abstract, even if the teacher has a view of knowledge as more diffuse. It is at the graduate level where the idea that knowledge is diffuse is more likely to be acknowledged (Smeby 1998). Rowland (1996) suggests that an interactive approach to teaching that looks at research knowledge in a critical way can enhance research and is most effective for this. He argues that where the teacher encourages students to deconstruct the argument of the lecture, there is a 'direct payoff' for the research, because it leaves the subject open to further inquiry:

> Where knowledge is seen as being absolute, specialized and unrelated to wider perspectives or experiences of life, then working with less knowledgeable students is unlikely to stimulate research. However, where the knowledge which research produces is seen (and is offered to students) as being tentative, open to reinterpretation or containing insights which can be applied more widely, then the ways that students relate to this knowledge is potentially significant to the lecturer's own research.
>
> (Rowland 1996:15)

Yet we have seen that many undergraduate students are unaware of the research that their teachers are doing (Jenkins et al. 1998; Zamorski 2002). This suggests that there may be reluctance on the part of academics to share the learning that they do through research with their undergraduate students. This is perhaps understandable if the questioning of such students is likely to deeply challenge research findings and assumptions. However, I suggest that in the turbulent societal context in which we find ourselves, such challenges should be welcomed rather than feared.

▶ Conclusion

In this chapter we have seen that there is a general coming together of research and learning practice and that research has much to learn from attending to the teaching and learning domain. Yet this all seems very far removed from the context of research assessment, and indeed from the dominant research practices of universities. It also does not take account of who sets the agenda for research in universities. In the next chapter we will examine the contexts in which teaching and research take place and look at the factors that inhibit, and those that encourage, the kinds of developments suggested here; ones that would lead to the development of inclusive scholarly knowledge-building communities.

9   Culture and Context

Whether we consider the way teaching is integrated into research or the way research is integrated into teaching, this all takes place within, and is influenced by, a number of cultural and contextual factors. These include the extent to which individuals are able to integrate their research and their teaching within particular institutional contexts, university policies and strategies which enhance or inhibit integration as well as wider social and political factors that influence how universities operate.

Key questions in this chapter, then, are what are the optimum contextual conditions for the development of inclusive scholarly knowledge-building communities within higher education? What cultural and contextual conditions facilitate the development of such communities? What conditions discourage it?

The chapter looks at the nature of academic work and how it is evaluated before going on to consider institutional factors that can have a facilitating or an inhibiting effect on the development of a research enhanced higher education experience. Finally, it goes beyond the university to examine wider agendas to see how they influence the integration of teaching and research. The chapter also considers the implications of engaging in inquiry-led development for the practice of academic staff development.

▶ The nature of academic work

The nature of academic work is such that it is often difficult to see where one activity starts and another finishes. Studies have consistently shown that academic-staff beliefs about the existence of the link between teaching and research are much stronger than the correlational research evidence would suggest it should be (see, for example, Webster 1985; Neumann 1993). Rowland (1996) found in his interview study with heads of academic departments that there was variation in how the terms 'teaching' and 'research' were used. So, while some respondents interpreted 'teaching' as 'giving lectures' and 'research supervision' as an aspect of 'research', others saw 'giving lectures' as a way of disseminating research. Rowland concludes:

although people normally used the terms teaching and research in a relatively unproblematic fashion, once some of them began to think of their academic activity in more specific detail, the two terms became much more closely intertwined.

(Rowland 1996: 13)

Carol Colbeck's work is helpful in understanding why that may be so. Her study of how academics actually spend their time suggests that there is considerable variation in the extent to which academics engage in activities designed to serve the dual purposes of teaching and research. Contrary to the views of many academics that time taken up in teaching is time taken out of research, Colbeck (1998) suggests that the average amount of time that people spend on activities that advance both goals simultaneously is about one-fifth.

What is particularly interesting about Colbeck's data for our purposes here, however, is her analysis of the contextual factors that contribute to, or inhibit, the extent to which academics are able to integrate their research and their teaching in particular tasks. She suggests that academics working in more bureaucratic institutions or disciplinary areas where their roles are defined for them may have less opportunity to integrate their research and their teaching than people in contexts where role expectations are less clearly defined. So, for example, Colbeck found that faculty academics in disciplines where there was a high degree of paradigm consensus, where there was widespread agreement about curriculum content and high levels of research collaboration were less able to integrate their research and their teaching in classroom contexts than were academics in disciplinary areas where knowledge is recognised to be more diffuse, and where there is low paradigm consensus. Since the latter are characterised, for example, according to Becher (1989), by idiosyncratic curricula, where academics engage in research independently, academics have more freedom to engage in activities which serve both teaching and research purposes:

The knowledge and social structures of hard disciplines appear to define faculty work behavior more rigorously than the knowledge and social structures of soft disciplines. Faculty in hard disciplines, therefore, may have fewer opportunities to integrate teaching and research than faculty in soft disciplines.

(Colbeck 1998: 651)

This largely accords with Rowland (1996: 14), who found that heads of department considered that a 'broad' approach to research where there was either a fundamental critique in a disciplinary area, or interdisciplinary research or research which applied the area to social or technical contexts, was more closely related to teaching because it was closer to the students' interests than narrower, more specialised areas; a point with which Smeby (1998), writing from a Norwegian perspective, concurs.

Rowland suggests that the approach to teaching also appears to influence whether an academic is able to integrate their research and their teaching:

> In more interactional settings, such as projects, tutorials and seminars the relationship between teaching and research was held to be much closer. This was not only because it provided an opportunity for the lecturer to teach their own speciality, but because the students' contributions offered new perspectives on the lecturer's own field of research, at times even challenging its assumptions.
>
> (Rowland 1996:14)

On this point, Colbeck found that the purpose of the teaching (whether classroom instruction or training students to conduct research) was more influential in whether academics integrated their teaching and research activities than the level of the students. So, for example, the closely knit communities of science provided more opportunities for research and teaching to be integrated where the teaching was oriented towards research training and development. The 'softer' more individualistic ways of working in the humanities tended, where research training is concerned, to work against the integration of research and teaching. Colbeck found that this was the case irrespective of the level of the student. This work ties in with work on research training and supervision development where it has been found that some academics consider supervision as an aspect of their research while others consider it to be an aspect of their teaching (see Chapter 8).

Rowland (1996) speculates that gender may be a factor in determining whether an academic integrates their research and their teaching. In his study, some of his male respondents described research as requiring single-mindedness, 'drive', 'stickability'; attributes that, he suggests, conform to male stereotypes, while teaching was described as requiring qualities represented by female stereotypes such as 'openness', 'concern for students', and 'caring'. Rowland suggests that 'such a perspective is no doubt self-reinforcing of the male hierarchy which produced it' (Rowland 1996:10) and Colbeck has identified issues of gender as a fruitful avenue for further research (Colbeck 2004).

What is also interesting in Colbeck's work are the ways in which the departmental and institutional context combines with these disciplinary factors and differing purposes of teaching to influence the extent to which academics feel able to integrate research and teaching activities. So, for example, she suggests that the ways in which research is evaluated in institutions can either promote or inhibit academics' capacity to integrate their research and their teaching. In a university where research is defined broadly, perhaps encompassing the scholarship of teaching, creative works, textbooks and the like, greater opportunities for academics to combine teaching and research activities are provided (Colbeck 1998: 660). Indeed, Neumann (1992) came to a similar conclusion in her study of senior administrators and Zetter (2002: 2) suggests that broad definitions of research enable 'consultancy-based knowledge' to be used in teaching. Colbeck also found that the extent to which academics are able to participate in departmental-level decisions about what they teach is related to their capacity to integrate their research and their teaching. So, for example, where academics are involved in the decision-making process, they are able to choose to teach their current research interests or at least incorporate aspects of their current work in their courses. Where they are allocated teaching without exercising much choice, it is more difficult. Colbeck found that the way in which departmental decision making was done had more influence on academics' capacity to integrate their research and their teaching than overall university policies.

One hotly debated question is whether a university's capacity to integrate research and teaching is dependent on the capacity of teaching staff to integrate their own research into their teaching by being research active, however 'research active' is defined. Neumann (1992: 162) reports that the senior administrators in her study indicated that only active researchers are able to teach at advanced levels and that students are disadvantaged if academics are not involved in research. She also found a belief that only those actively engaged in research are able to develop new researchers. Zetter (2002) argues, in contrast, that it is not necessary for all staff in a department to be research active. What is important, he suggests is to be an effective academic professional and that means developing awareness of and currency of the research others are doing, actively engaging with practitioners engaged in evidence-based practice.

It should be the case that in an environment where teachers are leading the research field, student learning should be more up to date than where teachers are not so engaged. However, there is by no means a clear view as to the effects on students' learning experiences, nor whether it results in better or more research based education. Neumann (1992: 167) argues, for example, that there is a cumulative benefit of being taught by active researchers; her senior administrators expressing the belief that therefore it is important for active researchers to teach at the first-year undergraduate level. This, they believed would ensure that students would be motivated to engage in postgraduate work and that they would acquire critical questioning skills and have a 'vision of what is possible'. While I agree that it is important to develop critical skills and motivate students towards awareness of, and chances to participate in, research at the first- and second-year undergraduate levels, it is by no means clear that senior researchers are necessary for this. Indeed, there appears to be a growing trend for senior researchers in possession of research grants to buy themselves out of teaching by using research grants to hire casual or part-time teachers.

There is no doubt that considerations of research-enhanced education need to be seen in the context of changing work roles and responsibilities. These include increases in hybrid roles, in teaching-only positions, in instructional design roles and in the numbers of administrators who also have a research function. A worrying trend, however, is the effect of casualisation on universities' ability to integrate research and teaching. For academics from performance and artistic areas, the predominance of casual teaching staff enables leading performers to be involved in teaching. This is in contrast to, for example, science, where casual staff tend to be neither leading practitioners nor researchers. This together with the lack of tenure, increasing difficulty of gaining promotion, experienced professionals taking up senior posts, and where it is becoming increasingly difficult for those in high-level management positions in universities to maintain research, all have an effect on a university's capacity and willingness to integrate research and teaching.

New working conditions and changes in types of position do not in themselves signal a cleft between research and teaching. Yet if such a divide is to be avoided, there is a need to think creatively about how new positions may contribute to research-enhanced education. This may include, for example, encouraging postgraduate students working as tutors and demonstrators to share their research with undergraduates and providing opportunities for them to do so, involving casual staff in supporting inquiry-based, problem-based curricula, inviting key researchers to talk about their research to junior-level students in student-based conferences, and so on.

Indeed, new kinds of positions provide creative opportunities to rethink relationships within institutions of higher education. I have already drawn attention to the divide between academics and students, with both occupying separate domains within the university. If we are to work towards the idea of universities as encompassing scholarly knowledge-building communities, other old academic divisions need to be broken down; for example, those which define academics and administrative/technical 'support' or 'general' staff as occupying separate facilities, with different rules and levels of commitment to the institution, on the one hand, and privileged 'academic' staff on the other. Inquiry-based learning can ultimately break down distinctions between different categories of people in higher education through the development of collaborative initiatives including allied as well as academic staff and students. It is not just that students are involved in inquiry in their courses, but rather that inquiry becomes an integral part of academic practice (see Chapter 11).

▶ Institutional climate

There is no doubt that a strong clear statement of intent to integrate research and teaching in some way is the cornerstone of initiatives to develop inclusive scholarly knowledge-building communities within specific universities. Drawing upon the Boyer Commission (1999) set of strategies for developing research-based learning in research-intensive universities, Jenkins, Breen, Lindsay and Brew (2003), enumerate a number of strategies both to encourage research and teaching to be linked and to align the organisation of teaching with research practices. These include:

- developing institutional awareness and institutional mission through, for example, putting the linking of teaching and research central to the institutional mission and formulating strategies and plans to support it, and organising events, research studies and publications to raise institutional awareness;
- developing curricula to support the nexus through, for example, development, planning and audit of teaching policies, and strategies;
- developing research to support the nexus by, for example, developing and auditing research policies, and ensuring links between research centres, the curriculum and student learning;
- developing staff and university structures to support the nexus by, for example, ensuring it is central to induction, staff development, promotion and reward policies and strategies, and ensuring effective synergies between units, committees and structures for teaching and research.

(Jenkins et al. 2003: 81–2)

This section is not concerned to explore how to implement such strategies. Rather, the focus is on the issues they raise. Institutional strategies and policies necessarily presuppose and also encourage particular views of the nature of academic work and the kind of relationships between academics and students that are possible and appropriate. The institutional climate is crucial in any consideration of how teaching and research are to be brought together in universities. The challenge at an institutional level is to ensure that policies and strategies to develop the relationship between teaching and research do not result in change only at superficial levels, but can accommodate and encourage people to ask and discuss the big questions. So how are different perspectives, needs and interests accommodated in institutional strategies to bring research and teaching together?

Policies necessarily tread a thin line between different perspectives and approaches that exist within the particular university community. It is interesting to witness the ways in which, once a policy has been formulated, individual academics and groups in their faculties, schools and departments negotiate and come to understand its implications. Indeed, the discussions which take place in the formulation and implementation of policy are an important aspect of a university's developing awareness of the complexity, but also the possibilities of a research-enhanced education. For example, at the University of Sydney, a research-intensive university in Australia, the marriage of different perspectives is evident in the statement outlining what is meant in the university by 'research-led teaching' that has been adopted as university policy (see Chapter 3). The statement includes university rhetoric such as: 'The University's strong research record and large number of active researchers is the foundation for research-led teaching.' It includes the beliefs of some of the faculty academics who assisted in drafting it: 'As far as possible, students are also expected to engage in research activity of some kind. The nature of such activities will vary at different levels.' It also includes aspects of the vision for research-led teaching that I have been developing: 'Research-led teaching emphasises the partnership of academics and students as they engage in the critical challenge of open exploratory inquiry' (University of Sydney 2004). These statements reveal different views of the scope and possibilities of research-led teaching which have had to be accommodated.

Another example comes from Southampton Solent University in the United Kingdom. It has defined its mission in terms of the development of 'advanced scholarship' (Southampton Institute 2004). There is a good deal of educational work being undertaken amongst academics and managers to explore the range and scope of activities that come under the advanced scholarship umbrella, and discussions about how academics can utilise the advanced scholarship initiative as a means of integrating teaching and research. Successful implementation of institutional policy is inescapably implemented in such multi-perspectival contexts.

Even within institutions where the mission represents the view of the chief executive officer or senior executive group rather than arising from academic community consensus, such policies and strategies are likely to represent a marriage of different views and interpretations of the overall mission. While, as indicated earlier, there is no contradiction in institutions that are not research intensive engaging in research-enhanced teaching, there is, I believe, a contradiction in institutions where decision making is of a managerial type endeavouring to move to a research-enhanced education. This is because a dimension of leadership in a research-enhanced institution is an openness to the spirit of inquiry across all its domains, including at the highest levels. Such openness is inconsistent with a managerial approach.

Even in collaborative collegial institutions, there is a danger that the views of strong and influential members of powerful groups can confine the university, faculty or department to simply renaming traditional prac-tices. There is research evidence that extended discussion of the relationship is productive of changed ideas about what is possible and desirable (see Jen-kins and Zetter 2003). Indeed, as important as the development of policies and strategies themselves are the discussions that take place at numerous levels of the university as a result of them. To open up research strategies to provide research-based undergraduate education and support and develop undergraduate research requires radical mind-shifts. Progress is dependent on discussion supported by the continual feeding in of ideas and suggestions derived from an informed understanding of the issues in the research litera-ture. It takes a lot of work and discussion to shift thinking and practice further. In this regard, I hope this book can help.

Of importance, too, are structures for implementation. For example, some universities have been working to develop research-enhanced teaching through cross-faculty working groups (see, for example, Brew and Prosser 2003; Wuetherick et al. 2004). Other universities have organised forums to consider issues; set up research projects to examine students' experiences and disseminate these to staff; used the Boyer Commission framework as a basis for a suite of strategies; set up criteria for award schemes for outstand-ing teaching and for promotion which emphasise scholarship in teaching; or performance indicators to measure the extent to which the integration of research and teaching have taken place (see, for example, Hattie 2001; Brew and Prosser 2003).

Targeted funding is also important to support any such strategies. For example in the context of an overall teaching performance indicator system, the University of Sydney has developed strategies to further the scholarship of teaching including the allocation of a portion of the university's teaching budget according to what is known as *The Scholarship Index*. This rewards departments for scholarly activity related to teaching and learning, according to a set of weighted criteria: for example, a qualification in university teach-ing (ten points); a national teaching award (finalist) (five points), a pub-lished refereed article on university teaching (two points) and so on.

In all of this there is often a tendency for policies and strategies to be focused on the teaching side of things. Even if there is high level leadership support on the teaching side, how are research bodies in institutions to be encouraged to view the bringing together of research and teaching as of ben-efit to them? For example, at the University of Sydney, we found initially that teaching policies, particularly recently formulated ones, included substantial references to the importance of linking research and teaching. However, research policies made scant reference to teaching. This may reflect the fact that initiatives to bring research and teaching together were largely being driven by the Pro-Vice-Chancellor (Teaching and Learning), not by the Pro-Vice-Chancellor (Research). An important issue is how, at the institutional level, research communities can be encouraged to see the bringing together of research and teaching as benefiting both research and teaching. In this regard the role of funding bodies in setting research agendas is a critical inhibiting or facilitating factor, as we shall see later in the chapter.

▶ Initiatives at faculty, school and departmental levels

School and department encouragement for aligning research and teaching is likely to vary within each institution. Again, Jenkins and colleagues (2003) suggest a number of implementation strategies, including: developing disciplinary (and departmental) understanding of teaching and research relations; making them a central consideration in hiring new staff and in appraising and developing existing staff; developing synergies between research centres, course planning teams and postgraduate and undergraduate teaching; auditing and reviewing courses structures and policies; developing effective synergies between teaching and research strategies, etc. (Jenkins et al. 2003:120).

Academics, faculties and departments have many and varied reasons for wanting to develop the relationship between teaching and research and varied conceptions of what that involves, not all of which are aligned with university rhetoric, nor with the requirements of good pedagogy. Whatever stage of implementation a particular faculty or department is at, the challenge is how to move thinking forward. It is all too easy for traditional practices to simply be redefined in the language of research enhanced education. If students are to benefit from engaging in scholarly knowledge-building communities, moving the discourse forward, though important, in itself is not enough. Educative strategies are needed to extend academics' thinking about the scope and possibilities for research-enhanced teaching and learning. As we saw in Chapter 7, courses that encourage a re-evaluation of educational values are important even though they present considerable challenges for academics.

I have suggested that school and department encouragement for aligning research and teaching will, of course, vary across any one university. As we have seen, the departmental and institutional context combines with disciplinary factors and differing purposes of teaching to influence the extent to which academics feel able to integrate research and teaching activities.

Audits of practice help to raise questions about what is understood by a research-enhanced education. Performance indicators provide a mechanism for auditing progress, but they focus on aspects that are relatively easy to measure. Such indicators are not neutral, but are constituted within existing ways of working and ways of organising that work. Specifically, they foreground atomistic strategies for the development of the relationship between teaching and research, and make more holistic perspectives appear distant and unachievable. They tend to be reductive and can only accommodate the complexity and multi-dimensional character of research-enhanced education with difficulty. Measurement heightens the visibility of an activity, but the most measurable aspects are not necessarily the most important ones (Fairweather in Colbeck 2002).

However, in developing performance indicators, academics develop understanding of research-enhanced education and may share many and diverse practices across different disciplinary contexts. They may include indicators focused on student awareness of, and active engagement with, research; on the capacity of academic staff to integrate research and teaching; on the extent to which the curriculum is designed to engage students in a variety of research-based activities, induct them into the research community and develop their awareness of research; and on departmental, faculty and overall university encouragement for, and commitment to, aligning research and teaching.

Once indicators are established, work can progress on collecting data on them. Our experience at the University of Sydney suggests that this can give a major impetus to initiatives to develop a research-enhanced education. The very act of collecting the data within faculties can itself be generative of developing understanding among faculty academics of the meaning, scope and opportunities for bringing research and teaching together. We are dealing with a dynamic fast-changing situation. Our ability to measure it will always lag behind where any faculty or department is at. Indeed, at the University of Sydney, by the time our report on findings was ready, there was evidence that the agreed indicators had already become outdated.

▶ **Beyond the institution to wider agendas**

The importance of national agendas and international trends on efforts to bringing teaching and research closer together must not be underestimated. The ways in which universities are funded, and national quality assurance processes, send messages to institutions about the relative value of research and teaching, indicating what to focus on (Willis 2001). In New Zealand, an act of parliament requires universities to ensure that 'research and teaching are closely interdependent and that programs are taught mainly by people engaged in research' (Willis, Harper and Sawicka 1999: 1; Willis 2001). There, and also in Australia, academic audit is being used to monitor, and indeed strengthen, the links between teaching and research. This is in spite of governmental regimes that provide separate funding for teaching and for research activities.

I have already mentioned disquiet within the academic community in the United Kingdom and Australia regarding the effects of national funding models on the capacity of institutions to develop both research and teaching. I have also alluded to the effects of a dual funding system on the relationship. If research and teaching are seen as distinct and funded separately as they are in these and a number of other countries, then efforts to integrate teaching and research already begin with disadvantages.

However, this is not the place to review the ways in which universities are funded. My concern here is with what is facilitative of the development of an inclusive research-based higher education and what inhibits such development. Jenkins and colleagues (2003) again present a number of strategies to increase the chances for institutions to integrate research and teaching. These include: building it into the statutory and legal definitions of higher education institutions, degree and professional requirements; ensuring there are limited negative impacts from research assessment and providing tangible support for research areas that strengthen the nexus; funding and supporting all institutions and staff to engage in scholarly activity; and developing national and international organisations and projects to support the relationship (Jenkins et al. 2003:148–9).

When considering institutional strategies, I suggested that policy and strategies are likely to be a compromise between many different views. The same is also true of government organisations which support and fund teaching and research activities. Once the need to provide an education for students that will develop a broad range of attributes, including research skills, is recognised, universities have to find a way to bring teaching and research together. Indeed, although governments separately fund teaching and research, it is not possible for institutions to keep the funding of activities separate. At some level, be it faculty or departmental level, the two overlap. As Colbeck's studies amply demonstrate, academics spend up to one-fifth of their time on activities that pursue both teaching and research objectives. Departments routinely utilise equipment, specialist library resources, collections and data bases purchased with research funds for undergraduates.

The implementation of strategies such as those suggested by Jenkins and colleagues (2003) is highly dependent on political will to bring research and teaching together; something that may be considered a luxury in an era of mass higher education on the one hand and the high cost of research on the other. When governments desire to be internationally competitive in research, it may be considered that this can only be achieved by concentrating research funding on those universities that are already strong in research. This leads to the unfortunate conclusion that teaching and research institutions should be separate. Perhaps paradoxically, the threat of teaching-only institutions being established in the United Kingdom has resulted in increasing concern about the relationship. What is interesting, and perhaps surprising in the context of governments' seeming unwillingness to accept that each university should engage in research, is that institutions are increasingly defining their missions in terms of the large research universities (Shulman 2000c). There is 'mission creep' in this regard, as French (2004) suggests from his experience of Hong Kong.

The extent to which there is political will to bring research and teaching together is demonstrated in the missions, aims and strategies of national research-funding bodies. For example, the role of the UK Economic and Social Research Council (ESRC) is stated as:

- to promote and support by any means, high-quality basic, strategic and applied research and related postgraduate training in the social sciences;
- to advance knowledge and provide trained social scientists who meet the needs of users and beneficiaries, and thereby contribute to the economic competitiveness of the United Kingdom, the effectiveness of public services and policy, and the quality of life;
- to provide advice on, and disseminate knowledge and promote public understanding of the social sciences.

(ESRC no date)

There is no reference here to teaching or undergraduate education, either in the Council's aims or in its strategic plans (apart from the use of the term 'education' as a field of study). The UK Engineering and Physical Sciences Research Council (EPSRC) also aims to generate public awareness and to communicate research outcomes, encourage public engagement and dialogue as well as to disseminate knowledge. Public engagement with research is one of its five overarching strategic objectives (EPSRC no date), but there is again no link into education in general nor higher education in particular. The UK Biotechnology and Biological Sciences Research Council shares similar aims and objectives (BBSRC no date).

Similarly, the mission of the Australian Research Council (ARC) is to advance Australia's research excellence to be globally competitive and 'deliver benefits to the community'. However, when we consider what such benefits are and how they are going to be delivered, once again mention is made of using its communications strategy to develop and improve public understanding and appreciation of the contribution that research makes to the economic, social and cultural benefit of the community; to promote the relevance and value of research as a career; and enhance understanding and support among the community of the outcomes and benefits of Australian research. However, no mention is made of the influence of research on, or relationship with, education at any level apart from its influence on research education and training of postgraduate students and in providing career opportunities for the brightest and best researchers (ARC 2003). The

National Health and Medical Research Council (NH&MRC) also aims to promote awareness of the Australian community about the benefits of health and medical research and promote research that engages the community in influencing and encouraging changes in health policy and practice. However, again there is no indication of how this might affect education except for the 'education of the research workforce' (NH&MRC 2003).

Given such a lack of encouragement to integrate research and teaching as demonstrated by these research councils, it is little wonder there is a perception that research and teaching are quite separate in these countries. In contrast, in the United States, the mission of the National Science Foundation, the principle body responsible for US governmental expenditure on academic research is stated as: 'To promote the progress of science; to advance the national health, prosperity, and welfare; . . . and to initiate and support basic scientific research and programs to strengthen scientific research potential *and science education programs at all levels*' (National Science Foundation Act of 1950, my italics). This is achieved within its programmes through the integration of research and education:

> Effective integration of research and education at all levels infuses learning with the excitement of discovery. Joining together research and education also ensures that the findings and methods of research are quickly and effectively communicated in a broader context and to a larger audience.
>
> (National Science Foundation 2001)

Thus the educative process is put at the heart of programmes to develop research within American higher education. This is pursued by the requirement for research teams to establish in their proposals how their research will reach a broad consistency within the country, and also through the funding of excellence in teaching scholars. While the language is of the spread of 'education' rather than the integration of 'teaching', and while such initiatives have to be seen within the context of a higher education system which values research over and above teaching, as exhibited by Boyer (1990) among others, such policies and strategies do appear to have the effect of reducing some of the problematic elements of the relationship between teaching and research within US higher education that are noted in other contexts.

▶ The role of the professional bodies

In considering how and whether courses can be enhanced by the integration of research, the requirements of professional bodies have to be taken into account since professional bodies have an influence on curricula which, in many cases, can be quite substantial. In a conversation a group of academics discussing the relationship between research, teaching and consultancy in the built-environment disciplines (Jenkins and Zetter 2003) work to dovetail their desires to move to inquiry-based approaches to teaching and learning with what they consider their professional bodies will accept as adequate and appropriate preparation for professional accreditation. This conversation is based on my notes at an actual meeting and I believe it to be typical of those between academics from new professional areas when working to integrate research and teaching. I have changed the names to protect the identity of the individuals concerned.

Paul: The building blocks of an applied discipline such as planning are the social sciences. But when you apply social science to the world of planning, things become more complex because students need to go beyond the theory to address particular practical problems; planning problems. So all the time, you have to balance theoretical social scientific questions, with questions at a policy level. Students have to learn to operationalise their understanding. This is a difficult challenge. Practice-based knowledge is a different kind of knowledge. You need to be able to define different kinds of research questions.

Janice: I know what you mean. My area is property and estate management. It's a very young discipline. If you do a literature search, you will almost certainly find that it is empty. The area is grossly under-explored. There just isn't the research history. I think that this presents us with a problem and also with an opportunity. We have to explore the nature of the discipline and what constitutes knowledge within property and estate management, and we have to do this with the students.

Eric: That's really interesting, and I think that we're all implicitly operating with different values about what constitutes good research and what is relevant research in terms of teaching and we convey that to the students; not directly, I don't mean that, but in the ways we present our own area to them. We make assumptions about other areas.

Ahmed: Yes. We're making different value judgments about what's important. You have to get across to students how knowledge is socially produced. The issue of values is important to students' understandings of what research is. Architecture for example is more about aesthetics. In planning, we have to draw on a whole heap of policy documents. It's social science, but we have to take account of the political dimension; like when consultants give the government the answers that they want.

Paul: Each discipline has a different set of value criteria.

Eric: But it's even more complicated than that, isn't it? I'm a building surveyor. Surveying isn't traditionally an academic discipline. My background is in practice and so is that of many of my colleagues. There is quite a lot of suspicion of the social scientists in surveying. We have to get over this. We're trying to get students to get in touch with the research side of things, but because our background is in practice many of us are suspicious about what social scientific research is telling us and about how it relates to practice. We don't, well some of us don't, feel confident about getting into research, let alone getting our students to engage with it.

John: My background is in sociology and I don't see planning as having a strong systematic basis in research. Social science is about investigating empirically. Planning is the practice knowledge of the locality. Planning doesn't give us any knowledge. Practice is not informed by research very much. Our conceptions of what knowledge is are therefore very relevant to the whole question of how we are to bring research, teaching and consultancy together.

Paul: Yes we're dealing with more subjects that are, well, derivative. Some of the more profound kinds of conceptual social scientific questions just don't come into our research agendas at all.

Marie: So what are the implications for students, do you think?

Paul: Well one of the problems is that professional organisations don't encourage students to ask any of the profound questions. They ask for things which divert students away from understanding things that would really get them involved in the subject at a deep level; things that I think they would actually find better in terms of developing their professionalism. I think that the way we are driven by our professional bodies is actually quite damaging in terms of the development of students' knowledge and understanding.

Janice: Yes it's unfortunate. Students are not now engaging with the deeper questions about the nature of knowledge. But they should be. We should be encouraging this.

Ahmed: The curriculum is more practice-based at present. Well, more practice-based than I think it should be. We're trying to combine teaching students to have a deep conceptual understanding on the one hand, and because of pressure from the professional bodies, employers and so on, to also develop their practice-based skills. I think things have swung rather too far on the practice side, unfortunately. So it's not now about developing a corpus of knowledge.

Paul: But there isn't a fixed basis of conceptual knowledge for students to acquire. Concepts are under challenge. So there is a tension between the two levels.

John: The whole thing is dogged by the fact that the culture is not research-led. A lot of what we teach is policy evaluation.

Janice: a lot of our teachers are practitioners and are a bit frightened by academic knowledge.

Here we see academics coming to terms with the implications for students of learning about the discipline in relatively new areas where there are not the traditionally strong research bases on which to build a curriculum. In this case the professional bodies are viewed as inhibiting the development of the very professionalism that they are set up to foster. While this is clearly not the case with all professional bodies, the point to note is that research-enhanced education is ultimately dependent upon academics coming to terms with the marriage of their ideas about knowledge with what is appropriate for their students and with the requirements of professional bodies.

▶ **Implications for academic development**

This chapter has explored factors that enhance or inhibit universities in going beyond the research and teaching divide at the level of the individual academic, at the level of the department, faculty and school, and at the level of the university. We have noted how such factors are influenced by the wider contexts of research funding and professional bodies. This all suggests that in universities committed to bringing research and teaching together, there is important work to be done by those with a role to enhance the skills, knowledge and attributes of academic staff, those with a responsibility to bring about organisational change, those charged with assisting in the implementation of strategic university initiatives, and/or those with curriculum development responsibilities. Many university managers, heads of department and faculty staff are involved in this. However, finally in this chapter, I want to look at specific implications for professional academic/staff/faculty developers. Developers have a role in encouraging research-enhanced teaching, but they also have a responsibility for encouraging teaching-enhanced research and that means working with faculty academics to understand what it might mean and where it might lead them to change their approaches to, and conceptions of, research.

If research and teaching are to be closely aligned, research and academic development also need to be brought closely together. On one level, this means doing research which is useful in academic development work and using research in development activities. On another level, it means that academic development work needs to be grounded in a research-based approach and to conform to high standards of academic behaviour. On yet another level, it means using research to enhance the quality of development work and using research in development activities (Brew 2003a). Academic developers have to be credible researchers if they are to be credible as agents for change within research-enhanced education. This will only happen if they can hold their own as researchers within their own field of study; that is, higher education. 'A key requirement is that developers engage in research which is professional and rigorous in execution, presentation and dissemination and that is credible in whatever ways count in their institution' (Brew 2003a: 6).

Since teaching development needs to be evidence based, developers need to be able to provide leadership in teaching and learning research. There appear to be five areas of research that it is appropriate for developers to pursue:

1. Research into the policies, practices, strategies of higher education in general.
2. Basic research into student learning, teaching methods and their effectiveness, conceptions of teaching, conceptions of the subject matter held by students and their teachers, effects of particular aspects of the learning environment on students' learning experiences, and so on.
3. Institutional research and evaluation of policy and strategy, student course perceptions and evaluation of students' experiences and outcomes.
4. Action research as an integral part of professional practice including working with academics who are researching the effects of their interventions on their own students or developers researching their own practice.
5. Research into methodologies for educational research to provide leadership in developing ideas about what research can be.

(Brew 2003a: 6–7)

Developers need to be ready to respond to managers' requests for data. However, there is a dilemma for individual developers in balancing how much time to spend providing information for institutional managers and how much to spend on research which will bring the credibility rewards needed for promotion and career advancement. These competing tensions between different agendas have to be resolved on every level, with every research project, in every research context, by every individual researcher or developer, and every research and development team.

Developers have an important role in encouraging academics to work towards developing inclusive scholarly knowledge-building communities with students. In order to encourage such initiatives, developers need to inform themselves about inquiry-based learning and to have a repertoire of responses when academics ask for examples. Developers must also work towards integrating research and teaching by encouraging academics to work towards developing academic professionalism among students. Developers have to be mindful of ways in which what we know about good teaching can inform the research process; they have a role in encouraging researchers and their students to focus on the processes of research and helping them to develop new forms and conceptions of research. If they are to do this, then developers must themselves participate in some of the same scholarly communities (Brew 2003b).

Yet perhaps developers' most important function is in assisting academics to develop a reflexive critique of practice. As we saw in Chapter 7, reflexivity in a Bourdieuian sense means becoming aware of aspects of how we think about, for example, the underlying assumptions that are made about the nature of higher education, what is appropriate as research, what students are capable of and so on. In developing a reflexive critique, teaching and learning become not simply aspects of practice to improve, but objects of study in their own right. We saw in Chapter 7 how, in developing an understanding of how their students learn and how they themselves teach, academics are led to question the basic assumptions that drive their practice and to develop new theories and understandings of that practice.

The scholarship of teaching and learning provides a method of analysis of higher education phenomena and pedagogical theories provide frameworks that assist understanding. Yet as we saw with Kreber's analysis of the ways in which academics reflect on their practice, the scholarship of university teaching can be carried out at technical, communicative or emancipatory levels. If individuals and institutions are to go beyond the divide between teaching and research, developers need to provide opportunities for academics to move from the technical to the emancipatory levels of reflection, for only then will the kind of changes to higher education that are needed for the establishment of inclusive, scholarly knowledge-building communities to be realised.

10 Dimensions of a Research-Enhanced Higher Education

Throughout this book I have suggested that in order to go beyond the divide between research and teaching, we have to question some of the assumptions within the academic habitus that limit capacity to develop scholarly knowledge-building communities. In this chapter, I want to bring the arguments together to examine how to tell whether, within any particular institution, progress is being made. What are the criteria that can be used to decide on the extent to which specific pedagogies and strategies are leading us beyond the teaching and research divide, and how would we know whether what we are doing is going in that direction? How would we evaluate it? What are the indicators that suggest we might be going in the opposite direction?

A higher education where teaching and research are integrated should, by its very nature, be dynamic, creative and organic. Yet the act of trying to specify the extent to which research and teaching are being brought together within any particular institution raises issues about how the level of integration is to be measured. The danger of too close attention to quantitative measures, as we saw in Chapter 9, is of trapping initiatives in a static state. Measurement without vision may result in a reiteration of the *status quo* and a failure to move forward. The extent to which there is integration of research and teaching depends on the direction from which we do the looking. Different universities, departments and individuals will have different views even when looking at essentially similar situations. This chapter represents a summary of ideas presented throughout this book that suggest what institutions need to attend to if they are to go beyond the divide. In examining the dimensions of such a higher education, my aim is to raise issues and ask questions that might be helpful in thinking how an institution, faculty, department or indeed individuals might move towards the development of inclusive scholarly knowledge-building communities.

In some ways it is easier to set up criteria to examine the extent to which teaching has been enriched by integrating research, than it is to enumerate criteria for examining whether research has been enriched by teaching. Both must be developed.

▶ Research activity

Questions about the nature of research activity and who is engaged in research are fundamental to determining the extent to which there are inclusive scholarly knowledge-building communities in any particular context. Key questions that need to be addressed are: who defines what counts as research, who is doing the research in the university and what encouragement is there for all to be involved in some form of inquiry, research and/or scholarship no matter what their position or role?

Chapter 8 considered the question of whether a university's capacity to integrate research and teaching is dependent upon the capacity of teaching staff to integrate their own research into their teaching by being research active. I suggested that it was by no means clear that research-active staff are critical to a research-enhanced higher education when looked at from the students' perspective and that while it might be expected that courses taught by researchers would be more up to date than those of teachers not engaged in research, research evidence that would support this assumption is lacking.

Chapter 9 noted that how research is defined in an institution can enhance or inhibit academics' capacity to integrate their research and their teaching. What is most effective for integration is if research is defined broadly and includes, for example, scholarly work leading to the production of textbooks, published output in pedagogical research, creative and artistic works, and so on. Yet demands for performativity (Lyotard 1984) within higher education which have led to research assessment exercises are currently distorting the nature of research, and influencing how and whether scholarly work is published. Such measures are also having a pernicious effect on recruitment in universities and driving academics to seek ways to escape from their teaching. They do not enhance a university's capacity to integrate research and teaching.

Encouraging academics to engage in and publish pedagogical research in their disciplinary area, however, is an important way to develop departmental capacity to integrate research and teaching, and I suggested in Chapter 7 that students should be involved in this too. Academics need to take a keen interest in the responsibility they have for continually updating and changing their teaching in the light of new circumstances. Researching their teaching and their students' learning is one of the most effective ways to meet this challenge.

Ideally, in a university committed to going beyond the research and teaching divide, a faculty, school or department would have a balance of high-quality researchers in the subject discipline, together with high-quality researchers concerned with subject-specific and generic pedagogical research and scholarship; each academic being active in researching and publishing; that is, working in at least one of these areas not simply to meet performance requirements, but in order to advance the subject and enhance their students' learning. Some would be active in both. There may also be academics whose focus is on the study of existing scholarly work in the disciplinary area and integrating that knowledge into their teaching and their students' learning.

I have suggested in this book that there is a need to extend the scope of participation in research, beyond the tenured full- and part-time academics and postgraduate and honours research students, to undergraduate education, even to the lower levels. Research schemes that provide opportunities and funding for undergraduates to collaborate with academics in real research projects do this, but they need to be extended. Departments need to ensure that student researchers and scholars are working collaboratively with academic researchers in partnership.

In Chapter 9 we also saw that research-enhanced education needs to be seen in the context of changing work roles and responsibilities. I argued that there is a need to think creatively about how new positions may contribute to research-enhanced education; that such positions provide creative opportunities to rethink relationships within institutions of higher education. Once we begin to shift mindsets towards thinking of all as being engaged in some form of learning through scholarly inquiry, new kinds of university policy suggest themselves. We move from questions about whether staff are research active to questions about whether all are engaged in some form of inquiry through which they learn. This implies what has been termed a learning culture or a learning community. Staff development is carried out through inquiry. Teaching and learning are carried out through inquiry-based approaches. Students and academics engage meaningfully in research together. All come to participate in inclusive scholarly knowledge-building communities, where each person's contribution is valued.

This may be a long way off for many institutions. However, serious attempts to integrate research and teaching will be working towards it. So, in order to determine whether an institution is committed to such a motive, it is not so much a question of whether the academic staff are research active, but it is the questions that are being asked about the research activity within the institution as a whole and within its departments specifically that are key indicators of the extent to which the institution takes seriously the drive to bring teaching and research together.

▶ **Evidence-based teaching**

In many areas of professional life there is a growing awareness of the need for evidence-based decision making. Evidence-based teaching and learning means taking account of findings from empirical and theoretical research in higher education. Not withstanding different understandings of the nature of evidence in educational contexts, there is a need for curriculum decisions to be based on informed knowledge of the literature on teaching and learning in higher education, together with well-founded evidence of students' responses, learning experiences and outcomes.

The higher education teaching and learning literature abounds with case studies, exemplars of teaching and learning strategies, speculative pieces, and small-scale qualitative studies such that the evidence-base of many developments in teaching and learning is too often small. Competing theories and conjectures, as well as fashionable trends, also make the literature hard to interpret. (This is the case, for example, with the use of information and communications technology in teaching and learning, the effectiveness of which has yet to be established in spite of vast expenditure on such developments.) Nevertheless, basing curriculum decisions on anecdote, hearsay or intuitive feelings about how students are responding is becoming a thing of the past. It is important that higher education teachers, and perhaps also their students, grapple with the evidence base of curriculum decisions.

Yet, if higher education teachers are going to base curriculum decisions on evidence, they need to carry out pedagogical research on an on-going basis. Chapters 6 and 7 discussed issues in the scholarship of teaching and learning, and I suggested that students need to be collaboratively involved in such processes. In other words, there is a need to extend the range and number of academics involved in pedagogical scholarship and to extend the range of people who are involved in carrying out such research. Teaching should become a process of research.

But the scholarship of teaching and learning, as we have seen, takes academics further. Inquiring into their own teaching leads to the development of a critique not only of their own practice, but also of the basic values and assumptions that underlie it. It challenges teachers' epistemological and ontological beliefs and assumptions and it provides a way for them to engage in the reflexivity of the unrecognised ideas lying behind what we think and how we act (Bourdieu and Wacquant 1992). Aspects of the academic habitus that were hitherto hidden come to light. Yet reflexivity can be disorienting. It may mean confronting aspects of the academic world, of one's position in a particular university, or a situation with regard to one's students that one would rather not know about. It is likely to mean changing one's fundamental beliefs and it is likely to mean changing oneself.

A university that is serious about developing evidence-based curriculum decision making would be taking seriously the need to develop pedagogical research among disciplinary academics. It may set up research grant schemes to encourage academics to carry out research on teaching, reward scholarly outputs in teaching and learning research through funding or through the promotions process, and it is likely to sponsor staff to attend courses where they will learn how to research their teaching.

► A research-based curriculum

We have seen that in many examples of research-enhanced teaching, the curriculum mirrors research processes and activities. In their learning and in the activities carried out for assessment, students are increasingly working in research-based ways or participating in curricula that simulate research approaches. However, we noticed in Chapters 4 and 5 that what students are asked to research and to learn is more often than not confined to the fringes of research action. Students are either spectators, or they engage in research tasters. What they learn is likely to be carefully prescribed. Students are by and large kept at a distance from the research culture. Collaborative research is encouraged, but more often than not this is collaborative research among students in the same year group.

The separation between what undergraduate students are doing and what academics are doing presents one of the most important overall challenges in developing a research-based higher education curriculum. I have argued in this book that assumptions about the student not being ready or worthy of engaging in research need to be seriously and systematically challenged. Ideas about students in higher education and what they are capable of need to change. The new model of the relationship between teaching and research proposed in Chapter 2 posits a close relationship between students and teachers as both engage in scholarly knowledge-building communities. To develop research-based curricula is to go beyond atomistic thinking of engaging students in one-off research-based activities within traditional courses, to considering the whole student experience and how that experience dovetails with academics' research and scholarship. Universities that are systematically doing this are on the way to bridging the divide.

Research-based curricula that integrate student learning with academic work do not happen within traditional departmental contexts, for such contexts enshrine many cultural practices which, among other things, tend to exclude students. Seriously developing a research-based curriculum means opening up spaces and creating places where students and academics can meet, areas where discussions can take place on research projects; reversing the trend to take over physical spaces intended for both staff and student use (i.e., tea rooms) for other needs seen to be more pressing. Events, too, need to be opened up to undergraduate students, for example departmental seminars and research meetings. Opening up research achievements and spaces to make research more visible to everybody is also desirable and there is a need to open up the language of higher education to provide a sense of belonging for everyone who is participating in the university's educative ventures. We return to this idea in the final chapter.

▶ A culture of inquiry

To say that higher education institutions should develop a culture of inquiry almost seems to be a truism. For, of course, in so far as they carry out research, they develop cultures of inquiry. Yet we have seen that universities embody a number of mechanisms to closely prescribe who is allowed to do research. If, as we saw in Chapter 8, research is a process of learning, in considering the extent to which a particular university fosters a culture of inquiry, we might usefully ask who are the learners in the institution.

If research and learning share activities in common, it should be a small matter to integrate academics' research and students' learning. Yet, as we have seen, the academic hierarchy exists to preserve privilege. Allowing students to participate in activities with high academic capital, such as research, flies in the face of this.

So an institution committed to integrating research and teaching will make efforts both to redefine who the researchers are and open up to a wider range of people who are the learners in higher education. Yet recognising that they are learners is something that researchers may resist. In my study of conceptions of research, a question about whether they would call the activities they had defined as research 'learning', was met with some resistance by the senior researchers who were interviewed. Most researchers could list skills, techniques and knowledge that they learnt through engaging in research, but most also resisted the idea that they were learners. This is like the workers in Boud and Solomon's (2003) study. As a research participant in their study said:

> Well I do [learn] but I wouldn't present myself as a learner because that would suggest that you didn't know what you were doing. You've always got to present with some kind of approach that's got a professionalism about it.
>
> (Boud and Solomon 2003: 330)

In the academy, such attitudes are translated into strengthening the hierarchy and preserving the distance between academics (seen as researchers) and students (viewed as learners).

In this book we have seen that there is a need to be open to undergraduate students becoming engaged in research right from the beginning of their higher education experience. A critical element of a research-enhanced context is a self-reflexive culture; one which takes an enquiry-based approach to understanding itself, to examining how it makes decisions, how students are integrated and how disciplinary understanding can contribute to knowledge of its practices. So where research and teaching are being integrated, there will routinely be debates and discussions within departments and faculties on such questions as: what can our disciplinary knowledge and theories contribute to our understanding of teaching and learning issues? How can disciplinary research inform teachers' understanding of their teaching and their students' learning? What is the nature of knowledge in our subject/s? What can the methodological approaches we adopt in researching our subject tell us about teaching and learning? How are we learning together? There may be critical questioning of the way research in the area is informing both the process of research and the teaching and learning. Within a research-based higher education, students would be involved in such discussions as a routine matter.

Another important question is the extent to which students are able to define the questions that they are to investigate for themselves. How can higher education teachers devise ways to work with students to develop relevant questions that will be useful in developing a high level of disciplinary understanding? In order to develop a higher education that goes beyond the divide between teaching and research we need to go beyond the separate notions of teaching and learning to stress the more integrative notions of education and of pedagogy. A culture of inquiry thus means not only research activity among staff, or students engaged in research in order to learn, but it involves research-based decision making and self-reflection on its activities and relationships among all of its constituents at all levels of the institution. I return to this idea in Chapter 11.

▶ Communities of scholars

The question of who are the learners might alternatively be phrased as, 'who are the scholars'? I have argued that the goal is to establish inclusive scholarly knowledge-building communities. Inclusivity means acknowledging that different participants have different things to contribute as well as to learn. Inclusive does not mean equal, but it does mean valuing the contributions of each person no matter what their level of prior knowledge and understanding. Different people will have different things to learn and different things to contribute. Some will contribute expertise. Some will contribute critical questioning. Some will contribute the capacity to explain. Some will contribute resources. Others will contribute enthusiasm and youthful excitement. All will contribute time. Inclusivity means trusting participants to carry out the work that they have agreed to do. This means being aware of the power issues that define different positions within the university hierarchy and taking steps to minimise their affects. We have seen that when students are engaged in their normal practices of undergraduate study they are treated differently to the way they are treated when they engage as research associates in an undergraduate research scheme.

A community of professional scholars in a university where research and teaching are integrated involves not only academics but also students, because communities of scholars in such an institution would be inclusive. We have seen how, currently, a kind of apartheid exists within higher education, where the students are separate from the academics and even occupy separate physical spaces, and I have argued that we need to be vigilant about how these are, perhaps inadvertently, maintained. Although it has not been a particular focus of discussion in this book, we have noted a similar divide between academic and support or general staff. University organisation sustains these divisions. Instead, to go beyond the research and teaching divide, structures, systems and strategies need to be created so as to eliminate them. We need to develop communities of practice drawing on the skills, abilities and knowledge of all members of the university community. The challenge is to create universities that are places where communities of scholars work together on common interests; people currently defined as 'students', 'staff', and 'faculty' or 'academics' and also 'general' or 'support' staff. Bearing in mind the discussion of communities in Chapter 2, communities of scholars must be seen as relatively tight-knit groups or networks of people engaged in a common task. This might, following Nowotny, Scott and Gibbons (2001) include professionals and others from outside the university.

There are, of course, challenges with the numbers of students entering higher education and the need to provide a broad education to meet diverse needs and abilities. However, it is important to find ways to integrate students at different levels. Universities committed to the integration of research and teaching will be exploring ways of organising student groups that do not depend on hierarchies of year groups and will be examining more efficient ways of carrying out scholarly work.

I have argued that no matter what profession students are going to enter when they graduate, and no matter how their lives pan out in the future, it is important for them to develop the skills of professionalism embedded in ideas of scholarship. This draws attention to key aspects of generic graduate attributes including paying attention to detail, being rigorous, learning to be systematic, to be able to multi-task; and it means having the specialist skills and knowledge of tools and techniques necessary to engage in inquiry within a particular profession.

What is really important is that students should become involved as participants in ongoing research programmes with a sense of belonging to a community of researchers. Assessment of the extent to which students engage in a student-based community of scholars, has to be viewed alongside measures being taken to break down the barriers with academic research and inquiry. To what extent are those employed within the institution maintaining separate communities which exclude students, particularly undergraduates? What steps are they taking to ensure that students are welcomed into, and invited to share, the otherwise elite communities of scholars of academics and researchers?

▶ Research-aligned teaching

The next dimension to be considered is research-aligned teaching and learning. To talk of research-aligned teaching is to take us to the heart of the ways universities are organised. In my book *The Nature of Research: Inquiry in Academic Contexts*, I presented a fictitious account of someone coming to work and study in quite a different kind of department within an institution: the Department of Fear (Brew 2001a: 1–3). The narrative serves to show that there is nothing inevitable in the ways in which our academic units are currently organised. Academic departments reflect the historical development of ideas about different domains of knowledge. Such domains are constantly shifting and changing and new research areas are causing new departments to emerge; witness, for example, the growth in microbiological and genetics departments, or departments of informatics, or feminist or cultural studies in the second half of the twentieth century.

Research-aligned teaching refers to the ways in which faculties may be organised around research strengths and interests, and about how this links with the way the curriculum is organised. If the curriculum is aligned with the research strengths of the staff (including pedagogical research), the learning needs of the students can be aligned with the learning needs of the academics. So the more research-aligned the faculty is, the more pervasive is the influence of these research areas on the curriculum, as in the example of the School of Biology at the University of Edinburgh mentioned in Chapter 8.

I suggested earlier that it is research which has the greater academic capital within institutions of higher education and also with governments and the wider community. Yet research, particularly in the sciences, is often organised according to something akin to fiefdoms, with key researchers leading laboratories which may have a number of research staff and technicians as well as post doctoral fellows and postgraduates. Given that the leaders of such groups are likely to be in possession of large amounts of money from research grants and foundations, they may have considerable power to protect themselves from the demands of undergraduate education and may, as a consequence, be quite unconnected to the work of undergraduates. We have seen how in the United States, a key research granting body, the National Science Foundation (2001), demands that research grantees demonstrate the way their research links to education 'at all levels'. This creates an incentive for the work of research teams to be integrated into the curriculum and for the work of the team to be open to undergraduates to participate, which as we have seen they do in large numbers within undergraduate research schemes in the United States.

Some universities have been set up with the express purpose of breaking down traditional boundaries around academic fields of study and opening up opportunities for different kinds of inquiry (e.g., Essex and Keele Universities in the United Kingdom). It is not the place here to discuss the merits of different kinds of university organisation. However, in thinking about how to tell if an institution is serious about developing inclusive scholarly knowledge-building communities, questions to ask may be about the extent to which the learning needs of both academics and students are being met by the way the university, or indeed particular faculties and departments are organised. It may mean, for example, re-examining the opportunities that there are for cross-disciplinary and transdisciplinary exchanges, and it may mean taking steps to provide opportunities for multi-disciplinary research.

With these questions, we confront the issue of the different time scales that academics and students are on. Students typically spend three years taking a broad-based university course through a series of modules or units of study. Academics are likely to be studying a narrow field of study over a long period of time. Most university departments that are set up to research and to teach represent a compromise between their need to accommodate these extremes. Yet there is always more that could be done to bring these different needs together, and here the question that needs to be asked is whether the institution is actively seeking to examine its structures and systems to maximise opportunities for research and curriculum alignment.

▶ **Teaching-enhanced research**

In this book I have focused principally on the way research may be integrated into the process of educating undergraduates. However, we have also seen that teaching enhances research and has useful things to teach it.

Chapter 8 examined how teaching stimulates disciplinary research through questioning by students, and through the results of the research and inquiry projects that students engage in. We also noted that teaching stimulates pedagogical research projects as academics question the effectiveness of teaching strategies and approaches and the learning experiences of their students. Thinking about how teaching links to research has also raised questions about what we understand by research. We have seen that different academics have different understandings of research and noted the importance of extending the repertoire of understandings in order to open up more possibilities for integrating research and teaching. We have also seen how reflective practice in research changes the character of research making it more participatory, more linked to personal and professional issues, and making researchers more aware of its ethical, political and social dimensions.

Critical elements in this are the requirements of research funding bodies, as these greatly influence the ways in which universities view the relationship between research and teaching when considering the needs of research in the institution. The ways in which policy at a national level is interpreted is going to determine whether, for example, teaching is viewed alongside the development of research policy in a particular institution, whether research is predominantly viewed alongside teaching initiatives, or whether the relationship between teaching and research is viewed as a matter for both the development of research and its policy, and the development of teaching and its policy. We have seen that while teaching policies include references to the importance of linking research and teaching, research policies in the same institution may make scant reference to teaching. Initiatives to bring research and teaching together may be driven by senior members of the university with responsibility for teaching and learning, not by the individuals with responsibility for research.

Undoubtedly, strong high-level leadership together with a strong climate of teaching development is a facilitative context for the development of research/teaching linkages. However, in Chapter 8 we also noted the importance of examining the structures, such as the existence of separate committees for teaching and for research matters, which require systematic linking of research and teaching to continually be mindful of this and to circumvent it. An important issue is how, at the institutional level, both teaching and research committees can be encouraged to see the bringing together of research and teaching as benefiting both research and teaching.

Further, if what I am suggesting as the development of inclusive scholarly knowledge-building communities is to be seriously entertained in the institution, questions need to be asked about the extent to which teaching and research are jointly supportive of each other, both in policies and in structures and strategies for implementation.

▶ Conclusion

Academics, faculties and departments have many and varied reasons for wanting to go beyond the divide between teaching and research and varied conceptions of what that involves. I have argued in this book that discussion and conversation is a key way to move practice towards inclusive scholarly knowledge-building communities. In the final chapter, I consider some of the aspects of higher education that are pulling in the opposite direction before exploring how new kinds of university, with new relationships, can most effectively be progressed.

11 Vision for the Future

A paradox faced throughout this book is the fact that in order to examine how to go beyond the divide between teaching and research, I have had to assume that divide. Yet to assume the divide is inevitably to reinforce it. So, what do we mean by going beyond the divide? This is the focus of this final chapter. I want to examine what a higher education would be like when the dual activities of teaching and research come together in such a way that any separation between them is unrecognisable. We saw in Chapter 1 that there were different motivations for bringing research and teaching together, particularly in different types of university. I have suggested throughout this book that bridging the divide between teaching and research is in the interests of students and academics in any kind of university. I have pursued a vision of university education where research and teaching are integrated as involving the growth of scholarly knowledge-building communities because I am convinced that this is to create a more inclusive higher education necessary for life in the twenty-first century.

▶ Going in the opposite direction

Any vision of universities where research and teaching are integrated needs to take account of some of the aspects of higher education and its funding that appear to be pulling in the opposite direction. If research and teaching are to be truly integrated, we need to take the dilemmas that this poses seriously.

The economic model of higher education has driven policies, strategies and actions in higher education institutions in recent years. At the same time as responding to economic demands on higher education practices, academics are also having to manage the fallout from crises in academic knowledge (Barnett and Griffin 1997); shifts in power and questions of legitimacy changing who decides what counts as knowledge in society (Gibbons et al. 1994; McNair 1997); and critical questioning of research practices and findings by an educated public (Brew 2001a, Nowotny et al. 2001). A key question for all who work in universities is how to maintain autonomy and integrity within such contexts.

Earlier, it was noted that teaching and research practices are being driven by the economics of higher education funding; that funding teaching and research separately simplifies the granting of monies to universities, but it strengthens rather than diminishes the divide. Similarly, we have noted that the accountability requirements of universities, where teaching and research are evaluated separately, also run counter to the integration of teaching and research even when there are attempts to measure such integration.

As can be seen from examples in different countries, when research funding bodies define their criteria in terms of the wider impacts of research on education, when they reward the involvement of both undergraduate as well as postgraduate students on research projects, and when research assessment exercises focus on outputs showing collaborative research between academics and students, then undergraduates appear to be more likely to be engaged in research leading to new knowledge.

We saw earlier that how academics view research influences how they believe research and teaching can be brought together, and I suggested there is a need to extend the range of ways individual academics consider integrating their research and their teaching. Yet changing ideas of individual academics about the possibilities for research-based higher education can only go so far. We have seen that structures and systems (for example, how teaching and research are rewarded; how university committees are structured; how university space is arranged; and the availability of library resources and so on) may limit possibilities for action even inadvertently. Thus students may carry out their own research collaboratively with their peers, but not be linked into the research of the department, nor that of their lecturers, nor to the wider research community. I am not suggesting that this is not desirable in higher education; only that if we are to integrate research and teaching, we need to go further.

Structural hierarchies also work against the integration of teaching and research. These influence the different ways undergraduates, graduates and postgraduates are treated and even the different ways undergraduate students at different stages (first years, second years and so on) are viewed. In spite of the existence of numerous mature-age students in higher education, levels appear frequently to be equated with age, so it is often assumed that the first years are younger than the second years, followed by the third years and then the postgraduates. In this book we have seen these different levels as aspects of the ways in which universities work to reinforce status and privilege (Bourdieu 1988, 1990, 1998) and have recognised the importance of patronage in the progression from one level to another. On the other hand we have noted that organising the curriculum around different year groups is not inevitable. I have suggested that in moving towards a more research- and inquiry-based higher education, there is a need to free up structures so that students mingle and work on common tasks with other individuals and groups at different stages of their education. This implies that shifts in power relationships, the inclusion of different kinds of knowledge, and of learning becoming a collaborative process of engagement in a joint enterprise need to be considered.

In today's higher education institutions, even though students are more often than not required to learn what is specified in unit or subject outlines, modular course structures have widened students' course choices. Students' satisfaction with their courses is known to be associated with having a clear idea about what it is intended they should learn (see, for example, Wilson, Lizzio and Ramsden 1997). Indeed, it has been claimed that improvements in the specification of learning outcomes have enhanced students' satisfaction (see for example, Trigwell, Prosser and Waterhouse 1999; Gordon and Debus 2002). On the other hand, there is growing uneasiness both with learning outcomes specification and with modular course structures, the argument being that they tend to curtail students' capacity to carry out a piece of work of personal interest and relevance to them over a relatively long period of time; necessary if they are to engage in sustained inquiry and research.

Similarly, the move in higher education in the last 30 years or so away from summative examinations that require students to integrate their learning over a period of time, to continuous formative assessment within individual modules is now being critically questioned. Opportunities to utilise research-based assessment processes, where students are able to integrate their learning around a question central to their studies, are being encouraged (see Boyer Commission 1999).

Another dilemma that has often been raised when I have presented ideas about research-based learning to academics, is students' perceived preference for traditional lecture-based approaches to teaching. This is frequently attributed to students having grown up within an economic rationalist model of higher education which has taught students to act like customers (Morley 2003). How students view research in the university, the experiences of research they have, how and whether they consider that their learning experiences and outcomes can be enhanced and what effect their views have on the quality of their experiences of research are central to developing a research-enhanced education. Claims that teaching is integrated with research do not seem credible where students have negative or no ideas about the university as a research environment, nor of the relationship between what they are learning and research.

▶ A different kind of university

Barnett (2000) argues that research should teach us how to live. It needs to produce socially useful knowledge, and to have the potential to transform those who engage in it. Maxwell (1984: 73) similarly argued that the outcome of academic inquiry should be: 'our enhanced capacity to solve our fundamental problems of living'. If this were the cornerstone of higher education in the twenty-first century, being a student would mean learning how to address real problems of the world, the country or the local community, and developing the capacity, in turn, to address the problems of an unknown future. The basis of an inquiry-based higher education, I suggest, needs to be the questions students bring about the problems of twenty-first-century society; for example, how to solve world poverty or ways to reduce greenhouse gases, or more locally, how to reduce drug-related crime in their neighbourhood or solve the traffic problems of the city in which they live. Students would then need to develop the skills, tools, techniques and knowledge related to the particular domain of knowledge appropriate to their chosen specialisms, at the same time as developing new insights for the benefit of themselves and of society.

In considering the variation in academics' understandings of research in Chapter 3, it was noted that while some academics consider research to be a way in which they develop their understanding of themselves and their place in, and ways of responding to, the world in which they live, others do not consider this aspect of research when thinking about how to integrate their research and their teaching. We saw in Chapter 5 that by engaging in research in a concentrated way over the course of just a few weeks, students develop their skills, their personal epistemologies and the emotional dimension of their lives. Research can thus have both personal as well as social dimensions for students. Making this explicit within a university education would mean that through the process of inquiry students' and academics' individual growth and personal development would become an integral part of their university study.

We have seen that learning to engage in the scholarship of teaching and learning can mean learning to articulate and solve issues related to students' learning; to make teaching more like research. Yet, as we have also seen, this is likely to encourage academics to develop a reflexive critique of their teaching and of higher education more generally, and challenge their epistemological assumptions. It can also challenge their identity as a teacher. Reflexivity can cause teachers to re-evaluate values and assumptions. It can cause them to come face to face with conflicts in their values. In some cases it can cause them to come face to face with themselves.

I have explored the idea that central to understanding one's personal identity as an academic is a capacity to critique the academic habitus; that is, those tacit and implicit assumptions that determine the distinctions that are made about what is appropriate and what is inappropriate, what is useful or useless, and what is good or bad. Yet why should this idea of reflexivity be confined to the learning and teaching domain? Going beyond the research-teaching divide suggests extending the domains of inquiry beyond the disciplinary research laboratory, the library or the field site, to address not only pedagogical issues, but also the endemic as well as the day-to-day problems of academic practice.

The complex challenges within our universities that are thrown up by competing interests and demands on an overstretched academic workforce suggest the need for inquiry-based solutions. Not only students but also their teachers need to be engaged in research and inquiry in order to live their lives in the twenty-first century. Bringing research and teaching together suggests that academic practice should itself be the subject of ongoing inquiry. The ways in which academics carry out research, the skills that they utilise in research – the posing of appropriate questions, the examination of evidence, the linking of research evidence to what is previously known and so on – should, I suggest, usefully be utilised in solving the problems and issues that arise within an academic environment:

> Restructuring the tertiary landscape entails a changing field dynamic, with destabilization of power balances, and intensification of power struggles. Shifting academic habitats create crises for many staff whose livelihoods, values and identities embody the field. In Bourdieu's terms, there are new trumps to play, and alliances to negotiate, in struggles over the very rules of the game of power within the field.
>
> (Zipin 1999: 32)

This 'restructuring' is central to the vision of inclusive scholarly knowledge-building communities. Without it, old hierarchies and privileged ways of being within university communities may go unchallenged; research may remain esoteric and separate from society and, indeed, from undergraduate students; academic practices may remain stagnant; and teaching and learning may have limited capacity for emancipatory critique.

▶ Towards inclusive scholarly knowledge-building communities

In this book we have noted that when students engage in undergraduate research schemes they become research associates and as such tend to be treated quite differently to the way they are treated in their courses. They are perhaps more likely to be engaged in discussions of a democratic nature. Brookfield and Preskill (1999) suggest that in democratic discussions the dispositions that are particularly important are:

Hospitality. Mutual receptiveness of new ideas and perspectives and a willingness to question even the most widely accepted assumptions.

Widespread participation. By everyone involved.

Mindfulness. Listening closely and carefully to what others have to say.

Humility. Acting on the assumption that one's own ideas are limited and incomplete.

Mutuality. Caring about everyone's self development as much as one's own.

Deliberation. Different points of view are aired and only abandoned in the light of compelling evidence.

Appreciation. Expressing appreciation for the contributions of others.

Hope. Recognising that people can work through problems in a supportive environment.

Autonomy. The ability to take a stand and argue for it but to accept the challenges of changing ideas.

(adapted from Brookfield and Preskill 1999: 7)

These, I suggest, are key elements of inclusive scholarly knowledge-building communities. Yet, while they may be characteristic of the best research teams, they are a long way from describing the typical undergraduate educational experience. So what happens when a teacher has a desire to build an inclusive scholarly community with students?

During the writing of this book, I was invited to discuss an example of the integration of research and teaching at University College, London. At the meeting were Hasok Chang, Jason Davis, Katherine Jackson, Alan Jenkins and Stephen Rowland. The conversation highlighted some important challenges in moving towards inclusive scholarly knowledge-building communities. (See Chapter 5 for a fuller discussion of what the students were doing.)

> *Hasok*: What I'm trying to do is to build a community of scholars. The aim is to make sure that students do what we do; that they build new knowledge. They get a real kick out of emailing famous researchers, especially when they get a response from them.
>
> *Angela*: So how does what they're doing relate to your own research.
>
> *Hasok*: As I indicated in my paper [Chang 2005], I think that it's important that I'm not an expert in the topic. I can then say that I don't know. If they thought that they were just researching something that I already knew, I don't think they would take

it so seriously. The idea is of a community that builds on the work of other students. Each group of students inherits knowledge from the earlier generation; in this case, the students who researched this topic in previous years. They come to treat each other as experts.

Angela: So they're contacting the experts and they're also becoming experts themselves.

Hasok: Yes.

Stephen: But this issue of Hasok not being an expert ... actually he does have general knowledge about the topic.

Katherine: I think you are an expert in a sense. There are points of contact with your research that make the chlorine (what the students are researching) work; that make it quite a good fit.

Jason: It's a small but significant area that plugs in.

Katherine: Actually, you have a lot of expertise in the history and philosophy of science in a general sense, but also, importantly, you have a large amount of expertise in methodology.

Angela: Well, I'd be interested to hear, Hasok, what you think your expertise is in.

Hasok: Well, I suppose I'd say the history and philosophy of science with a special focus on the history of physics and chemistry in the last two centuries. So it's very broad.

Angela: So it does fit in.

Hasok: Well I had noticed a few very interesting things about chlorine along the way.

Jason: I'm actually wondering if part of the success of the project is the topic. I mean, how transferable would this be to other disciplines; other contexts?

Hasok: The topic does work well. It's a very mixed group of students. Some are from chemistry, some from the history of chemistry. Others are from philosophy. Very mixed.

Alan: So Hasok knows where the relevant experts are.

Stephen: Yes. But is it Hasok's community of practice that the students are tapping into? What is the community of practice here? Who defines it? How do you see your role? You're not just a facilitator. What are you?

Hasok: I see myself as a director; like a film director.

Stephen: But on what basis are you making decisions about how to intervene with students; how to answer their questions?

Hasok: Well, I'm improvising really; just responding. When there are obvious questions, I'm facilitating. Sometimes I sit down with a group of students and we work through how to solve a particular issue so in that sense we work together. Sometimes there are tougher questions; for example, when a student insists 'there's nothing out there'. There was one student who just couldn't see a theme in her notes. She couldn't make sense of it. So I took her notes home over the weekend and I noticed that there was a key issue staring me in the face.

Angela: So it seems as if sometimes you're working like you do when you supervise a doctoral student and sometimes you're having to teach in a more conventional undergraduate sense.

Hasok: Yes. There's an ambiguity in the relationship. I'm just feeling my way. I think what is also interesting is the way the students relate to each other. In the exam I include references to other students' work. So they come to appreciate each other as experts. So, for example, it might say 'Describe David X's view of . . . whatever'; David X being a previous student.

Alan: So you're not only changing their relationships to each other, you're also changing their relationships to the exam.

Hasok: Yes. But I'm not creating the community of practice for them. The students are as much creating it for themselves in the way they contact and use expert researchers and their work, and how they relate to and use each other's work. Each person's community is different.

Angela: So developing scholarly communities means negotiating new relationships. Like we're doing here. We're all feeling our way.

Alan: In many ways it's like going on geography field courses. When academics and students go away for field courses, the whole relationship between staff and students shifts. People investigate different things and they bring it together at the end of the time. Sometimes there's an element of handing over to the next group of students too, in the form of a paper that might get published.

Jason: But there's just no way that students are going to be able to publish in journals in some subjects. Elite research communities are difficult to get into. There are the experts and the expert journals and there are the students, and even if there are student journals there's no way that they are going to be able to bridge the gap between them. In some areas the gap is enormous.

Hasok: What I'm interested in doing is blurring the bifurcation between the community and the experts.

Stephen: Yes, if you're going to engage students in research, you need to take account of these social and cultural aspects.

The first issue that the group addresses is the relationship of the topics the students are researching to the expertise of their teacher. It becomes clear that the area that the students are researching is an area that comes under the general expertise of the teacher, but is not synonymous with it. The question of whether the teacher has expertise in the topic being researched by students is a key question when considering the extent to which research-based learning is possible where teachers are not active researchers. As Hasok suggests, if students are genuinely going to engage in developing new knowledge, what they are researching is likely to be unknown, even by their teacher.

However, as Jason suggests, the definition of an appropriate topic is vital. The history of chlorine lends itself to a number of topics, none of which has been extensively researched. Students are able to contact the very few experts on their chosen topic and in so doing build up their own community of experts in which they themselves play an important role. The process of passing on notes and findings to the next group of students develops that sense of a community of experts. Importantly, as Hasok notes, he is not creating a community of practice for the students in this instance. They do not join a pre-existing community. They are creating scholarly communities for themselves; ones which may include other students, but also experts in other parts of the world whom they contact via email. This shifts thinking away from the idea of students joining academic communities to which their teachers belong, to the idea of building contacts and negotiating networks for themselves.

In this kind of more inclusive higher education where students engage in research, relationships between students and their teachers are subject to change. The idea that students might be invited to participate in negotiating knowledge, as suggested in the idea of a democratic discussion and demonstrated in this conversation extract, is likely to be quite an alien concept to many people in higher education. As we have seen, according to Bourdieu (1998), social spaces are sites of contestation and debate, the structures of which are determined by the way different kinds of capital (social, political or, for example, academic) are distributed. As we have seen throughout this book, since academics hold academic capital they have privileged status within particular domains, particularly where the subjects of discussion are within their areas of expertise. However, when students are invited to engage in more inclusive scholarly work, their relationship with their teachers and with each other changes. There is a shift in status as they are listened to by experts in the field. Hasok admits to ambiguity in his relationship with his students. Sometimes he works in a similar way to working with doctoral students and at other times he is teaching in a more conventional undergraduate sense. He is 'feeling his way' as the students develop their own academic capital through their engagement with their research topic and as they develop their scholarly community.

Academic communities share a common purpose, namely, to come to understand an aspect or aspects of the world better. As such, higher education becomes a participatory activity, where people are enabled to develop their identity through their particular contributions to the knowledge-building enterprise. As Jason points out in the above conversation, some academic communities are elite and exclusive. In contrast, an inclusive scholarly community is, I suggest, distinguishable by the fact that each person's contributions are valued. Such communities are not likely to be all rosy as we have seen. They provide sites for sharing perspectives, some of which may be radically different from each other, and for challenging old hierarchies. In this instance the elements of democratic discussion become very important. The capacity to listen to what others are contributing, to treat others with respect and integrity and to put in place mechanisms for dealing with interpersonal conflict are, I believe, vital.

As can be seen from the conversation, inclusive scholarly knowledge-building communities are not exclusive. They are likely to go beyond the particular university community to embrace experts in other institutions, participants from the professions and from other walks of life. Nowotny and colleagues (2001) argue that essentially segregated, tightly knit research communities, traditionally characterised by strong collectivist beliefs and organisation where researchers essentially communicate almost exclusively with each other, are opening up. This is the challenge that Hasok's initiative presents. Nowotny and colleagues argue that research communities are themselves becoming more integrated within society because individual researchers are becoming more free to communicate with people from different social arenas. These more 'individualistic relationships' (p. 104) are leading to greater integration and, in turn, to the development of different kinds of hierarchical relationships and to trans-disciplinarity; suggesting that even the elite communities to which Jason refers are in the process of change.

However, Nowotny and colleagues' notion of the 'agora' is helpful in showing how far from genuine communities of practice we typically are with students, particularly undergraduates. The agora is a kind of marketplace where ideas are exchanged and developed. They suggest that in a Mode 2 society (see Chapter 2), academics, professionals and other people in society negotiate knowledge in what they term 'transaction spaces' (p. 103). In such spaces, academics, who may have particular specialist knowledge, work with other professionals, experts, politicians and lay people in order to negotiate and generate knowledge. Our meeting above represents just such a transaction space. The expansion of the higher education system and a proliferation of sites where research can be pursued, together with an increase in both the supply of researchers and in the demand for knowledge create such transaction spaces within the wider society. Research directions, Nowotny and colleagues suggest, arise in the multiple processes of interaction with people in a multiplicity of contexts and it is the people in their many contexts who need to be taken account of in the research of a Mode-2 society. Members of society are able to participate in discussions that take place concerning particular knowledge ideas and objects (Nowotny et al. 2001). The idea of scholarly knowledge-building communities is a reminder that this also needs to apply in the undergraduate domain. It recognises this shift in the way knowledge is generated in society and brings undergraduate as well as postgraduate students into this endeavour.

We noted earlier that students become research associates when they engage in summer research programmes, thus removing the connotations of subordination tied to the concept of 'student'. This suggests that going beyond the divide between teaching and research may require changes to be made in the language we use to describe people and their relationships to each other. Changing the discourse, I suggest, is an important prerequisite to breaking down unhelpful distinctions. At the very least, awareness of the language and the unintended connotations of current practice is indicated.

This brings us back to the role that reflexivity plays in suggesting how teachers and researchers and managers and administrators can go forward in ways that transcend the divide between research and teaching. The application of a critical, inquiry-based approach to academic practice including teaching and learning and curriculum decision making, which does not stop at examining the underlying values and assumptions that are made in academic contexts of teaching, research and learning, is, I suggest, the starting point for the development of inclusive scholarly knowledge-building communities. It is to begin the process of going beyond the research and teaching divide and it may begin at any level in an institution. Individuals may begin the process of critically examining their practice in a research-based way. Whole departments or faculties may take a decision to implement research-based approaches to strategic decision making in regard to particular aspects of academic practice. Whole institutions may work towards an ethic of research-based practice.

I have sketched a framework of some of the elements of inclusive scholarly knowledge-building communities, but what this would mean in any particular context is a matter for investigation and discussion. I do not offer recipes for action. In this book I have suggested that conversations in particular contexts are an important element in thinking through how to move forward. I do not underestimate the difficulties in doing so, but they too are a matter for investigation and discussion.

▶ Conclusion

In this book I set out on a quest to explore, through various conversations and in discussion, what a university seriously committed to developing the relationship between teaching and research would look like. I have explored different dimensions of the relationship between teaching and research and have, I hope, developed understanding of both how to bring research and teaching closer together and how to recognise institutional imperatives, intentions and strategies which are aimed at going beyond the teaching and research divide. I have asked the question as to why we would want to do this, and have suggested there is a need to do it in order to meet the demands of today's society and to prepare students for a world which is uncertain, super-complex, unpredictable and, indeed, terrifying. I have suggested that to seriously bring teaching and research together is to define a new kind of higher education in which students, academics and others who work in universities progressively work towards the development of inclusive scholarly knowledge-building communities of practice.

Yet let us be clear. There is no golden city that is 'beyond the divide'. What is important is the journey we take; the processes of putting into practice the values and aspirations of an inclusive, scholarly higher education community. My aim has been to present issues for discussion that will feed into new conversations that people in universities might have about future directions for their particular contexts. My hope is that such conversations would begin the process of going beyond the divide between teaching and research.

Once I met a man who had walked around the world. A little child said, 'How can you walk around the world? It's a long way round the world.' The man replied, 'Each step makes the next step possible.' By starting these conversations we have taken the first steps. We have begun the journey. The book is now finished, but the conversations continue.

Bibliography

Aldersey-Williams, H. (13 September 1999). The back half: The misappliance of science. *New Statesman*. Available at: http://www.newstatesman.co.uk/199909130038.htm [12 December 2004].

Annan, N. G. (1974). *Report of the Disturbances in the University of Essex* [The Annan Enquiry]. Colchester: University of Essex.

ARC. (2003). *Australian Research Council Strategic Plan 2003–2005* [Web Page]. URL www.arc.gov.au/publications/strategic.plan.htm [29 November 2004].

Baillie, C. (2004). Personal communication.

Barg, A. M., Crawford, A. K., Fekete, A. A., Greening, A. T., Hollands, A. O., Kay, A. J., and Kingston, A. J. (2000). Problem-based learning for foundation computer science courses. *Journal of Computer Science Education*, 10 (2): 1–20.

Barnett, R. (1997). *Higher Education: A Critical Business*. Buckingham: Society for Research into Higher Education and the Open University Press.

Barnett, R. (2000). *Realizing the University: In an Age of Super-Complexity*. Buckingham: Society for Research into Higher Education and the Open University Press.

Barnett, R. (2003). Learning for an unknown future. Keynote address to Learning for an Unknown Future: Annual Conference of the Higher Education Research and Development Society of Australasia. University of Canterbury, New Zealand, 6–9 July.

Barnett, R., and Griffin, A. (Eds). (1997). *The End of Knowledge in Higher Education*. London: Cassell.

Barrie, S. C. (2003). *Conceptions of Generic Graduate Attributes: A phenomenographic investigation of academics' understandings of generic graduate attributes in the context of contemporary university courses and teaching*. Unpublished doctoral dissertation, University of Technology, Sydney, Australia.

Barrie, S. C. (2004). A research-based approach to generic graduate attributes policy. *Higher Education Research and Development*, 23 (3): 261–75.

Barrie, S. C. (in press). Academics' understandings of generic graduate attributes: a conceptual base for lifelong learning. In P. Hager and S. Holland

(Eds), *Graduate Attributes, Learning and Employability.* Dortrecht, NL: Springer, pp. 80–90.

Baxter Magolda, M., Boes, L., Hollis, M. L., and Jaramillo, D. L. (1998). *Impact of the Undergraduate Summer Scholar Experience on Epistemological Development.* Miami: University of Miami.

BBSRC. (no date) *Biotechnology and Biological Sciences Research Council* [Web Page]. URL www.bbsrc.ac.uk/about/plans.reports/bbsrc.vision.pdf [29 November 2004].

Becher, T. (1989). *Academic Tribes and Territories: Intellectual Enquiry and the Cultures of Disciplines.* Buckingham: Society for Research into Higher Education and the Open University Press.

Becher, T., and Trowler, P. (2001). *Academic Tribes and Territories: Intellectual Enquiry and the Cultures of Disciplines* (2nd edn). Buckingham: Society for Research into Higher Education and the Open University Press.

Benjamin, J. (2000). The scholarship of teaching in teams: What does it look like in practice? *Higher Education Research and Development,* 19 (2): 191–204.

Bereiter, C. (2002). *Education and the Mind in the Knowledge Age.* Mahwah, NJ: Lawrence Erlbaum Associates.

Biggs, J. (1996). Enhancing teaching through constructive alignment. *Higher Education,* 32: 1–18.

Biggs, J. (1999). *Teaching for Quality Learning at University.* Buckingham: Society for Research into Higher Education and the Open University Press.

Blackmore, P., and Cousin, G. (2003). Linking teaching and research through research-based learning. *Educational Developments,* 4 (4): 24–7.

Boud, D. (1985). Problem-based learning in perspective. In D. Boud (Ed.), *Problem-Based Learning in Education for the Professions.* Sydney, NSW: Higher Education Research and Development Society of Australasia, pp. 13–18.

Boud, D., and Feletti, G. I. (1997). *The Challenge of Problem-Based Learning* (2nd edn). London: Kogan Page.

Boud, D., and Solomon, N. (2003). 'I don't think I am a learner': Acts of naming learners at work. *Journal of Workplace Learning,* 15 (7/8): 326–31.

Boud, D., Keogh, R., and Walker, D. (Eds) (1985). *Reflection: Turning Experience into Learning.* London: Kogan Page.

Bourdieu, P. (1982). Quoted in 'Lecture on the lecture'. In P. Bourdieu (1990). *The Logic of Practice.* Cambridge: Polity Press. Quoted in P. Bourdieu and L. J. D. Wacquant (1992). *An Invitation to Reflexive Sociology.* Cambridge, UK: Polity Press, p. 40.

Bourdieu, P. (1988). *Homo Academicus,* translated from the French by P. Collier. Cambridge: Polity Press.

Bourdieu, P. (1998). *Practical Reason.* Oxford: Polity Press.

Bourdieu, P., and Passeron, J.-C. (1977). *Reproduction in Education, Society and Culture*, translated from the French by R. Nice. London: Sage.

Bourdieu, P., and Wacquant, L. J. D. (1992). *An Invitation to Reflexive Sociology*. Cambridge: Polity Press.

Boyer Commission. (1999). *Reinventing Undergraduate Education: A Blueprint for America's Research Universities*. Stony Brook, NY: Carnegie Foundation for University Teaching.

Boyer, E. (1990). *Scholarship Reconsidered: Priorities for the Professoriate*. Princeton, NJ: Carnegie Foundation for the Advancement of Teaching, University of Princeton.

Boyer, E. L. (1996). The scholarship of engagement. *Journal of Public Service and Outreach*, 1 (1): 11–20.

Brew, A. (1993). Unlearning through experience. In D. Boud, R. Cohen and D. Walker, *Using Experience for Learning*. Buckingham: Society for Research into Higher Education and The Open University Press, pp. 87–98.

Brew, A. (1999a). Research and teaching: Changing relationships in a changing context. *Studies in Higher Education*, 24 (3): 291–301.

Brew, A. (1999b). The value of scholarship. Paper presented at the Annual Conference of the Higher Education Research and Development Society of Australasia, Melbourne, July.

Brew, A. (2001a). *The Nature of Research: Inquiry in Academic Contexts*. London: RoutledgeFalmer.

Brew, A. (2001b). Conceptions of research: A phenomenographic study. *Studies in Higher Education*, 26 (2): 271–85.

Brew, A. (2003a). Research and the academic developer: A new agenda. *International Journal for Academic Development*, 7 (2): 112–22.

Brew, A. (2003b). Teaching and research: New relationships and their implications for inquiry-based teaching and learning in higher education. *Higher Education Research and Development*, 22 (1): 3–18.

Brew, A. (2003c). *The Future of Research and Scholarship in Academic Development*. In H. Eggins and R. MacDonald (Eds), *Research and Scholarship in Academic Development in Higher Education*. Buckingham: Society for Research into Higher Education and the Open University Press, pp. 165–81.

Brew, A., and Barrie, S. C. (1999). Academic development through a negotiated curriculum. *International Journal for Academic Development*, 3 (1): 34–42.

Brew, A., and Boud, D. (1995). Teaching and research establishing the vital link with learning. *Higher Education*, 29 (3): 261–73.

Brew, A., and Peseta, T. (2004). Changing supervision practice: A program to encourage learning through feedback and reflection. *Innovations in Education and Teaching International*, 41 (1): 5–22.

Brew, A., and Phillis, F. (1997). Is research changing? Conceptions of successful researchers. Proceedings of the Higher Education Research and Development Society of Australasia Conference (pp. 131–5) Adelaide.

Brew, A. and Prosser, M. (2003). Integrating quality practices in research-led teaching and institutional priorities. In S. Nair and R. Harris (Eds), *National Quality in a Global Context: Proceedings of the Australian Universities Quality Forum*. Melbourne: Australia, pp. 113–16.

Brew, A., McShane, K., and Peseta,T. (2003). Encouraging the scholarship of teaching: Reflections on challenges and paradoxes. Workshop presented at the Annual Conference of the Higher Education Research and Development Society of Australasia. University of Canterbury, New Zealand, 6–9 July.

Brookfield, S., and Preskill, S. (1999). *Discussion as a Way of Teaching: Tools and Techniques for University Teachers.* Buckingham: Society for Research into Higher Education and the Open University Press.

Burgoyne, S. (2002). Refining questions and renegotiating consent. In P. Hutchings (Ed.), *Ethics of Inquiry: Issues in the Scholarship of Teaching and Learning*. Menlo Park, CA: Carnegie Publications, pp. 35–45.

Calandra, R. (2002). Teaching to learning: scientists who balance teaching and research enjoy rewards and recharging. *The Scientist,* 16 (17): 51.

Caswell, D., Johnston, C., Douglas, D., Eggermont, M., Howard, D., and Deacon, P. (2004). ENGG 251/253 – Fostering creative problem solving in a multi-disciplinary environment. Keynote presentation to the Society for Teaching and Learning in Higher Education Annual Conference, Ottawa, Canada, 16–19 June.

Centra, J. A. (1983). Research productivity and teaching effectiveness. *Research in Higher Education,* 18 (4): 379–89.

Chang, H. (2005). Turning an undergraduate class into a professional research community. *Teaching in Higher Education,* 10 (3): 387–94.

Chen, T. F., Crampton, M., Krass, I., and Benrimoj, S. I. (1999a). Collaboration between community pharmacists and GPs' medication review process. *Journal of Social and Administrative Pharmacy,* 16: 134–44.

Chen, T. F., Crampton, M., Krass, I., and Benrimoj, S. I. (1999b). Impact of a training programme and medication review meetings on communication between community pharmacists and GPs. *Journal of Social and Administrative Pharmacy,* 16: 76–7.

Colbeck, C. (1998). Merging in a seamless blend: How faculty integrate teaching and research. *The Journal of Higher Education,* 69 (6): 647–71.

Colbeck, C. (2002). Balancing teaching with other responsibilities: Integrating roles or feeding alligators. Paper presented at the annual meeting of the American Educational Research Association, New Orleans, Penn State University.

Colbeck, C. (2004). A cybernetic systems model of teaching and research production: Impact of disciplinary differences. Invited paper presented at

'Research & Teaching: Closing the Divide? An International colloquium', Marwell, Hampshire, 17–19 March 2004 [Web Page]. URL http://www.solent.ac.uk/rtconference/ [13 December 2004].

Cosgrove, D. (1981). Teaching geographical thought through student interviews. *Journal of Geography in Higher Education*, 5 (1): 19–22.

Council on Undergraduate Research. (2003) *Slide Show 'All about CUR'* [Web Page]. URL *http://www.cur.org/slide/cur.html* [28 October 2004].

Davies, P. (1999). What is evidence-based education? *British Journal of Educational Studies*, 47 (2): 108–21.

Dearn, J., Fraser, K., and Ryan, Y. (2002). *Investigation into the Provision of Professional Development for University Teaching in Australia: A Discussion Paper*. Canberra: Department of Education, Skills and Training.

Deer, C. (2003). Bourdieu on higher education: The meaning of the growing integration of educational systems and self-reflective practice. *British Journal of Sociology of Education*, 24 (2): 195–207.

DFES. (2003). *The Future of Higher Education*. London: Department for Education and Skills.

Diamond, R. M., and Adam, B. E. (1995). *The Disciplines Speak: Rewarding the Scholarly, Professional, and Creative Work of Faculty. Forum on Faculty Roles and Rewards*. Washington, DC: American Association for Higher Education, [FGK01523].

Dwyer, C. (2001). Linking research and teaching: A staff-student interview project. *Journal of Geography in Higher Education*, 25 (3): 357–66.

Elton, L. (1986). Research and teaching: Symbiosis or conflict? *Higher Education*, 15 (34): 299–304.

Elton, L. (1992). Research, teaching and scholarship in an expanding higher education system. *Higher Education Quarterly*, 46 (3): 252–67.

Entwistle, N. (1997). Introduction: Phenomenography in higher education. *Research and Development in Higher Education*, 16 (2): 127–34.

EPSRC. (no date). *Engineering and Physical Sciences Research Council Mission Statement* [Web Page]. URL www.epsrc.ac.uk/AboutEPSRC/MissionStatement.htm [29 November 2004].

ESRC. (no date). *Mission of the Economic and Social Research Council* [WebPage]. URL www.esrc.ac.uk/PublicationsList/strategic/ESRC%20-%20Strategic%20Plan%202001–2006.htm [29 November 2004].

Etkina, E., and Ehrenfeld, D. (2000). Helping ecology students to read: The use of reading reports. *Bioscience*, 50 (7): 602–8. Quoted in S. Jones and L. Barmuta (2002). Challenging students to think critically: A science unit focussing on generic skills. *Proceedings of the Annual Conference of the Higher Education Research and Development Society of Australasia*. Canberra: Higher Education Research and Development Society of Australasia.

Fallows, S., and Steven, C. (Eds). (2000). *Integrating Key Skills in Higher Education*. London: Kogan Page.

Feldman, K. A. (1987). Research productivity and scholarly accomplishment of college teachers as related to their instructional effectiveness: a review and exploration. *Research in Higher Education*, 26 (3): 227–98.

Feyerabend, P. (1978). *Science in a Free Society*. London: Verso.

French, N. J. (2004). The higher education teaching/research nexus: The Hong Kong experience. Paper presented at 'Research and Teaching: Closing the Divide? An International Colloquium', Marwell, Hampshire, 17–19 March 2004 [Web Page]. URL http://www.solent.ac.uk/rtconference/[13 December 2004].

Gaskin, S. (no date) *Abstracting Research Papers* [Web Page]. URL www.gees.ac.uk/linktr/Gaskin.htm [14 October 2004].

Gibbons, M., Limoges, C., Nowotny, H., Schwartzman, S., Scott, P., and Trow, M. (1994). *The New Production of Knowledge: The Dynamics of Science and Research in Contemporary Societies*. London: Sage.

Gibbs, G., and Coffey, M. (2004). The impact of training of university teachers on their teaching skills, their approach to teaching and the approach to learning of their students. *Active Learning in Higher Education*, 5 (1): 87–100.

Gibbs, G., and Jenkins, A. (1992). *Teaching Large Classes in Higher Education*. London: Kogan Page.

Gilbert, A., and Foster, S. F. (1997). Experiences with problem-based learning in business and management. In D. Boud, and G. Feletti (Eds), *The Challenge of Problem-Based Learning* (2nd edn). London: Kogan Page, pp. 244–52.

Glassick, C. E., Huber, M. T., and Maeroff, G. I. (1997). *Scholarship Assessed: Evaluation of the Professoriate*. An Ernest L. Boyer Project of the Carnegie Foundation for the Advancement of Teaching. San Franscisco: Jossey-Bass.

Gordon, C., and Debus, R. (2002). Developing deep learning approaches and personal teaching efficacy within a preservice teacher education context. *British Journal of Educational Psychology*, 72: 483–511.

Griffiths, R. (2004). Knowledge production and the research-teaching nexus: the case of the built environment disciplines. *Studies in Higher Education*, 29 (6): 709–26.

Groundwater-Smith, S., and Hunter, J. (2000). Whole school inquiry: evidence-based practice. *Journal of In-Service Education*, 26 (3): 583–600.

Habermas, J. (1987). *Knowledge and Human Interests*. London: Polity Press.

Haggis, T. (2004). Meaning, identity and 'motivation': Expanding what matters in understanding learning in higher education. *Studies in Higher Education*, 29 (3): 335–52.

Hattie, J. (2001). Performance indicators for the interdependence of research and teaching. In *Towards Understanding the Interdependence of Research and Teaching: Occasional papers from the vice-chancellor's symposium on the research teaching nexus*. Palmerston North, NZ: Massey University, pp. 50–2.

Hattie, J., and Marsh, H. W. (1996). The relationship between research and teaching: A meta-analysis. *Review of Educational Research.* 66 (4): 507–42.

Healey, M. (2000). Developing the scholarship of teaching in higher education: A discipline-based approach. *Higher Education Research and Development,* 19 (1): 169–89.

Huber, M. T. (2000). Disciplinary styles in the scholarship of teaching: Reflections on the Carnegie Academy for the Scholarship of Teaching and Learning. In C. Rust (Ed.), *Improving Student Learning Through the Disciplines: Proceedings of the 1999 7th International Symposium.* Oxford: Oxford Centre for Staff and Learning Development, pp. 20–31.

Huber, M. T., and Morreale, S. P. (2003). *On the Road with Disciplinary Styles in the Scholarship of Teaching and Learning* [Web Page]. URL http:// aahebulletin.com/member/articles/styles.asp [28 July 2003].

Hutchings, P. (Ed). (2002). *Ethics of Inquiry: Issues in the Scholarship of Teaching and Learning.* Menlo Park, CA: Carnegie Publications.

Hutchings, P., and Shulman, L. (1999). The scholarship of teaching: New elaborations, new developments. *Change,* 31 (5): 10–15.

Hutchings, P., Babb, M., and Bjork, C. (2002). *An Annotated Bibliography of the Scholarship of Teaching and Learning in Higher Education.* Menlo Park, CA: The Carnegie Foundation for the Advancement of Teaching.

Institute for Teaching and Learning. (2001). *Vice-Chancellor's Showcase of Scholarly Inquiry in Teaching and Learning: Program and Abstracts.* Sydney, NSW, Australia: Institute for Teaching and Learning, The University of Sydney. Available at: http://www.itl.usyd.edu.au/RLT/usydproject/ initiatives.htm [13 December 2004].

Jaakkola, T. (2003). Does network-supported collaborative learning promote learning of research methodology? Paper presented at the Annual Conference of the European Association for Research on Learning and Instruction, Padua, Italy, 26–30 August.

Jenkins, A. (2002). *Designing a Curriculum that Values a Research-Based Approach to Student Learning* [Web Page]. URL www.brookes.ac.uk/ genericlink/publications.htm! [14 October 2004].

Jenkins, A., and Zetter, R. (2003). *Linking Research and Teaching in Departments.* York: LTSN Generic Centre.

Jenkins, A., Blackman, T., Lindsay, R., and Paton-Saltzberg, R. (1998). Teaching and research: Student perspectives and policy implications. *Studies in Higher Education,* 23, (2): 127–41.

Jenkins, A., Breen, R., Lindsay, R., and Brew, A. (2003). *Reshaping Teaching in Higher Education: Linking Teaching with Research.* London: Kogan Page.

Jensen, J.-J. (1988). Research and teaching in the universities of Denmark: Does such an interplay really exist? *Higher Education,* 17: 17–26.

Jones, S., and Barmuta, L. (2002). Challenging students to think critically: A science unit focussing on generic skills. *Proceedings of the Annual Conference of the Higher Education Research and Development Society of Australasia.* Canberra: Higher Education Research and Development Society of Australasia. Available at: http://www.surveys.canterbury.ac. nz/herdsa03/pdfsnon/N1096.pdf

Kellett, M., Forrest, R., Dent, N., and Ward, S. (2004). 'Just teach us the skills please, we'll do the rest': Empowering ten-year-olds as active researchers. *Children and Society,* 18 (5): 329–43.

Kemmis, S., and McTaggart, R. (2000). Participatory action research. In N. Denzin, and Y. Lincoln (Eds), *The SAGE Handbook of Qualitative Research* (2nd edn). Thousand Oaks, CA: Sage Publications, p. 567–605.

Kemp, I. J., and Seagraves, L. (1995). Transferable skills – can higher education deliver. *Studies in Higher Education,* 20 (3): 315–28.

Kirov, S. M. (2003). Teaching and research: Impossible or essential link? *Microbiology Australia,* 24 (4): 12–13.

Kreber, C. (2002). Controversy and consensus on the scholarship of teaching. *Studies in Higher Education,* 27: 151–67.

Kreber, C. (2004). An analysis of two models of reflecton and their implications for educational development. *International Journal for Academic Development,* 9 (1): 29–50.

Kreber, C., and Cranton, P. A. (2000). Exploring the scholarship of teaching. *The Journal of Higher Education,* 71 (4): 476–95.

Kyvik, S., and Smeby, J.-C. (1994). Teaching and research: The relationship between the supervision of graduate students and faculty research performance. *Higher Education,* 28 (2): 227–39.

Lave, J., and Wenger, E. (1993). *Situated Learning: Legitimate Peripheral Participation.* Cambridge: Cambridge University Press.

Leatherman, C. (1990). Definition of faculty scholarship must be expanded to include teaching, Carnegie Foundation says. *Chronicle of Higher Education,* pp. 16–17.

Lenzen, M., and Dey, C. (2001). Teaching equity and sustainabiltiy in the context of climate change: A personal approach. Institute for Teaching and Learning. *Vice-Chancellor's Showcase of Scholarly Inquiry in Teaching and Learning: Program and Abstracts.* Sydney: Institute for Teaching and Learning, The University of Sydney.

Lenzen, M., and Smith, S. (1999–2000). Teaching responsibility for climate change: Three neglected issues. *Australian Journal of Environmental Education,* 15/16: 65–75.

Lueddeke, G. R. (2003). Professionalising teaching practice in higher education: A study of disciplinary variation and 'teaching-scholarship'. *Studies in
Higher Education,* 28 (2): 213–28.

Lyotard, J.-F. (1984). *The Postmodern Condition: A Report on Knowledge.*
Minneapolis: University of Minnesota Press.

MacAllister, S., and Pascoe, B. (Eds) (1999). *Homeric Hymns: A Project in
Creation.* Sydney: Department of Classics, University of Sydney.

MacDonald, G. (2001). What they need to know, what they want to know: The
challenge of relevance at the 1st year level. In Institute for Teaching and
Learning (2001). *Vice-Chancellor's Showcase of Scholarly Inquiry in Teaching and Learning: Program and Abstracts.* Sydney: Institute for Teaching
and Learning, The University of Sydney, p. 70.

Marsh, H.W., and Hattie, J. (2002). The relation between research productivity and teaching effectiveness: Complementary, antagonistic, or independent constructs. *Journal of Higher Education,* 73 (5): 603–14.

Marton, F. (1981). Phenomenography: Describing conceptions of the world
around us. *Instructional Science,* 10: 177–200.

Marton, F., Hounsell, D., and Entwistle, N. (Eds). (1997). *The Experience of
Learning* (2nd edn). Edinburgh: Scottish Academic Press.

Maxwell, N. (1984). *From Knowledge to Wisdom: A Revolution in the Aims and
Methods of Science.* London: Basil Blackwell.

McAlpine, L., and Weston. C. (2002). Reflection: Issues related to improving
professors' teaching and students' learning. In N. Nativa, and P. Goodyear
(Eds), *Teacher Thinking, Beliefs and Knowledge in Higher Education.* Dortrecht, NL: Kluwer Academic Publishers, pp. 59–78.

McKenzie, J. (2003). *Variation and Change in Ways of Experiencing Teaching.*
Unpublished doctoral dissertation, University of Technology, Sydney.

McKenzie, J. (2004). Critical aspects and dimensions of variation: Extending
understandings of ways of experiencing teaching. Paper presented at
Improving Student Learning International Symposium. Oxford: Oxford
Centre for Staff and Learning Development, Oxford Brookes University.

Mclean, M., and Barker, H. (2004). Students making progress and the
'research-teaching nexus' debate. *Teaching in Higher Education,* 9 (4):
407–19.

McNair, S. (1997). Is there a crisis? Does it matter? In Barnett R., and
Griffin A. (Eds), *The End of Knowledge in Higher Education.* London: Cassell, pp. 27–38.

Mooney, C. J. (1990). Higher-education conferees applaud Carnegie plan to
broaden the definition of faculty scholarship. *Chronicle of Higher Education,* p. 16.

Morley, L. (2003). *Quality and Power in Higher Education.* Buckingham:
Society for Research into Higher Education and the Open University Press.

Morse, K. (2003). Broadening the scope of undergraduate research. Plenary address to *NSF Workshop: Exploring the Concept of Undergraduate Research Centers,* 31 March–1 April. [Web page] urc.arizona.edu/morse.cfm [12 November 2004]

Murtonen, M. (2005). University students' research orientations: Do negative attitudes exist toward quantitative methods? *Scandinavian Journal of Educational Research,* 49 (3): 263–80.

National Science Foundation (2001). GPRA Strategic Plan: IV Strategy. www.nsf.gov/publs/2001/nsf0104/strategy.htm [26 November 2004]

Neumann, R. (1992). Perceptions of the teaching-research nexus: A framework for analysis. *Higher Education,* 23 (2): 159–71.

Neumann, R. (1993). Research and scholarship: Perceptions of senior academic administrators. *Higher Education,* 25: 97–110.

Neumann, R. (1994). The teaching-research nexus: Applying a framework to university students' learning experiences. *European Journal of Education,* 29 (3): 323–38.

NH&MRC. (2003). *National Health and Medical Research Council Strategic Plan 2003–2006* [Web Page]. URL www.nhmrc.gov.au/publications/pdf/nh46.pdf [29 November 2004].

Nicholls, G. (2004). Scholarship in teaching as a core professional value: What does this mean to the academic? *Teaching in Higher Education,* 9 (1): 29–42.

Nowotny, H., Scott, P., and Gibbons, M. (2001). *Re-Thinking Science: Knowledge and the Public in an Age of Uncertainty.* Cambridge: Polity Press.

Paulsen, M. B., and Feldman, K. A. (1995). Toward a reconceptualization of scholarship: A human action system with functional imperatives. *Journal of Higher Education,* 66 (6): 615–40.

Pearson, M., and Brew, A. (2002). Research training and supervision development. *Studies in Higher Education,* 27 (1): 135–50.

Perry, W. (1999). *Forms of Ethical and Intellectual Development in the College Years: A Scheme* (2nd edn). San Francisco: Jossey Bass.

Petersson, G. (2005). Medical and nursing students' development of conceptions of science during three years of study in higher education. *Scandinavian Journal of Educational Research,* 49 (3): 281–96.

Popper, K. R. (1972). *Objective Knowledge.* Oxford: Clarendon Press.

Prosser, M., and Trigwell, K. (1999). *Understanding Learning and Teaching: The Experience in Higher Education.* Buckingham: Society for Research into Higher Education and the Open University Press.

Quinn, J. (2003). A theoretical framework for professional development in a South African University. *International Journal for Academic Development,* 8: 61–76.

Rades, T., and Norris, P. (2003). Research-informed teaching in pharmaceutical sciences and pharmacy practice at the University of Otago.

Proceedings of the Annual Conference of the Australasian Pharmaceutical Science Association, University of Sydney, 2 December.

Ramsden, P. (1991). A performance indicator of teaching quality in higher education: The course experience questionnaire. *Studies in Higher Education*, 16 (2): 129–50.

Ramsden, P. (2001). Strategic management of teaching and learning. In C. Rust (Ed.), *Improving Student Learning Strategically. Proceedings of the 2000 8th International Symposium on Improving Student Learning*. Oxford: Oxford Centre for Staff and Learning Development, pp. 1–10.

Ramsden, P. (2003). *Learning to Teach in Higher Education* (2nd edn). London: RoutledgeFalmer.

Ramsden, P., and Moses, I. (1992). Associations between research and teaching in Australian higher education. *Higher Education*. 23 (3): 273–95.

Reeders, E. (2000). Scholarly practice in work-based learning: Fitting the glass slipper. *Higher Education Research and Development*, 19 (2): 205–20.

Refshauge, K., Shirley, D., Latimer, J., and Maher, C. (2001 Changing knowledge, beliefs and attitudes of physiotherapy students to depression in patients with back pain. In Institute for Teaching and Learning, *The Vice-Chancellor's Showcase of Scholarly Inquiry in Teaching and Learning Program and Abstracts*. Sydney: Institute for Teaching and Learning, p. 73.

Rice, R. E. (1992). Towards a broader conception of scholarship: The American context. In T. G. Whiston, and R. L. Geiger (Eds), *Research and Higher Education: The United Kingdom and the United States*. Buckingham: Society for Research into Higher Education and The Open University Press, pp. 117–29.

Rice, R. E. (1996). Making a place for the new American scholar. New Pathways: Faculty Career and Employment for the 21st Century Working Paper Series, Inquiry #1. American Association for the Advancement of Science, Washington, DC. [FGK01540].

Rice, R. E. (2004). Rethinking scholarship and engagement: The struggle for new meanings. Invited paper presented at 'Research and Teaching: Closing the Divide? An International Colloquium', Marwell, Hampshire, 17–19 March 2004 [Web Page]. URL http://www.solent.ac.uk/rtconference/[13 December 2004].

Robertson, J. (2002). *Research and Teaching in a Community of Inquiry*. Unpublished doctoral dissertation, University of Canterbury, New Zealand.

Robertson, J., and Bond, C. (2001). Experiences of the relation between teaching and research: What do academics value? *Higher Education Research and Development*, 20 (1): 5–19.

Roth, W.-M. (2003). Contradictions in 'Learning Communities'. Keynote paper presented at the Annual Conference of the European Association for Research on Learning and Instruction, Padua, Italy, 26–30 August.

Rowland, S. (1996). Relationships between teaching and research. *Teaching in Higher Education*, 1 (1/96): 7–20.

Rowland, S. (2000). *The Enquiring University Teacher.* Buckingham: The Society for Research into Higher Education and the Open University Press.

Ruscio, K. P. (1987). The distinctive scholarship of the selective liberal arts college. *Journal of Higher Education*, 58 (2): 205–22.

Sachs, J. (2002). *The Activist Teaching Profession.* Buckingham: Open University Press.

Sainsbury, E. (2003). The many faces of teaching research. Proceedings of the Annual Conference of the Australasian Pharmaceutical Science Association. University of Sydney.

Sainsbury, E., McLachlan, A., and Aslani, P. (2001). Tools of the trade: Preparing pharmacists for professional practice. In *Vice-Chancellor's Showcase of Scholarly Inquiry in Teaching and Learning: Program and Abstracts.* Sydney, NSW, Australia: Institute for Teaching and Learning, The University of Sydney, p. 74.

Schenkel, A. (2002). *Communities of Practice or Communities of Discipline: Managing Deviations at the Øresund Bridge.* Unpublished doctoral dissertation, Stockholm School of Economics, Stockholm.

Schön, D. A. (1995). The new scholarship requires a new epistemology. *Change,* 27 (6): 26–34.

Schönwetter, D. J., Sokal, L., Friesen, M., and Taylor, K. L. (2001). Teaching philosophies reconsidered: A conceptual model for the development and evaluation of teaching philosophy statements. *International Journal for Academic Development,* 7 (1): 83–97.

Scott, D. K., and Awbrey, S. M. (1993). Transforming scholarship. *Change,* 25 (4): 38–43.

Serow, R. C. (2000). Research and teaching at a research university. *Higher Education,* 40 (4): 449–63.

Seymour, E., Hunter, A. B., Laursen, S. L., and Deantoni, T. (2004). Establishing the benefits of research experiences for undergraduates in the sciences: First findings from a three-year study. Published online in *Wiley InterScience (www.interscience.wiley.com)*, DO1 10.1002/sce.10131.

Shore, B., Pinkler, S., and Bates, M. (1990). Research as a model for university teaching. *Higher Education,* 19: 21–35.

Shulman, L. (1993). Teaching as community property: Putting an end to pedagogical solitude. *Change,* 25 (6): 6–7.

Shulman, L. (1999). Taking learning seriously. *Change,* 31 (4): 11–17.

Shulman, L. (2000a). From Minsk to Pinsk: Why a scholarship of teaching and learning. *The Journal of Scholarship of Teaching and Learning,* 1 (1): 48–52.

Shulman, L. (2000b). Teacher development: Roles of domain expertise and pedagogical knowledge. *Journal of Applied Developmental Psychology,* 21 (1): 129–35.

Shulman, L. (2000c). Vision of the possible: Models for campus support of the scholarship of teaching and learning [Web Page]. Available at: http://www.carnegiefoundation.org/elibrary/docs/printable/ visions.htm [21 July 2003].

Smeby, J. C. (1998). Knowledge production and knowledge transmission: The interaction between research and teaching at universities. *Teaching in Higher Education,* 3 (1): 5–20.

Smith, R., and Coldron, J. (2000). How does research affect pre-service students' perceptions of their practice? Paper presented at Annual meeting of AERA, New Orleans, 25 April.

Southampton Institute. (2004) *Strategic Plan 2004–2008,* [Web Page]. URL http://www.solent.ac.uk/ExternalUP/318/advanced.scholarship.strategy.1. doc [12 December 2004].

Southorn, N. (1999). Case studies in learning and assessment: Experience with agricultural engineering applications. Paper presented at the 4th Northumbria Assessment Conference, Newcastle upon Tyne.

Spanier, B. B. (1995). *Im/partial Science: Gender Ideology in Molecular Biology.* Bloomington and Indianapolis: Indiana University Press.

Stoecker, J. L. (1993). The Biglan classification revisited. *Research in Higher Education,* 34 (4): 451–64.

Sundre, D. L. (1992). The specification of the content domain of faculty scholarship. *Research in Higher Education,* 33 (3): 297–315.

Takacs, D. (2002). Using students work as evidence. In P. Hutchings (Ed.), *Ethics of Inquiry: Issues in the Scholarship of Teaching and Learning.* Menlo Park, CA: Carnegie Publications, pp. 27–34.

Trigwell, K., and Shale, S. (2004). Student learning and the scholarship of university teaching. *Studies in Higher Education,* 29 (4): 523–36.

Trigwell, K., Prosser, M., and Taylor, P. (1994). Qualitative differences in approaches to teaching first-year university science. *Higher Education,* 27: 75–84.

Trigwell, K., Prosser, M., and Waterhouse, F. (1999). Relations between teachers' approaches to teaching and students' approaches to learning. *Higher Education,* 37: 57–70.

Trigwell, K., Martin, E., Benjamin, J., and Prosser, M. (2000). Scholarship of teaching: A model. *Higher Education Research and Development,* 19 (2): 155–68.

University of Sydney. (2004) *Academic Board Statement on Research-Led Teaching and Scholarship of Teaching* [Web Page]. URL http://www.usyd. edu.au/su/ab/Research-Led.Teaching.Statement.pdf [15 December 2004].

Warren-Smith, A. K., McLean, A. N., Nicol, H. I., and McGreevy, P. D. (2004). Variations in the timing of reinforcement as a training technique for foals (*Equus caballus*). Thirteenth Annual Conference of the International Society for Anthrozoology (ISAZ).

Watson, J. D. (1969). *The Double Helix*. Harmondsworth: Penguin, Mentor Books.

Webb, J., Shirato, T., and Danaher, G. (2002). *Understanding Bourdieu*. London: Sage.

Webster D S. (1985). Does research productivity enhance teaching? *Educational Record*, 66: 60–3.

Weimar, M. (1993). The disciplinary journals on pedagogy. *Change*, 25 (6): 44–52.

Wenger, E. (1998). *Communities of Practice: Learning, Meaning and Identity*. Cambridge: Cambridge University Press.

Westergaard, J. (1991). Scholarship, research and teaching: A view from the social sciences. *Studies in Higher Education*, 16 (1): 23–8.

Willis, D. (2001). Building local partnerships between teaching and research: The impact of national policy and audit. Paper presented at the Annual conference of the Higher Education Research and Development Society of Australasia.

Willis, D., Harper, J., and Sawicka, T. (1999). Putting the worms back in the can: Encouraging diversity in the teaching research nexus. In *Cornerstones: What do We Value in Higher Education?* Canberra: Higher Education Research and Development Society of Australasia.

Wilson, D., Lizzio, A., and Ramsden, P. (1987) The development, validation and application of the course experience questionnaire. *Studies in Higher Education*, 22 (1): 33–52.

Winn, S. (1995). Learning by doing: Teaching research methods through student participation in a comissioned research project. *Studies in Higher Education*, 20: 203–314.

Wong, F., You, J., Baker, N., and Duke, C. (2001). Pharmaceutical drug analytical profile laboratory exercise. In Institute for Teaching and Learning, *The Vice-Chancellor's Showcase of Scholarly Inquiry in Teaching and Learning Program and Abstracts*. Sydney: Institute for Teaching and Learning, The University of Sydney, p. 88.

Woolgar, S. (1988). *Knowledge and Reflexivity: New Frontiers in the Sociology of Knowledge*. London: Sage.

Wuetherick, B., Yonge, O., Kachanoski, G., Connor, B., Cormack, L., Robinson, R., Chacko, T., Erlit, E., Varnhagen, C., Hoddinot, J., Haughey, M., Swaters, G., Brechtel, M., and Skallerup, L. (2004). Serving students: Connecting research and teaching at the University of Alberta. Poster presented at the Annual Conference of the Society for Teaching and Learning in Higher Education, University of Ottawa, 16–19 June.

Zamorski, B. (2000). *Research-Led Teaching and Learning in Higher Education*. Norwich: University of East Anglia.

Zamorski, B. (2002). Research-led teaching and learning in higher education: A case. *Teaching in Higher Education*, 7 (4): 411–27.

Zetter, R. (2002). Getting from Perkins to Jenkins: Filling the implementation gap. *Teaching News, the Newsletter of Oxford Brookes University*, pp. 5–6.

Zetter, R. (2003) *Urban Land and Vulnerability of the Urban Poor Workshop* [Web Page]. URL www.brookes.ac.uk/schools/planning/LTRC/outputs/Cat3.htm! [14 October 2004].

Zetter, R. (no date). FDTL 65/99 Linking teaching with research and consultancy in the built environment: Examples of effective teaching practice, example number 14.

Zipin, L. (1999). Simplistic fictions in Australian higher education policy debates: A Bourdieuan analysis of complex power struggles. *Discourse: Studies in the Cultural Politics of Education*, 20 (1): 21–39.

Index